DIRECTIONS IN DEVELOPMENT

Evaluating the Impact of Development Projects on Poverty

A Handbook for Practitioners

Judy L. Baker

The World Bank
Washington, D.C.

Library of Congress Cataloging-in-Publication Data

Baker, Judy L., 1960–
   Evaluating the impact of development projects on poverty : a handbook
for practitioners / Judy L. Baker
      p.   cm. — (Directions in development)
   Includes bibliographical references.
   ISBN 0-8213-4697-0
   1. Economic development projects—Evaluation—Handbooks, manuals, etc.
2. Poor—Developing countries. I. Title   II. Directions in development
(Washington, D.C.)

HD75.9 .B35 2000
338.9'0068'4—dc21   00–028325

Contents

Annexes

Foreword

Despite the billions of dollars spent on development assistance each year, there is still very little known about the actual impact of projects on the poor. There is broad evidence on the benefits of economic growth, investments in human capital, and the provision of safety nets for the poor. But for a specific program or project in a given country, is the intervention producing the intended benefits and what was the overall impact on the population? Could the program or project be better designed to achieve the intended outcomes? Are resources being spent efficiently? These are the types of questions that can only be answered through an impact evaluation, an approach that measures the outcomes of a program intervention in isolation of other possible factors.

Many governments, institutions, and project managers are reluctant to carry out impact evaluations because they are deemed to be expensive, time consuming, and technically complex, and because the findings can be politically sensitive, particularly if they are negative. Many evaluations have also been criticized because the results come too late, do not answer the right questions, or were not carried out with sufficient analytical rigor. A further constraint is often the limited availability and quality of data.

Yet with proper and early planning, the support of policymakers, and a relatively small investment compared with overall project cost, a rigorous evaluation can be very powerful in assessing the appropriateness and effectiveness of programs. Evaluating impact is particularly critical in developing countries where resources are scarce and every dollar spent should aim to maximize its impact on poverty reduction. If programs are poorly designed, do not reach their intended beneficiaries, or are wasteful, with the right information they can be redesigned, improved, or eliminated if deemed necessary. The knowledge gained from impact evaluation studies will also provide critical input to the appropriate design of future programs and projects.

This handbook seeks to provide project managers and policy analysts with the tools needed for evaluating project impact. It is aimed at readers with a general knowledge of statistics. For some of the more in-depth statistical methods discussed, the reader is referred to the technical literature on the topic. Chapter 1 presents an overview of concepts and methods, Chapter 2 discusses key steps and related issues to consider in implementation, Chapter 3 illustrates various analytical techniques through a case study, and Chapter 4 includes a discussion of lessons learned from a rich set of "good practice" evaluations of poverty projects that have been reviewed for this handbook. The case studies, included in Annex I, were selected from a range of evaluations carried out by the World Bank, other donor agencies, research institutions, and private consulting firms. They were chosen for their methodological rigor, in an attempt to cover a broad mix of country settings, types of projects, and evaluation methodologies. Also included in the Annexes are samples of the main components that would be necessary in planning any impact evaluation—sample terms of reference, a budget, impact indicators, a log frame, and a matrix of analysis.

Although the techniques used in impact evaluation are similar across sectors and population subgroups, the illustrations of methodologies and case examples in the handbook focus on assessing the impact of projects targeted to the poor. Poverty impact can include a wide range of projects and evaluation questions, such as measuring the impact of microfinance programs on household income, the impact of a training program on employment, the impact of a school feeding program on student attendance, or the impact of the construction of rural roads on household welfare.

Regardless of the project type or questions being addressed, the design of each impact evaluation will be unique, depending on factors such as the type of data available, local capacity, and timing and budget concerns. Finally, evaluations that will yield high-quality, credible, and generalizable results for policymakers will require strong financial and political support; early and careful planning; participation of stakeholders in the design of the objectives and approach of the study; adequate data; a suitable mix of methodologies, including both quantitative and qualitative techniques; the rigorous application of these techniques; and communication between team members throughout the process.

Acknowledgments

The preparation of this book benefited from the invaluable contributions of a core team. I would like to acknowledge both the written input, and helpful comments along the way, from the following team members: Gillette Hall (case studies, lessons learned), Julia Lane (case studies, lessons learned), Martin Ravallion (analytical methods case study), and Laura Rawlings (implementation issues, lessons learned); and the work on impact evaluation carried out by Kene Ezemenari, Gloria Rubio, Anders Rudqvist, and K. Subbarao. Background research was carried out by Matthew Fleming and Samir Stewart. The book was jointly supported by the Latin America and Caribbean Region and the Poverty Reduction and Economic Management Network of the World Bank under the leadership of Norman Hicks, Guillermo Perry, and Michael Walton. The work also benefited greatly from the comments received by Omar Arias, Sabina Alkire, Michael Bamberger, Soniya Carvalho, Wendy Cunningham, Norman Hicks, Shahidur Khandker, Norbert Schady, and Quentin Wodon.

Chapter 1
Defining Concepts and Techniques
for Impact Evaluation

A comprehensive evaluation is defined in the literature as an evaluation that includes monitoring, process evaluation, cost-benefit evaluation, and impact evaluation. Yet each of these components is distinctly different. Monitoring will help to assess whether a program is being implemented as was planned. A program monitoring system enables continuous feedback on the status of program implementation, identifying specific problems as they arise. Process evaluation is concerned with how the program operates and focuses on problems in service delivery. Cost-benefit or cost-effectiveness evaluations assess program costs (monetary or nonmonetary), in particular their relation to alternative uses of the same resources and to the benefits being produced by the program. And finally, impact evaluation is intended to determine more broadly whether the program had the desired effects on individuals, households, and institutions and whether those effects are attributable to the program intervention. Impact evaluations can also explore unintended consequences, whether positive or negative, on beneficiaries. Of particular interest for this handbook is the extent to which project benefits reach the poor and the impact that these benefits have on their welfare. Some of the questions addressed in impact evaluation include the following: How did the project affect the beneficiaries? Were any improvements a direct result of the project, or would they have improved anyway? Could program design be modified to improve impact? Were the costs justified?

These questions cannot, however, be simply measured by the outcome of a project. There may be other factors or events that are correlated with the outcomes but are not caused by the project. To ensure methodological rigor, an impact evaluation must estimate the counterfactual, that is, what would have happened had the project never taken place or what otherwise would have been true. For example, if a recent graduate of a labor training program becomes employed, is it a direct result of the program or would that individual have found work anyway? To determine the counterfactual, it is necessary to net out the effect of the interventions from other factors—a somewhat complex task. This is accomplished through the use of comparison or control groups (those who do not participate in a program or receive benefits), which are subsequently compared with the treatment group (individuals who do receive the intervention). Control groups are selected randomly from the same population as the program participants, whereas the comparison group is more simply the group that does not receive the program under investigation. Both the comparison and control groups should resemble the treatment group in every way, the only difference between groups being program participation.

Determining the counterfactual is at the core of evaluation design. This can be accomplished using several methodologies which fall into two broad categories, experimental designs (randomized), and quasi-experimental designs (nonrandomized). It is, however, quite tricky to net out the program impact from the counterfactual conditions that can be affected by history, selection bias, and contamination. Qualitative and participatory methods can also be used to assess impact. These techniques often provide critical insights into beneficiaries' perspectives, the value of programs to beneficiaries, the processes that may have affected outcomes, and a deeper interpretation of results observed in quantitative analysis. The strengths and weaknesses of each of these methods are discussed in more detail below. As the reader will find, no technique is perfect and thus the evaluator must make decisions about the tradeoffs for each method chosen. Early and careful planning will, however, provide many more methodological options in designing the evaluation.

Experimental Designs

Experimental designs, also known as randomization, are generally considered the most robust of the evaluation methodologies. By randomly allocating the intervention among eligible beneficiaries, the assignment process itself creates comparable treatment and control groups that are statistically equivalent to one another, given appropriate sample sizes. This is a very powerful outcome because, in theory, the control groups generated through random assignment serve as a perfect counterfactual, free from the troublesome selection bias issues that exist in all evaluations. The main benefit of this technique is the simplicity in interpreting results—the program impact on the outcome being evaluated can be measured by the difference between the means of the samples of the treatment group and the control group. One example is the Kenya textbooks evaluation in which evaluators selected a random allocation of program sites, administered a baseline survey, created control groups, and then administered the treatment, which in this case was the delivery of textbooks. Having control and treatment groups then allowed the evaluators to clearly determine the impact of textbooks on student learning.

While experimental designs are considered the optimum approach to estimating project impact, in practice there are several problems. First, randomization may be unethical owing to the denial of benefits or services to otherwise eligible members of the population for the purposes of the study. An extreme example would be the denial of medical treatment that can turn out to be lifesaving to some members of a population. Second, it can be politically difficult to provide an intervention to one group and not another. Third, the scope of the program may mean that there are no nontreatment groups such as with a project or policy change that is broad in scope—examples include an adjustment loan or programs administered at a national level. Fourth, individuals in control groups may change certain identifying characteristics during the experiment that could invalidate or contaminate the results. If, for example, people move in and out of a project area, they may move in and out of the treatment or control group. Alternatively, people who were denied a program benefit may seek it through alternative sources, or those being offered a program may not take up the intervention. Fifth, it may be difficult to ensure that assignment is truly random. An example of this might be administrators who exclude high-risk applicants to achieve better results. And finally, experimental designs can be expensive and time consuming in certain situations, particularly in the collection of new data.

With careful planning, some of these problems can be addressed in the implementation of experimental designs. One way is with the random selection of beneficiaries. This can be used to provide both a politically transparent allocation mechanism and the basis of a sound evaluation design, as budget or information constraints often make it impossible to accurately identify and reach the most eligible beneficiaries. A second way is bringing control groups into the program at a later stage once the evaluation has been designed and initiated. In this technique, the random selection determines *when* the eligible beneficiary receives the program, not *if* they receive it. This was done in the evaluation of a nutrition program in Colombia, which provided the additional benefit of addressing questions regarding the necessary time involved for the program to become effective in reducing malnutrition (McKay 1978). Finally, randomization can be applied within a subset of equally eligible beneficiaries, while reaching all of the most eligible and denying benefits to the least eligible, as was done with education projects in the El Chaco region for the Bolivia social fund evaluation (Pradhan, Rawlings, and Ridder 1998). However, if the latter suggestion is implemented, one must keep in mind that the results produced from the evaluation will be applicable to the group from which the randomly generated sample was selected.

Quasi-Experimental Designs

Quasi-experimental (nonrandom) methods can be used to carry out an evaluation when it is not possible to construct treatment and comparison groups through experimental design. These techniques generate comparison groups that resemble the treatment group, at least in observed characteristics, through econometric methodologies, which include matching methods, double difference methods, instrumental variables methods, and reflexive comparisons (see Box 1.2). When these techniques are used, the treatment and comparison groups are usually selected *after* the intervention by using nonrandom methods. Therefore, statistical controls must be applied to address differences between the treatment and comparison groups and sophisticated matching techniques must be used to construct a comparison group that is as similar as possible to the treatment group. In some cases a comparison group is also chosen before the treatment, though the selection is not randomized.

The main benefit of quasi-experimental designs is that they can draw on existing data sources and are thus often quicker and cheaper to implement, and they can be performed after a program has been implemented, given sufficient existing data. The principal disadvantages of quasi-experimental techniques are that (a) the reliability of the results is often reduced as the methodology is less robust statistically; (b) the methods can be statistically complex; and (c) there is a problem of selection bias. In generating a comparison group rather than randomly assigning one, many factors can affect the reliability of results. Statistical complexity requires considerable expertise in the design of the evaluation and in analysis and interpretation of the results. This may not always be possible, particularly in some developing country circumstances.

The third problem of bias relates to the extent to which a program is participated in differentially by subgroups of a target population, thus affecting the sample and ultimately the results. There are two types of bias: those due to differences in observables or something in the data, and those due to differences in unobservables (not in the data), often called selection bias (Box 1.1). An observable bias could include the selection criteria through which an individual is targeted, such as geographic location, school attendance, or participation in the labor market. Unobservables that may bias program outcomes could include individual ability, willingness to work, family connections, and a subjective (often politically driven) process of selecting individuals for a program. Both types of biases can yield inaccurate results, including under- and overestimates of actual program impacts, negative impacts when actual program impacts are positive (and vice versa), and statistically insignificant impacts when actual program impacts are significant and vice versa. (See, for example, LaLonde 1986, Fraker and Maynard 1987, LaLonde and Maynard 1987, and Friedlander and Robins 1995.) It is possible to control for bias through statistical techniques such as matching and instrumental variables, but it is very difficult to fully remove them which remains a major challenge for researchers in the field of impact analysis.

Among quasi-experimental design techniques, matched-comparison techniques are generally considered a second-best alternative to experimental design. The majority of the literature on evaluation methodology is centered around the use of this type of evaluation, reflecting both the frequency of use of matched comparisons and the many challenges posed by having less-than-ideal comparison groups. In recent years there have been substantial advances in propensity score matching techniques (Rosenbaum and Rubin 1985; Jalan and Ravallion 1998). This method is

---

Box 1.1 The Problem of Selection Bias

Selection bias relates to unobservables that may bias outcomes (for example, individual ability, preexisting conditions). Randomized experiments solve the problem of selection bias by generating an experimental control group of people who would have participated in a program but who were randomly denied access to the program or treatment. The random assignment does not remove selection bias but instead balances the bias between the participant and nonparticipant samples. In quasi-experimental designs, statistical models (for example, matching, double differences, instrumental variables) approach this by modeling the selection processes to arrive at an unbiased estimate using nonexperimental data. The general idea is to compare program participants and nonparticipants holding selection processes constant. The validity of this model depends on how well the model is specified.

A good example is the wages of women. The data represent women who choose to work. If this decision were made, we could ignore the fact that not all wages are observed and use ordinary regression to estimate a wage model. Yet the decision by women to work is not made randomly—women who would have low wages may be unlikely to choose to work because their personal reservation wage is greater than the wage offered by employers. Thus the sample of observed wages for women would be biased upward.

This can be corrected for if there are some variables that strongly affect the chances for observation (the reservation wage) but not the outcome under study (the offer wage). Such a variable might be the number of children at home.

Source: Greene (1997).

very appealing to evaluators with time constraints and working without the benefit of baseline data given that it can be used with a single cross-section of data. This technique is, however, dependent on having the right data because it relies on oversampling program beneficiaries during the fielding of a larger survey and then "matching" them to a comparison group selected from the larger core sample of the overall effort, often a national household survey. Given the growth in the applications of large surveys in developing countries, such as the multipurpose Living Standards Measurement Studies, this evaluation method seems particularly promising. A good example is the evaluation of a public works program, TRABAJAR, in Argentina (Jalan and Ravallion 1998, Annex 1.1, and chapter 4).

Box 1.2 Summary of Quantitative Methods for Evaluating Program Impact

The main methods for impact evaluation are discussed below. Because no method is perfect, it is always desirable to triangulate.

Experimental or Randomized Control Designs

- *Randomization*, in which the selection into the treatment and control groups is random within some well-defined set of people. In this case there should be no difference (in expectation) between the two groups besides the fact that the treatment group had access to the program. (There can still be differences due to sampling error; the larger the size of the treatment and control samples the less the error.)

Nonexperimental or Quasi-Experimental Designs

- *Matching methods or constructed controls*, in which one tries to pick an ideal comparison that matches the treatment group from a larger survey. The most widely used type of matching is *propensity score matching*, in which the comparison group is matched to the treatment group on the basis of a set of observed characteristics or by using the "propensity score" (predicted probability of participation given observed characteristics); the closer the propensity score, the better the match. A good comparison group

comes from the same economic environment and was administered the same questionnaire by similarly trained interviewers as
the treatment group.

- *Double difference or difference-in-differences* methods, in which one
compares a treatment and comparison group (first difference)
before and after a program (second difference). Comparators
should be dropped when propensity scores are used and if they
have scores outside the range observed for the treatment group.
- *Instrumental variables or statistical control* methods, in which one
uses one or more variables that matter to participation but not to
outcomes given participation. This identifies the exogenous variation in outcomes attributable to the program, recognizing that
its placement is not random but purposive. The "instrumental
variables" are first used to predict program participation; then
one sees how the outcome indicator varies with the predicted
values.
- *Reflexive comparisons*, in which a baseline survey of participants is
done before the intervention and a follow-up survey is done
after. The baseline provides the comparison group, and impact is
measured by the change in outcome indicators before and after
the intervention.

Qualitative Methods

Qualitative techniques are also used for carrying out impact evaluation
with the intent to determine impact by the reliance on something other
than the counterfactual to make a causal inference (Mohr 1995). The focus
instead is on understanding processes, behaviors, and conditions as they
are perceived by the individuals or groups being studied (Valadez and
Bamberger 1994). For example, qualitative methods and particularly participant observation can provide insight into the ways in which households and local communities perceive a project and how they are affected by it. Because measuring the counterfactual is at the core of impact
analysis techniques, qualitative designs have generally been used in conjunction with other evaluation techniques. The qualitative approach uses
relatively open-ended methods during design, collection of data, and
analysis. Qualitative data can also be quantified. Among the methodologies used in qualitative impact assessments are the techniques developed
for rapid rural assessment, which rely on participants' knowledge of the
conditions surrounding the project or program being evaluated, or par-

ticipatory evaluations in which stakeholders are involved in all stages of the evaluation—determining the objectives of the study, identifying and selecting indicators to be used, and participating in data collection and analysis. For a detailed discussion on participatory methods see World Bank (1996), *The World Bank Participation Sourcebook.*

The benefits of qualitative assessments are that they are flexible, can be specifically tailored to the needs of the evaluation using open-ended approaches, can be carried out quickly using rapid techniques, and can greatly enhance the findings of an impact evaluation through providing a better understanding of stakeholders' perceptions and priorities and the conditions and processes that may have affected program impact.

Among the main drawbacks are the subjectivity involved in data col-lection, the lack of a comparison group, and the lack of statistical robust-ness, given mainly small sample sizes, all of which make it difficult to generalize to a larger, representative population. The validity and relia-bility of qualitative data are highly dependent on the methodological skill, sensitivity, and training of the evaluator. If field staff are not sensi-tive to specific social and cultural norms and practices, and nonverbal messages, the data collected may be misinterpreted. And finally, without a comparison group, it is impossible to determine the counterfactual and thus causality of project impact.

Integrating Quantitative and Qualitative Methods

Although there is an extensive literature on quantitative versus qualita-tive methods in impact evaluation, there is also a growing acceptance of the need for integrating the two approaches. Impact evaluations using quantitative data from statistically representative samples are better suited to assessing causality by using econometric methods or reaching generalizable conclusions. However, qualitative methods allow the in-depth study of selected issues, cases, or events and can provide critical insights into beneficiaries' perspectives, the dynamics of a particular reform, or the reasons behind certain results observed in a quantitative analysis. There are significant tradeoffs in selecting one technique over another.

Integrating quantitative and qualitative evaluations can often be the best vehicle for meeting the project's information needs. In combining the two approaches, qualitative methods can be used to inform the key impact evaluation questions, survey the questionnaire or the stratifica-tion of the quantitative sample, and analyze the social, economic, and political context within which a project takes place, whereas quantitative methods can be used to inform qualitative data collection strategies, to design the sample to inform the extent to which the results observed in the qualitative work can be generalized to a larger population by using a statistically representative sample, and, statistical analysis can be used to control for household characteristics and the socio-economic conditions of different study areas, thereby eliminating alternative explanations of the observed outcomes.

There are several benefits of using integrated approaches in research discussed in Bamberger (2000) that also apply to impact evaluations. Among them:

- Consistency checks can be built in through the use of triangulation procedures that permit two or more independent estimates to be made for key variables (such as income, opinions about projects, reasons for using or not using public services, and specific impact of a project).
- Different perspectives can be obtained. For example, although researchers may consider income or consumption to be the key indicators of household welfare, case studies may reveal that women are more concerned about vulnerability (defined as the lack of access to social support systems in times of crises), powerlessness, or exposure to violence.
- Analysis can be conducted on different levels. Survey methods can provide good estimates of individual, household, and community-level welfare, but they are much less effective for analyzing social processes (social conflict, reasons for using or not using services, and so on) or for institutional analysis (how effectively health, education, credit, and other services operate and how they are perceived by the community). There are many qualitative methods designed to analyze issues such as social process, institutional behavior, social structure, and conflict.
- Opportunities can be provided for feedback to help interpret findings. Survey reports frequently include references to apparent inconsistencies in findings or to interesting differences between communities or groups that cannot be explained by the data. In most quantitative research, once the data collection phase is completed it is not possible to return to the field to check on such questions. The greater flexibility of qualitative research means that it is often possible to return to the field to gather additional data. Survey researchers also use qualitative methods to check on outliers—responses that diverge from the general patterns. In many cases the data analyst has to make an arbitrary decision as to whether a household or community that reports conditions that are significantly above or below the norm should be excluded (on the assumption that it reflects a reporting error) or the figures adjusted. Qualitative methods permit a rapid follow-up in the field to check on these cases.

In practice, the integration of quantitative and qualitative methods should be carried out during each step of the impact evaluation. Chapter 2 mentions many opportunities for doing this. For illustration, the Nicaragua School Autonomy Reform Case provides a good example of integrated methods. Quantitative methods following a quasi-experimental design were used to determine the relationship between decentralized management and learning and to generalize results for different types of schools. In addition, qualitative techniques, including a series of key informant interviews and focus group discussions with different school-based staff and parents, were utilized to analyze the context in which the reform was introduced, examine the decisionmaking dynamics in each school, and assess the perspectives of different school community actors on the autonomy process (see Annex 1.11).

Other Approaches to Impact Evaluation

Two other topics are particularly relevant to the discussion of evaluating the poverty impact of projects: (a) approaches to measuring the impact of structural adjustment programs, and (b) theory-based evaluations. Both incorporate many of the methodologies discussed above, but each uses a different approach.

Evaluating Structural Adjustment Programs. There has been substantial debate on the impact of structural adjustment programs on the poor. Much of the evidence used to support this debate is, however, based on deficient assumptions and methods. As with other projects, the policy changes under structural adjustment projects must be (a) compared with relevant counterfactuals that would respond to the same macroeconomic constraints, and (b) analyzed in the context of the local economic structure and based on empirical information from household surveys. This, however, is very difficult for three reasons. First, policy changes may have economy-wide impact, making it impossible to find comparison groups that are unaffected. Second, because of exogenous factors, lags, feedbacks, and substitutions, any changes in the well-being of the poor must be interpreted with extreme caution. And third, it is difficult to predict what would have happened if adjustment had not taken place—what alternative policies a government might have pursued and what the resulting impact would have been on the poor.

In the literature, several approaches have been used, each with its own shortcomings. The techniques are in many cases similar to those described in Box 1.2, though, as shown in Box 1.3, estimating the counterfactual requires vast assumptions that may substantially affect the validity of the results. This is most viably handled by isolating specific policy changes that would affect the population, such as exchange rate policies, trade policies, reductions in public expenditures, and reductions in public sector employment. Yet even with this approach it can be difficult to isolate the impact of specific policies. For examples, see Killick (1995), Poppele, Summarto, and Pritchett (1999), Bourguignon, de Melo, and Suwa (1991), and Sahn, Dorosh, and Younger (1996).

Box 1.3 Summary of Methods Used to Evaluate Adjustment Policies

Approaches with No Counterfactual

- Qualitative studies that assess conditions of the population (often identifying vulnerable subgroups) before, during, and after adjustment policies are implemented through focus groups, interviews, and other qualitative techniques.
- "Before and After," which compares the performance of key variables during and after a program with those prior to the program. The approach uses statistical methods to evaluate whether there is a significant change in some essential variables over time. This approach often gives biased results because it assumes that had it not been for the program, the performance indicators would have taken their pre-crisis-period values.

Approaches that Generate a Counterfactual Using Multiple Assumptions

- Computable general equilibrium models (CGEs) that attempt to contrast outcomes in treatment and comparison groups through simulations. These models seek to trace the operation of the real economy and are generally based on detailed social accounting matrices collected from data on national accounts, household expenditure surveys, and other survey data. CGE models do produce outcomes for the counterfactual, though the strength of the model is entirely dependent on the validity of the assumptions. This can be problematic as databases are often incomplete and many of the parameters have not been estimated by formal econometric methods. CGE models are also very time consuming, cumbersome, and expensive to generate.

(Box continues on the following page.)

Box 1.3 *(continued)*

- With and without comparisons, which compare the behavior in key variables in a sample of program countries with their behavior in nonprogram countries (a comparison group). This is an approach to the counterfactual question, using the experiences of the comparison group as a proxy for what would otherwise have happened in the program countries. It is, however, quite difficult to achieve a true comparison group. The method assumes that only the adoption of an adjustment program distinguishes a program country from the comparison group and that the external environment affects both groups the same.
- Statistical controls consisting of regressions that control for the differences in initial conditions and policies undertaken in program and nonprogram countries. The approach identifies the differences between program and nonprogram countries in the preprogram period and then controls these differences statistically to identify the isolated impacts of the programs in the postreform performance.

Theory-Based Evaluation. The premise of theory-based evaluations is that programs and projects are based on explicit or implicit theory about how and why a program will work. The evaluation would then be based on assessing each theory and assumptions about a program during implementation rather than at a midpoint or after the project has been completed. In designing the evaluation, the underlying theory is presented as many microsteps, with the methods then constructed for data collection and analysis to track the unfolding of assumptions. If events do not work out as expected, the evaluation can say with a certain confidence where, why, and how the breakdown occurred.

The approach puts emphasis on the responses of people to program activities. Theories direct the evaluator's attention to likely types of near-term and longer-term effects. Among the advantages are, first, that the evaluation provides early indications of program effectiveness during project implementation. If there are breakdowns during implementation, it is possible to fix them along the way. Second, the approach helps to explain how and why effects occurred. If events work out as expected, the evaluation can say with a certain confidence how the effects were generated. By following the sequence of stages, it is possible to track the microsteps that led from program inputs through to outcomes.

The shortcomings of the approach are similar to many of the other methodologies. In particular, (a) identifying assumptions and theories can be inherently complex; (b) evaluators may have problems in measuring each step unless the right instruments and data are available, (c) problems may be encountered in testing the effort because theory statements may be too general and loosely constructed to allow for clear-cut testing, and (d) there may be problems of interpretation that make it difficult to generalize from results (see Weiss 1998).

An example of theory-based technique is being piloted by the Operations and Evaluation Department of the World Bank to evaluate the impact of social investment funds on community-level decisionmaking processes, traditional power structures and relationships, and community capacity, trust, and well-being. This will be based on the theory that priority groups can effectively implement a project and operate and maintain the investment created by the project. A set of main assumptions and subassumptions has been set out and will be tested using existing household survey data, as well as a specially designed survey instrument for a smaller sample, and focus groups and other PRA techniques. The information from each of these data sources will be triangulated in the analysis.

Cost-Benefit or Cost-Effectiveness Analysis

While this type of analysis is not strictly concerned with measuring impact, it enables policymakers to measure program efficiency by comparing alternative interventions on the basis of the cost of producing a given output. It can greatly enhance the policy implications of the impact evaluation and therefore should also be included in the design of any impact evaluation. (For a more complete discussion of cost-benefit and cost-effectiveness analysis, see *Handbook on Economic Analysis of Investment Operations*, World Bank 1996.)

Cost-benefit analysis attempts to measure the economic efficiency of program costs versus program benefits, in monetary terms. For many projects, especially in the social sectors, it is not possible to measure all the benefits in monetary terms. For example, the benefits of a program to provide school inputs (textbooks, classroom furniture, preschool programs) would be increased learning. Instead of measuring monetary outcomes, learning achievement scores could be used to quantify the benefits. This would require cost-effectiveness analysis. The concepts for both types of analysis are the same.

The main steps of cost-benefit and cost-effectiveness analysis are to identify all project costs and benefits and then compute a cost-to-effectiveness ratio. In calculating costs, the value of the intervention itself should be included, as well as all other costs, such as administration, delivery, investment costs (discounted to the net present value), the monetary value of freely provided goods or services, social costs such as environmental deterioration, and health hazards. Benefits can be monetary, such as gain in income, or the number of units delivered, test scores, or health improvements. When benefits cannot be quantified, it is possible to use subjective indicators such as ranking or weighting systems. This approach, however, can be tricky in interpreting subjective scores.

Once the costs and benefits have been determined, the cost-effectiveness ratio (R) is then $R = cost/unit$ (or benefit). This ratio can then be compared across interventions to measure efficiency. In theory, this technique is quite straightforward. In practice, however, there are many caveats involved in identifying and quantifying the costs and benefits. It is important to ensure that appropriate indicators are selected, that the methodologies and economic assumptions used are consistent across ratios, and that the ratios are indeed comparable. And as with other techniques used in impact analysis, measuring cost-effectiveness can be best carried out when included in the evaluation design from the earliest stages. This allows for the collection of the necessary cost and benefit information and ensuring consistency.

Choosing a Methodology

Given the variation in project types, evaluation questions, data availability, cost, time constraints, and country circumstances, each impact evaluation study will be different and will require some combination of appropriate methodologies, both quantitative and qualitative. The evaluator must carefully explore the methodological options in designing the study, with the aim of producing the most robust results possible. Among quantitative methods, experimental designs are considered the optimal approach and matched comparisons a second-best alternative. Other techniques, however, can also produce reliable results, particularly with a good evaluation design and high-quality data.

The evidence from the "best-practice" evaluations reviewed for this handbook highlights that the choice of impact evaluation methodologies is not mutually exclusive. Indeed, stronger evaluations often combine methods to ensure robustness and to provide for contingencies in implementation. Joining a "with and without" approach with a "before and after" approach that uses baseline and follow-up data is one combination strongly recommended from a methodological perspective (Subbarao and others 1999). Having baseline data available will allow evaluators to verify the integrity of treatment and comparison groups, assess targeting, and prepare for a robust impact evaluation. This is true even for randomized control designs. Although randomization ensures equivalent treatment and comparison groups at the time of randomization, this feature should not influence evaluators into thinking that they do not need baseline data. Indeed, baseline data may be crucial to reconstructing why certain events took place and controlling for these events in the impact assessment.

Incorporating cost-benefit or cost-effectiveness analysis is also strongly recommended. This methodology can enable policymakers to compare alternative interventions on the basis of the cost of producing a given output. This is particularly important in the developing-country context in which resources are extremely limited.

Finally, combining quantitative and qualitative methods is the ideal because it will provide the quantifiable impact of a project as well as an explanation of the processes and interventions that yielded these outcomes. Although each impact evaluation will have unique characteristics requiring different methodological approaches, a few general qualities of a best-practice impact evaluation include:

- An estimate of the counterfactual has been made by (a) using random assignment to create a control group (experimental design), and (b) appropriately and carefully using other methods such as matching to create a comparison group (quasi-experimental design).
- To control for pre- and postprogram differences in participants, and to establish program impacts, there are relevant data collected at baseline and follow-up (including sufficient time frame to allow for program impacts).
- The treatment and comparison groups are of sufficient sizes to establish statistical inferences with minimal attrition.
- Cost-benefit or cost-effectiveness analysis is included to measure project efficiency.
- Qualitative techniques are incorporated to allow for the triangulation of findings.

Chapter 2
Key Steps in Designing and Implementing Impact Evaluations*

Undertaking an impact evaluation study can be quite challenging and cost-ly, with implementation issues arising at every step of the way. These challenges highlight the importance of a well-designed study, a committed and highly qualified team, and good communication between the evaluation team members. By incorporating the evaluation early into the design of a project, it will be possible to obtain results in a timely way so that the findings can be used for midproject adjustments of specific components.

Regardless of the size, program type, or methodology used for the evaluation, there are several key steps to be carried out as outlined below (Box 2.1). This chapter will provide a discussion of these steps as well as a discussion of the many issues that may arise in implementation. The sequencing of these steps is critical, particularly in ensuring the collection of necessary data before the project begins implementation. Early planning provides the opportunity to randomize, to construct ex ante matched comparisons, to collect baseline data, and to identify upcoming surveys that could be used in a propensity score matching approach.

All of the design work and initial data collection should be done during project identification and preparation. Ideally, some results will be available during the course of project implementation so they can feed into improving the project design if necessary. A good example of how a project incorporated evaluation plans from the earliest stages is illustrated in the Uganda Nutrition and Early Childhood Development Project (see chapter 4).

Determining Whether or Not to Carry Out an Evaluation

A first determination is whether or not an impact evaluation is required. As discussed above, impact evaluations differ from other evaluations in that they are focused on assessing causality. Given the complexity and cost in carrying out impact evaluation, the costs and benefits should be assessed, and consideration should be given to whether another approach would be more appropriate, such as monitoring of key performance indicators or a process evaluation. (These approaches should not

---

* This chapter draws heavily on a paper prepared by Laura Rawlings, *Implementation Issues in Impact Evaluation,* Processed, 1999.

Box 2.1 Main Steps in Designing and Implementing Impact Evaluations

During Project Identification and Preparation

1. Determining whether or not to carry out an evaluation
2. Clarifying objectives of the evaluation
3. Exploring data availability
4. Designing the evaluation
5. Forming the evaluation team
6. If data will be collected:
    (a) Sample design and selection
    (b) Data collection instrument development
    (c) Staffing and training fieldwork personnel
    (d) Pilot testing
    (e) Data collection
    (f) Data management and access

During Project Implementation

7. Ongoing data collection
8. Analyzing the data
9. Writing up the findings and discussing them with policymakers and other stakeholders
10. Incorporating the findings in project design

be seen as substitutes for impact evaluations; indeed they often form critical complements to impact evaluations.) And perhaps the most important inputs to the decision of whether or not to carry out an evaluation are strong political and financial support.

The additional effort and resources required for conducting impact evaluations are best mobilized when the project is innovative, is replicable, involves substantial resource allocations, and has well-defined interventions. For example, the impact evaluation of the Bolivian Social Investment Fund met each of these criteria. First, the new social fund model introduced in Bolivia was considered innovative and replicable; second, the social fund has been responsible for roughly 25 percent of all public investments in Bolivia since the beginning of the evaluation; and third, the interventions were well-defined by the social fund menu of subprojects.

Impact evaluations should also be prioritized if the project in question is launching a new approach such as a pilot program that will later be under consideration for expansion based on the results of the evaluation, or the new World Bank Learning and Innovation Loans. This rationale made the Nicaraguan school autonomy reform a good candidate for an impact evaluation. The evaluation study accompanied the government's testing of a new decentralized school management model from its pilot stage in the mid-1990s through its expansion to almost all secondary schools and about half of all primary schools today. The evaluation was managed by a closely coordinated international team including local staff from the Ministry of Education's research and evaluation unit and the World Bank's Primary Education Project coordination office in Managua. Their involvement ensured that the evaluation informed key policy decisions regarding the modification and expansion of the pilot.

Another important consideration is to ensure that the program that is to be evaluated is sufficiently developed to be subject to an impact evaluation. Pilot projects and nascent reforms are often prone to revisions regarding their content as well as how, when, and by whom they will be implemented. These changes can undermine the coherence of the evaluation effort, particularly experimental designs and other types of prospective evaluations that rely on baseline and follow-up data of clearly established treatment and control groups. Where the policies to be evaluated are still being defined, it may be advisable to avoid using an impact evaluation in order to allow for flexibility in the project.

Gaining support from policymakers and financiers for an impact evaluation can be challenging but is a prerequisite for proceeding. They must be convinced that the evaluation is a useful exercise addressing questions that will be relevant to decisions concerning the evaluated program's refinement, expansion, or curtailment. They must also be convinced of the legitimacy of the evaluation design and therefore the results, particularly when the results are not as positive as anticipated.

Financing for an impact evaluation remains a difficult issue for program managers and client counterparts alike. The financing issue is compounded by the fact that data on evaluation costs are usually difficult to obtain. And perhaps the stickiest issue arises from the public good value of the evaluation: if the results of the evaluation are going to be used to inform policies applied outside of the national boundaries within which the evaluation is conducted, as is often the case, why should an individual country bear the cost of the evaluation? Among the case studies that had information on sources of funding, the information shows that countries often assume the majority, but not the entirety, of the evaluation costs. As is discussed more fully in chapter 4, many of the cases reviewed suggest that successfully implementing an impact evaluation requires not only a substantial resource commitment from the client countries but also the involvement of World Bank staff, or external researchers and consultants, necessitating resources beyond those provided by the country.

Clarifying Evaluation Objectives

Once it has been determined that an impact evaluation is appropriate and justified, establishing clear objectives and agreement on the core issues that will be the focus of the evaluation up front will contribute greatly to its success. Clear objectives are essential to identifying information needs, setting output and impact indicators, and constructing a solid evaluation strategy to provide answers to the questions posed. The use of a logical (log) framework approach provides a good and commonly used tool for identifying the goals of the project and the information needs around which the evaluation can be constructed.

The log frame, increasingly used at the World Bank, is based on a simple four-by-four matrix that matches information on project objectives with how performance will be tracked using milestones and work schedules, what impact project outputs will have on a beneficiary institution or system and how that will be measured, and how inputs are used to deliver outputs (see Annex 5 for examples). In other words, it is assumed that the project's intended impact is a function of the project's outputs as well as a series of other factors. The outputs, in turn, are a function of the project's inputs and factors outside the project. Quantifiable measures should then be identified for each link in the project cycle. This approach does not preclude the evaluator from also looking at the unintended impacts of a project but serves to keep the objectives of the evaluation clear and focused. Qualitative techniques are also useful in eliciting participation in clarifying the objectives of the evaluation and resulting impact indicators.

Although a statement of the objective would seem on the face of it to be one of the easiest parts of the evaluation process, it can be extremely difficult. For example, statements that are too broad do not lend themselves to evaluation. The objective statement in the Mexico PROBECAT evaluation (Annex 1.9) that the evaluation is about "the effect of the PROBECAT training program on labor market outcomes" would be more precise if it were narrowed down to the effect of PROBECAT on hours worked, hourly earnings, monthly salary, and time to first job placement for different types of workers. The Mexico PROGRESA evaluation provides a good example of creating a clear outline and delineating multiple objectives from the start with a separate discussion of each component—with objectives detailed in subcategories (Annex 1.10). This was particularly important because the intervention was quite complex, with the evaluation having to address not only the program impact but also aspects of program operations targeting and timing.

Reviewing other evaluation components such as cost-effectiveness or process evaluations may also be important objectives of a study and can complement the impact evaluation. Cost-effectiveness may be of particular concern for policymakers whose decision it will be to curtail, expand, or reform the intervention being evaluated. On issues related to service delivery, a process evaluation may be relevant to assess the procedures, dynamics, norms, and constraints under which a particular program is carried out.

Exploring Data Availability

Many types of data can be used to carry out impact evaluation studies. These can include a range from cross-sectional or panel surveys to qualitative open-ended interviews. Ideally this information is available at the individual level to ensure that true impact can be assessed. Household-level information can conceal intrahousehold resource allocation, which affects women and children because they often have more limited access to household productive resources. In many cases, the impact evaluation will take advantage of some kind of existing data or piggyback on an ongoing survey, which can save considerably on costs. With this approach, however, problems may arise in the timing of the data collection effort and with the flexibility of the questionnaire design. Box 2.2 highlights some key points to remember in exploring the use of existing data resources for the impact evaluation.

With some creativity, it may be possible to maximize existing information resources. A good example is the evaluation of the Honduran Social Investment Fund (see chapter 4). This study used a module from the national income and expenditure survey in the social fund questionnaire, thereby allowing social fund beneficiaries' income to be compared with national measures to assess poverty targeting (Walker and others 1999).

At the most basic level, data on the universe of the population of interest will be required as a basis from which to determine sample sizes, construct the sampling frame, and select the sample. Other types of data that may be available in a given country and can be used for different impact evaluations include (see Valadez and Bamberger 1994): household income and expenditure surveys; Living Standards Measurement Studies (LSMSs); labor market surveys; records of cooperatives, credit unions, and other financial institutions; school records on attendance, repetition, and examination performance; public health records on infant mortality,

Box 2.2 Key Points for Identifying Data Resources for Impact Evaluation

- Know the program well. It is risky to embark on an evaluation without knowing a lot about the administrative and institutional details of the program; that information typically comes from the program administration.
- Collect information on the relevant "stylized facts" about the setting. The relevant facts might include the poverty map, the way the labor market works, the major ethnic divisions, and other relevant public programs.
- Be eclectic about data. Sources can embrace both informal, unstructured interviews with participants in the program and quantitative data from representative samples. However, it is extremely difficult to ask counterfactual questions in interviews or focus groups; try asking someone who is currently participating in a public program: "What would you be doing now if this program did not exist?" Talking to program participants can be valuable, but it is unlikely to provide a credible evaluation on its own.
- Ensure that there is data on the outcome indicators and relevant explanatory variables. The latter need to deal with heterogeneity in outcomes conditional on program participation. Outcomes can differ depending, for example, on whether one is educated. It may not be possible to see the impact of the program unless one controls for that heterogeneity.
- Depending on the methods used, data might also be needed on variables that influence participation but do not influence outcomes given participation. These instrumental variables can be valuable in sorting out the likely causal effects of nonrandom programs (box 1.2).
- The data on outcomes and other relevant explanatory variables can be either quantitative or qualitative. But it has to be possible to organize the information in some sort of systematic data structure. A simple and common example is that one has values of various variables including one or more outcome indicators for various observation units (individuals, households, firms, communities).
- The variables one has data on and the observation units one uses are often chosen as part of the evaluation method. These choices

(Box continues on the following page.)

Box 2.2 *(continued)*

should be anchored to the prior knowledge about the program (its objectives, of course, but also how it is run) and the setting in which it is introduced.

- The specific source of the data on outcomes and their determinants, including program participation, typically comes from survey data of some sort. The observation unit could be the household, firm, or geographic area, depending on the type of program one is studying.
- Survey data can often be supplemented with useful other data on the program (such as from the project monitoring database) or setting (such as from geographic databases).

incidence of different infectious diseases, number of women seeking advice on contraception, or condom consumption; specialized surveys conducted by universities, nongovernmental organizations (NGOs), and consulting groups; monitoring data from program administrators; and project case studies.

Using Existing Survey Data. Many surveys may also be in the planning stages or are ongoing. If a survey measuring the required indicators is planned, the evaluation may be able to oversample the population of interest during the course of the general survey (for example, to use for the propensity score matching approach) as was done for the Nicaraguan Social Investment Fund evaluation and the Argentine TRA-BAJAR workfare program evaluation (Jalan and Ravallion 1998). Conversely, if a survey is planned that will cover the population of interest, the evaluation may be able to introduce a question or series of questions as part of the survey or add a qualitative survey to supplement the quantitative information. For example, the Credit with Education program in Ghana included a set of qualitative interviews with key stakeholders as well as with nonparticipant and participant focus groups that provided qualitative confirmation of the quantitative results (Annex 1.6). The evaluation assessed the impact of the program on the nutritional status and food security of poor households. Quantitative data included specific questions on household income and expenditure and skills level, whereas qualitative data focused on women's empowerment—status and decisionmaking in the household, social networks, self-confidence, and so forth.

Designing the Evaluation

Once the objectives and data resources are clear, it is possible to begin the design phase of the impact evaluation study. The choice of methodologies will depend on the evaluation question, timing, budget constraints, and implementation capacity. The pros and cons of the different design types discussed in chapter 1 should be balanced to determine which methodologies are most appropriate and how quantitative and qualitative techniques can be integrated to complement each other.

Even after the evaluation design has been determined and built into the project, evaluators should be prepared to be flexible and make modifications to the design as the project is implemented. In addition, provisions should be made for tracking the project interventions if the evaluation includes baseline and follow-up data so that the evaluation effort is parallel with the actual pace of the project.

In defining the design, it is also important to determine how the impact evaluation will fit into the broader monitoring and evaluation strategy applied to a project. All projects must be monitored so that administrators, lenders, and policymakers can keep track of the project as it unfolds. The evaluation effort, as argued above, must be tailored to the information requirements of the project.

Evaluation Question. The evaluation questions being asked are very much linked to the design of the evaluation in terms of the type of data collected, unit of analysis, methodologies used, and timing of the various stages. For example, in assessing the impact of textbooks on learning outcomes, it would be necessary to tailor the evaluation to measuring impact on students, classrooms, and teachers during a given school year. This would be very different than measuring the impact of services provided through social fund investments, which would require data on community facilities and households. The case studies in Annex I provide the other examples of how the evaluation question can affect the evaluation design.

In clarifying the evaluation questions, it is also important to consider the gender implications of project impact. At the outset this may not always be obvious, however; in project implementation there may be secondary effects on the household, which would not necessarily be captured without specific data collection and analysis efforts.

Timing and Budget Concerns. The most critical timing issue is whether it is possible to begin the evaluation design before the project is implemented and when the results will be needed. It is also useful to identify up front at which points during the project cycle information from the evaluation effort will be needed so that data collection and analysis activities can be linked. Having results in a timely manner can be crucial to policy decisions—for example, during a project review, around an election period, or when decisions regarding project continuation are being made.

Some methods require more time to implement than others. Random assignment and before-and-after methods (for example, reflexive comparisons) take longer to implement than ex-post matched-comparison approaches. When using before-and-after approaches that utilize baseline and follow-up assessments, time must be allowed for the last member of the treatment group to receive the intervention, and then usually more time is allowed for postprogram effects to materialize and be observed. Grossman (1994) suggests that 12 to 18 months after sample enrollment in the intervention is a typical period to allow before examining impacts. In World Bank projects with baselines, waiting for both the intervention to take place and the outcomes to materialize can take years. For example, in the evaluation of the Bolivian Social Investment Fund, which relied on baseline data collected in 1993, follow-up data was not collected until 1998 because of the time needed for the interventions (water and sanitation projects, health clinics, and schools) to be carried out and for effects on the beneficiary population's health and education outcomes to take place. A similar period of time has been required for the evaluation of a primary education project in Pakistan that used an experimental design with baseline and follow-up surveys to assess the impact of community schools on student outcomes, including academic achievement.

The timing requirements of the evaluation cannot drive the project being evaluated. By their very nature, evaluations are subject to the time frame established by the rest of the project. Evaluations must wait on projects that are slow to disburse and generate interventions. And even if projects move forward at the established pace, some interventions take longer to carry out, such as infrastructure projects. The time frame for the evaluation is also sensitive to the indicators selected because many, such as changes in fertility rates or educational achievement, take longer to manifest themselves in the beneficiary population.

Implementation Capacity. A final consideration in the scale and complexity of the evaluation design is the implementation capacity of the evaluation team. Implementation issues can be very challenging, particularly in developing countries where there is little experience with applied research and program evaluations. The composition of the evaluation team is very important, as well as team members' experience with different types of methodologies and their capacity relative to other activities being carried out by the evaluation unit. This is particularly relevant when working with public sector agencies with multiple responsibilities and limited staff. Awareness of the unit's workload is important in order to assess not only how it will affect the quality of evaluation being conducted but also the opportunity cost of the evaluation with respect to other efforts for which the unit is responsible. There are several examples of evaluation efforts that were derailed when key staff were called onto other projects and thus were not able to implement the collection of data on schedule at the critical point in time (such as a point during the school year or during agricultural season). Such situations can be avoided through coordination with managers in the unit responsible for the evaluation to ensure that a balance is achieved with respect to the timing of various activities, as well as the distribution of staff and resources across these activities. Alternatively, it can be preferable to contract a private firm to carry out the evaluation (discussed below).

Formation of the Evaluation Team

A range of skills is needed in evaluation work. The quality and eventual utility of the impact evaluation can be greatly enhanced with coordination between team members and policymakers from the outset. It is therefore important to identify team members as early as possible, agree upon roles and responsibilities, and establish mechanisms for communication during key points of the evaluation.

Among the core team is the evaluation manager, analysts (both economist and other social scientists), and, for evaluation designs involving new data collection, a sampling expert, survey designer, fieldwork manager and fieldwork team, and data managers and processors (for a comprehensive guide to designing and implementing surveys, see Grosh and Muñoz 1996). Depending on the size, scope, and design of the study, some of these responsibilities will be shared or other staffing needs may be added to this core team. In cases in which policy analysts may not have had experience integrating quantitative and qualitative approaches, it may be necessary to spend additional time at the initial team building stage to sensitize team members and ensure full collaboration. The broad responsibilities of team members include the following:

- Evaluation manager—The evaluation manager is responsible for establishing the information needs and indicators for the evaluation (which are often established with the client by using a logical framework approach), drafting terms of reference for the evaluation, selecting the evaluation methodology, and identifying the evaluation team. In many cases, the evaluation manager will also carry out policy analysis.

- Policy analysts—An economist is needed for the quantitative analysis, as well as a sociologist or anthropologist for ensuring participatory input and qualitative analysis at different stages of the impact evaluation. Both should be involved in writing the evaluation report.
- Sampling expert—The sampling expert can guide the sample selection process. For quantitative data, the sampling expert should be able to carry out power calculations to determine the appropriate sample sizes for the indicators established, select the sample, review the results of the actual sample versus the designed sample, and incorporate the sampling weights for the analysis. For qualitative data, the sampling expert should guide the sample selection process in coordination with the analysts, ensuring that the procedures established guarantee that the correct informants are selected. The sampling expert should also be tasked with selecting sites and groups for the pilot test and will often need to be paired with a local information coordinator responsible for collecting for the sampling expert data from which the sample will be drawn.
- Survey designer—This could be a person or team, whose responsibility is designing the data collection instruments, accompanying manuals and codebooks, and coordinating with the evaluation manager(s) to ensure that the data collection instruments will indeed produce the data required for the analysis. This person or team should also be involved in pilot testing and refining the questionnaires.
- Fieldwork manager and staff —The manager should be responsible for supervising the entire data collection effort, from planning the routes for the data collection to forming and scheduling the fieldwork teams, generally composed of supervisors and interviewers. Supervisors generally manage the fieldwork staff (usually interviewers, data entry operators, and drivers) and are responsible for the quality of data collected in the field. Interviewers administer the questionnaires. In some cultures, it is necessary to ensure that male and female interviewers carry out the surveys and that they are administered separately for men and women.
- Data managers and processors—These team members design the data entry programs, enter the data, check the data's validity, provide the needed data documentation, and produce basic results that can be verified by the data analysts.

In building up the evaluation team, there are also some important decisions that the evaluation manager must make about local capacity and the appropriate institutional arrangements to ensure impartiality and quality in the evaluation results. First is whether there is local capacity to implement the evaluation, or parts of it, and what kind of supervision and outside assistance will be needed. Evaluation capacity varies greatly from country to country, and although international contracts that allow for firms in one country to carry out evaluations in another country are becoming more common (one example is the Progresa evaluation being carried out by the International Food and Policy Research Institute), the general practice for World Bank–supported projects seems to be to implement the evaluation using local staff while providing a great deal of international supervision. Therefore, it is necessary to critically assess local capacity and determine who will be responsible for what aspects of the evaluation effort. Regardless of the final composition of the team, it is important to designate an evaluation manager who will be able to work effectively with the data producers as well as the analysts and policymakers using the data and the results of the evaluation. If this person is not based locally, it is recommended that a local manager be designated to coordinate the evaluation effort in conjunction with the international manager.

Second is whether to work with a private firm or public agency. Private firms can be more dependable with respect to providing results on a timely basis, but capacity building in the public sector is lost and often private firms are understandably less amenable to incorporating elements into the evaluation that will make the effort costlier. Whichever counterpart or combination of counterparts is finally crafted, a sound review of potential collaborators' past evaluation activities is essential to making an informed choice.

And third is what degree of institutional separation to put in place between the evaluation providers and the evaluation users. There is much to be gained from the objectivity provided by having the evaluation carried out independently of the institution responsible for the project being evaluated. However, evaluations can often have multiple goals, including building evaluation capacity within government agencies and sensitizing program operators to the realities of their projects once these are carried out in the field. At a minimum, the evaluation users, who can range from policymakers in government agencies in client countries to NGO organizations, bilateral donors, and international development institutions, must remain sufficiently involved in the evaluation to ensure that the evaluation process is recognized as being legitimate and that the results produced are relevant to their information needs. Otherwise, the evaluation results are less likely to be used to inform policy. In the final analysis, the evaluation manager and his or her clients must achieve the right balance between involving the users of evaluations and maintaining the objectivity and legitimacy of the results.

Data Development

Having adequate and reliable data is a necessary input to evaluating project impact. High-quality data are essential to the validity of the evaluation results. As discussed above, assessing what data exist is a first important step before launching any new data collection efforts. Table 2.1 links the basic evaluation methodologies with data requirements. Most of these methodologies can incorporate qualitative and participatory techniques in the design of the survey instrument, in the identification of indicators, and in input to the identification of controls, variables used for matching, or in instrumental variables.

Table 2.1 Evaluation Methods and Corresponding Data Requirements

Method	Data requirement Minimal	Data requirement Ideal	Use of qualitative approach
Experimental or randomized controls	Single project cross-section with and without beneficiaries	Baseline and follow-up surveys on both beneficiaries and nonbeneficiaries. Allows for control of contemporaneous events, in addition to providing control for measuring impact. (This allows for a difference-in-difference estimation.)	• Inform design of survey instrument, sampling • Identify indicators • Data collection and recording using – Textual data – Informal or semi-structured interviews – Focus groups or community meetings – Direct observation – Participatory methods – Photographs – Triangulation – Data analysis
Nonexperimental designs a) Constructed controls or matching	Large survey, census, national budget, or LSMS type of surveyæt hat oversamples beneficiaries	Large survey, and smaller project-based household survey, both with two points in time to control for contemporaneous events	
b) Reflexive comparisons and double difference	Baseline and follow-up on beneficiaries	Time series or panel on beneficiaries and comparable non-	

Table 2.1 *(continued)*

| Method | Data requirement | | Use of qualitative approach |
	Minimal	Ideal	
		beneficiaries	
c) Statistical control or instrumental variable	Cross-section data representative of beneficiary population with corresponding instrumental variables	Cross-section and time series representative of both the beneficiary and nonbeneficiary population with corresponding instrumental variables	

Sources: Adapted from Ezemenari, Rudqvist, and Subbarao (1999) and Bamberger

For evaluations that will generate their own data, there are the critical steps of designing the data collection instruments, sampling, fieldwork, data management, and data access. This section does not outline the step-by-step process of how to undertake a survey but rather provides a brief discussion of these steps. Some of the discussion in this section, notably regarding sampling and data management, is more relevant to evaluations based on the collection and analysis of larger-scale sample surveys using quantitative data than for evaluations using qualitative data and small sample sizes.

Deciding What to Measure. The main output and impact indicators should be established in planning the evaluation, possibly as part of a logical framework approach. To ensure that the evaluation is able to assess outcomes during a period of time relevant to decisionmakers' needs, a hierarchy of indicators might be established, ranging from short-term impact indicators such as school attendance to longer-term indicators such as student achievement. This ensures that even if final impacts are not picked up initially, program outputs can be assessed. In addition, the evaluator should plan on measuring the delivery of intervention as well as taking account of exogenous factors that may have an effect on the outcome of interest.

Evaluation managers can also plan to conduct the evaluation across several time periods, allowing for more immediate impacts to be picked up earlier while still tracking final outcome measures. This was done in the Nicaragua School Reform evaluation, in which the shorter-term impact of the reform on parental participation and student and teacher attendance was established and the longer-term impacts on student achievement are still being assessed.

Information on the characteristics of the beneficiary population not strictly related to the impact evaluation but of interest in the analysis might also be considered, such as their level of poverty or their opinion of the program. In addition, the evaluator may also want to include cost measures in order to do some cost-effectiveness analysis or other complementary assessments not strictly related to the impact evaluation.

The type of evaluation design selected for the impact evaluation will also carry data requirements. These will be specific to the methodology, population of interest, impact measures, and other elements of the evaluation. For example, if an instrumental variable approach (one of the types of matched-comparison strategies) is to be used, the variable(s) that will serve as the instrument to separate program participation from the outcome measures must be identified and included in the data collection. This was done for the Bolivian Social Investment Fund impact evaluation, in which knowledge of the social fund and the presence of NGOs were used as instrumental variables in assessing the impact of social fund interventions.

It can be useful to develop a matrix for the evaluation, listing the question of interest, the outcome indicators that will be used to assess the results, the variable, and the source of data for the variable. This matrix can then be used to review questionnaires and plan the analytical work as was done in the evaluation of the Nicaragua Emergency Social Investment Fund (see Annex 6).

Developing Data Collection Instruments and Approaches. Developing appropriate data collection instruments that will generate the required data to answer the evaluation questions can be tricky. This will require having the analysts involved in the development of the questions, in the pilot test, and in the review of the data from the pilot test. Involving both the field manager and the data manager during the development of the instruments, as well as local staff—preferably analysts who can provide knowledge of the country and the program—can be critical to the quality of information collected (Grosh and Muñoz 1996.) It is also important to ensure thatthe data collected can be disaggregated by gender to explore the differential impact of specific programs and policies.

Quantitative evaluations usually collect and record information either in a numeric form or as precoded categories. With qualitative evaluations, information is generally presented as descriptive text with little or no categorization. The information may include an individual's responses to open-ended interview questions, notes taken during focus groups, or the evaluator's observations of events. Some qualitative studies use the precoded classification of data as well (Bamberger, 2000). The range of data collection instruments and their strengths and weaknesses are summarized in table 2.2—the most commonly used technique being questionnaires.

The responses to survey questionnaires can be very sensitive to design; thus it is important to ensure that the structure and format are appropriate, preferably undertaken by experienced staff. For example, the utility of quantitative data has often been severely handicapped for simple mechanical reasons, such as the inability to link data from one source to another. This was the case in a national education assessment in one country where student background data could not be linked to test score results, which made it impossible to assess the influence of student characteristics on performance or to classify the tests scores by students' age, gender, socioeconomic status, or educational history.

For both qualitative and quantitative data collection, even experienced staff must be trained to collect the data specific to the evaluation, and all data collection should be guided by a set of manuals that can be used as orientation during training and as a reference during the fieldwork. Depending on the complexity of the data collection task, the case examples show that training can range from three days to several weeks.

Pilot testing is an essential step because it will reveal whether the instrument can reliably produce the required data and how the data collection procedures can be put into operation. The pilot test should mimic the actual fieldwork as closely as possible. For this reason, it is useful to have data entry programs ready at the time of the pilot to test their functionality as well as to pilot test across the different populations and geographical areas to be included in the actual fieldwork.

Sampling. Sampling is an art best practiced by an experienced sampling specialist. The design need not be complicated, but it should be informed by the sampling specialist's expertise in the determination of appropriate sampling frames, sizes, and selection strategies. (The discussion on sampling included here refers primarily to issues related to evaluations that collect quantitative data from larger, statistically representative samples.) The sampling specialist should be incorporated in the evaluation process from the earliest stages to review the available information needed to select the sample and determine whether any enumeration work will be needed, which can be time consuming.

As with other parts of the evaluation work, coordination between the sampling specialist and the evaluation team is important. This becomes particularly critical in conducting matched comparisons because the sampling design becomes the basis for the "match" that is at the core of the

Table 2.2 Main Data Collection Instruments for Impact Evaluation

Technique	Definition and use	Strengths	Weaknesses
Case studies	Collecting information that results in a story that can be descriptive or explanatory and can serve to answer the questions of how and why	– Can deal with a full variety of evidence from documents, interviews, observation – Can add explanatory power when focus is on institutions, processes, programs, decisions, and events	– Good case studies are difficult to do – Require specialized research and writing skills to be rigorous – Findings not generalizable to population – Time consuming – Difficult to replicate
Focus groups	Holding focused discussions with members of target population who are familiar with pertinent issues before writing a set of structured questions. The purpose is to compare the beneficiaries' perspectives with abstract concepts in the evaluation's objectives.	– Similar advantages to interviews (below) – Particularly useful where participant interaction is desired – A useful way of identifying hierarchical influences	– Can be expensive and time consuming – Must be sensitive to mixing of hierarchical levels – Not generalizable
Interviews	The interviewer asks questions of one or more persons and records the respondents' answers. Interviews may be formal or informal, face-to-face or by telephone, or closed- or open-ended.	– People and institutions can explain their experiences in their own words and setting – Flexible to allow the interviewer to pursue unanticipated lines of inquiry and to probe into issues in depth	– Time consuming – Can be expensive – If not done properly, the interviewer can influence interviewee's response

Method	Description	Advantages	Disadvantages
		– Particularly useful where language difficulties are anticipated – Greater likelihood of getting input from senior officials	
Observation	Observing and recording situation in a log or diary. This includes who is involved; when, where, what happens; and how events occur. Observation can be direct (observer watches and records), or participatory (the observer becomes part of the setting for a period of time).	– Provides descriptive information on context and observed changes	– Quality and usefulness of data highly dependent on the observer's observational and writing skills – Findings can be open to interpretation – Does not easily apply within a short time frame to process change
Questionnaires	Developing a set of survey questions whose answers can be coded consistently	– Can reach a wide sample, simultaneously – Allow respondents time to think before they answer – Can be answered anonymously – Impose uniformity by asking all respondents the same things – Make data compilation and comparison easier	– The quality of responses highly dependent on the clarity of questions – Sometimes difficult to persuade people to complete and return questionnaire – Can involve forcing institutional activities and people's experiences into predetermined categories – Can be time consuming
Written document analysis	Reviewing documents such as records, administrative databases, training materials, and correspondence.	– Can identify issues to investigate further and provide evidence of action, change, and impact to support respondents' perceptions – Can be inexpensive	

Source: Adapted from Taschereau (1998).

evaluation design and construction of the counterfactual. In these cases, the sampling specialist must work closely with the evaluation team to develop the criteria that will be applied to match the treatment and comparison groups. For example, in the evaluation of the Nicaragua school autonomy reform project, autonomous schools were stratified by type of school, enrollment, length of time in the reform, and location and matched to a sample of nonautonomous schools by using the same stratifications except length of time in the reform. This can be facilitated by having a team member responsible for the data collection work assist the sampling specialist in obtaining the required information, including data on the selected outcome indicators for the power calculations (an estimate of the sample size required to test for statistical significance between two groups), a list of the population of interest for the sample selection, and details on the characteristics of the potential treatment and comparison groups important to the sample selection process.

There are many tradeoffs between costs and accuracy in sampling that should be made clear as the sampling framework is being developed. For example, conducting a sample in two or three stages will reduce the costs of both the sampling and the fieldwork, but the sampling errors and therefore the precision of the estimates will be increased.

Once the outcome variables and population(s) of interest have been determined by the evaluation team, a first step for the sampling specialist would be to determine the power calculations (see Valadez and Bamberger 1994, pp. 382–84, for a discussion of the power calculation process). Since the power calculation can be performed using only one outcome measure, and evaluations often consider several, some strategic decisions will need to be made regarding which outcome indicator to use when designing the sample.

After developing the sampling strategy and framework, the sampling specialist should also be involved in selecting the sample for the fieldwork and the pilot test to ensure that the pilot is not conducted in an area that will be included in the sample for the fieldwork. Often initial fieldwork will be required as part of the sample selection procedure. For example, an enumeration process will be required if there are no up-to-date maps of units required for the sample (households, schools, and so forth) or if a certain population of interest, such as malnourished children, needs to be pre-identified so that it can be selected for the purpose of the evaluation.

Once the fieldwork is concluded, the sampling specialist should provide assistance on determining sampling weights to compute the expansion factors and correct for sampling errors and nonresponse. (Grosh and Muñoz 1996 provide a detailed discussion of sampling procedures as part of household survey work. Kish 1965 is considered one of the standard textbooks in the sampling field.) And finally, the sampling specialist should produce a sampling document detailing the sampling strategy, including (a) from the sampling design stage, the power calculations using the impact variables, the determination of sampling errors and sizes, the use of stratification to analyze populations of interest; (b) from the sample selection stage, an outline of the sampling stages and selection procedures; (c) from the fieldwork stage to prepare for analysis, the relationship between the size of the sample and the population from which it was selected, nonresponse rates, and other information used to inform sampling weights; and any additional information that the analyst would need to inform the use of the evaluation data. This document can be used to maintain the evaluation project records and should be included with the data whenever it is distributed to help guide the analysts in using the evaluation data.

Questionnaires. The design of the questionnaire is important to the validity of the information collected. There are four general types of information required for an impact evaluation (Valadez and Bamberger 1994). These include

- Classification of nominal data with respondents classified according to whether they are project participants or belong to the comparison group;
- Exposure to treatment variables recording not only the services and benefits received but also the frequency, amount, and quality—assessing quality can be quite difficult;
- Outcome variables to measure the effects of a project, including immediate products, sustained outputs or the continued delivery of services over a long period, and project impacts such as improved income and employment; and
- Intervening variables that affect participation in a project or the type of impact produced, such as individual, household, or community characteristics—these variables can be important for exploring biases.

The way in which the question is asked, as well as the ordering of the questions, is also quite important in generating reliable information. A relevant example is the measurement of welfare, which would be required for measuring the direct impact of a project on poverty reduction. Asking individuals about their income level would not necessarily yield accurate results on their level of economic well- being. As discussed in the literature on welfare measurement, questions on expenditures, household composition, assets, gifts and remittances, and the imputed value of homegrown food and owner-occupied housing are generally used to capture the true value of household and individual welfare. The time recall used for expenditure items, or the order in which these questions are asked, can significantly affect the validity of the information collected.

Among the elements noted for a good questionnaire are keeping it short and focused on important questions, ensuring that the instructions and questions are clear, limiting the questions to those needed for the evaluation, including a "no opinion" option for closed questions to ensure reliable data, and using sound procedures to administer the questionnaire, which may indeed be different for quantitative and qualitative surveys.

Fieldwork Issues. Working with local staff who have extensive experience in collecting data similar to that needed for the evaluation can greatly facilitate fieldwork operations. Not only can these staff provide the required knowledge of the geographical territory to be covered, but their knowledge can also be critical to developing the norms used in locating and approaching informants. Field staff whose expertise is in an area other than the one required for the evaluation effort can present problems, as was the case in an education evaluation in Nicaragua that used a firm specializing in public opinion polling to conduct a school and household survey. The expertise that had allowed this firm to gain an excellent reputation based on its accurate prediction of improbable election results was not useful for knowing how to approach school children or merge quantitative data sets. This lack of expertise created substantial survey implementation problems that required weeks of corrective action by a joint team from the Ministry of Education and the World Bank.

The type of staff needed to collect data in the field will vary according to the objectives and focus of the evaluation. For example, a quantitative impact evaluation of a nutrition program might require the inclusion of an anthropometrist to collect height-for-weight measures as part of a survey team, whereas the impact evaluation of an educational reform would most likely include staff specializing in the application of achievement tests to measure the impact of the reform on academic achievement. Most quantitative surveys will require at least a survey manager, data manager, field manager, field supervisors, interviewers, data entry operators, and drivers. Depending on the qualitative approach used, field staff may be similar with the exception of data entry operators. The skills of the interviewers, however, would be quite different, with qualitative interviewers requiring specialized training, particularly for focus groups, direct observation, and so forth.

Three other concerns are useful to remember when planning survey operations. First, it is important to take into consideration temporal events that can affect the operational success of the fieldwork and the external validity of the data collected, such as the school year calendar, holidays, rainy seasons, harvest times, or migration patterns. Second, it is crucial to pilot test data collection instruments, even if they are adaptations of instruments that have been used previously, both to test the quality of the instrument with respect to producing the required data and to familiarize fieldwork staff with the dynamics of the data collection process. Pilot tests can also serve as a proving ground for the selection of a core team of field staff to carry out the actual survey. Many experienced data collectors will begin with 10 to 20 percent more staff in the pilot test than will be used in the actual fieldwork and then select the best performers from the pilot to form the actual data collection teams. Finally, communications are essential to field operations. For example, if local conditions permit their use, fieldwork can be enhanced by providing supervisors with cellular phones so that they can be in touch with the survey manager, field manager, and other staff to answer questions and keep them informed of progress.

Data Management and Access. The objectives of a good data management system should be to ensure the timeliness and quality of the evaluation data. Timeliness will depend on having as much integration as possible between data collection and processing so that errors can be verified and corrected prior to the conclusion of fieldwork. The quality of the data can be ensured by applying consistency checks to test the internal validity of the data collected both during and after the data are entered and by making sure that proper documentation is available to the analysts who will be using the data. Documentation should consist of two types of information: (a) information needed to interpret the data, including codebooks, data dictionaries, guides to constructed variables, and any needed translations; and (b) information needed to conduct the analysis, which is often included in a basic information document that contains a description of the focus and objective of the evaluation, details on the evaluation methodology, summaries or copies of the data collection instruments, information on the sample, a discussion of the fieldwork, and guidelines for using the data.

It is recommended that the data produced by evaluations be made openly available given the public good value of evaluations and the possible need to do additional follow-up work to assess long-term impacts by a team other than the one that carried out the original evaluation work. To facilitate the data-sharing process, at the outset of the evaluation an open data access policy should be agreed upon and signed, establishing norms and responsibilities for data distribution. An open data access policy puts an added burden on good data documentation and protecting the confidentiality of the informants. If panel data are collected from the same informants over time by different agencies, the informants will have to be identified to conduct the follow-up work. This requirement should be balanced against the confidentiality norms that generally accompany any social sector research. One possible solution is to make the anonymous unit record data available to all interested analysts but ask researchers interested in conducting follow-up work to contact the agency in charge of the data in order to obtain the listing of the units in the sample, thereby giving the agency an opportunity to ensure quality control in future work through contact with the researchers seeking to carry it out.

Analysis, Reporting, and Dissemination

As with other stages of the evaluation process, the analysis of the evaluation data, whether quantitative or qualitative, requires collaboration between the analysts, data producers, and policymakers to clarify questions and ensure timely, quality results. Problems with the cleaning and interpretation of data will almost surely arise during analysis and require input from various team members.

Some of the techniques and challenges of carrying out quantitative analysis based on statistical methods are included in chapter 3. There are also many techniques for analyzing qualitative data (see Miles and Huberman 1994). Although a detailed discussion of these methods is beyond the scope of this handbook, two commonly used methods for impact evaluation are mentioned—content analysis and case analysis (Taschereau 1998).

Content analysis is used to analyze data drawn from interviews, observations, and documents. In reviewing the data, the evaluator develops a classification system for the data, organizing information based on (a) the evaluation questions for which the information was collected; (b) how the material will be used; and (c) the need for cross-referencing the information. The coding of data can be quite complex and may require many assumptions. Once a classification system has been set up, the analysis phase begins, also a difficult process. This involves looking for patterns in the data and moving beyond description toward developing an understanding of program processes, outcomes, and impacts. This is best carried out with the involvement of team members. New ethnographic and linguistic computer programs are also now available, designed to support the analysis of qualitative data.

Case analysis is based on case studies designed for in-depth study of a particular group or individual. The high level of detail can provide rich information for evaluating project impact. The processes of collecting and analyzing the data are carried out simultaneously as evaluators make observations as they are collecting information. They can then develop and test explanations and link critical pieces of information.

Whether analyzing the quantitative or qualitative information, a few other general lessons related to analysis, reporting, and dissemination can also be drawn from the case examples in Annex 1.

First, analysis commonly takes longer than anticipated, particularly if the data are not as clean or accessible at the beginning of the analysis, if the analysts are not experienced with the type of evaluation work, or if there is an emphasis on capacity building through collaborative work. In the review of the case studies considered for this article, the most rapid analysis took approximately one year after producing the data and the longer analysis took close to two years. The case in chapter 3 illustrates some of the many steps involved in analysis and why it can take longer than anticipated.

Second, the evaluation manager should plan to produce several products as outputs from the analytical work, keeping in mind two elements. The first is to ensure the timing of outputs around key events when decisions regarding the future of the project will be made, such as mid-term reviews, elections, or closings of a pilot phase. The second is the audience for the results. Products should be differentiated according to the audience for which they are crafted, including government policymakers, program managers, donors, the general public, journalists, and academics.

Third, the products will have the most policy relevance if they include clear and practical recommendations stemming from the impact analysis. These can be broken into short- and long-term priorities, and when possible, should include budgetary implications. Decisionmakers will be prone to look for the "bottom line."

Finally, the reports should be planned as part of a broader dissemination strategy, which can include presentations for various audiences, press releases, feedback to informants, and making information available on the Web. Such a dissemination strategy should be included in the initial stages of the planning process to ensure that it is included in the budget and that the results reach the intended audience.

Chapter 3
Applying Analytical Methods for Impact Evaluation: A Case Study*

This case study is based on a hypothetical antipoverty program, PROSCOL, which provides cash transfers targeted to poor families with school-age children in one region of a given developing country. The case is intended to illustrate the analytical steps involved in carrying out an impact evaluation and the options an analyst may face, with the process applicable to any type of antipoverty program. In exploring how to go about evaluating the impact of the program, the policy analyst makes several common errors along the way, seeking input on specific topics from the specialized skills of colleagues—a statistician, an economist, an econometrics professor, and a sociologist.

Among the analytical steps that the analyst goes through in the case are identifying the questions to be addressed in the impact evaluation, assessing data resources, taking a first look at the data, understanding biases, learning about forgone income, adding control variables, understanding the importance of exogeneity, exploring better ways to form a comparison group (propensity score matching), learning about biases due to unobservables, reviewing what could have been done with a baseline survey (double differences), using instrumental variables, testing the various methodologies, incorporating input from the field, and planning for future work.

Description of the Hypothetical Program, PROSCOL

The PROSCOL program identifies families eligible for participation using various poverty proxies, which include the number of people in the household, the education of the head, and various attributes of the dwelling. PROSCOL pays a fixed amount per school-age child to all selected households on the condition that the children attend 85 percent of their school classes, which has to be verified by a note from the school. Households must keep their children in school until 18 years of age.

This program was introduced 12 months ago, is financed by the World Bank, and operates out of the Ministry of Social Development. In an effort

---

* This chapter draws heavily on a background paper by Martin Ravallion, *The Mystery of the Vanishing Benefits: Ms. Speedy Analyst's Introduction to Evaluation*, Policy Research Working Paper No. 2153, 1999.

to assess PROSCOL's impact on poverty in order to help determine whether the program should be expanded to include the rest of the country or be dropped, the World Bank has requested an impact evaluation by the Ministry of Finance. The request was to the Ministry of Finance so as to help assure an independent evaluation and to help develop capacity for this type of evaluation in a central unit of the government—close to where the budgetary allocations are being made.

Identifying the Questions to Be Addressed in the Impact Evaluation

The first step for the analyst in the Ministry of Finance assigned to the task of carrying out the PROSCOL evaluation is to clarify which project objectives will be looked at in evaluating impact. The project has two policy goals: the cash transfers aim to reduce current poverty, and by insisting that transfer recipients keep their kids in school the program aims to reduce future poverty by raising education levels among the current population of poor children. Two pieces of information would therefore be needed about the program to assess impact. First, are the cash transfers mainly going to low-income families? And second, how much is the program increasing school enrollment rates?

Assessing Data Resources

To carry out the evaluation the analyst has two main resources. The first is a report based on qualitative interviews with program administrators and focus groups of participants. It is not clear, however, whether those interviewed were representative of PROSCOL participants, or how poor they were relative to those who were not picked for the program and were not interviewed. The report says that the children went to school, but it is possible that they might have also gone to school if the program had not existed. Although this report is an important start, it does not tell the analyst how poor PROSCOL participants are and what impact the program has on schooling. The second resource is a recent independent national household survey carried out by the country's Bureau of Statistics, called the Living Standards Survey (LSS). The LSS included a random sample of 10,000 households and asked about household incomes by source, employment, expenditures, health status, education attainments, and demographic and other attributes of the family. The survey had incorporated a question on whether or not the sampled household had participated in PROSCOL and a line item for money received from PROSCOL in the listing of income sources.

Taking a First Look at the Data

The analyst then proceeds with obtaining the raw LSS data set to focus on assessing who is benefiting from the program. She uses a statistical software package such as SPSS or SAS to generate a cross-tabulation of the average amount received from PROSCOL by household deciles, where the deciles are formed by ranking all households in the sample according to their income per person. In calculating the latter, the analyst decides to subtract any monies received from PROSCOL as a good measure of income in the absence of the program with the intent of identifying who gained according to his or her preintervention income.

The cross-tabulation suggests that the cash transfers under the program are quite well-targeted to the poor. By the country's official poverty line, about 30 percent of the population in the Northwest is poor. From the table, calculations show that the poorest 30 percent of the survey sample receive 70 percent of the PROSCOL transfers. At first glance, this appears to be a positive result.

The next question is about the impact on schooling. This is looked at through a cross-tabulation of average school enrollment rates of various age groups for PROSCOL families versus non-PROSCOL families. This suggests almost no difference between the two; the average enrollment rate for kids aged 6 to 18 is about 80 percent in both cases. The analyst then calculates average years of schooling at each age, and the results are plotted separately for PROSCOL families and non-PROSCOL families. This shows that the two figures are not identical, but they are very close. At this stage, the analyst wonders whether there was really no impact on schooling, or whether the approach is wrong.

Understanding Biases

With this uncertainty the analyst next seeks input from a senior statistician to explore why the results suggest that PROSCOL children are no more likely to be in school than non-PROSCOLchildren. The statistician hypothesizes that the results may have a serious bias. In order to assess program impact, we need to know what would have happened without the program. Yet the analyst has not accounted for this; instead the non-PROSCOL families are used as the comparison group for inferring what the schooling of the PROSCOL participants would have been if the program had not existed.

In other words, P_i denotes PROSCOL participation of the ith child. This can take two possible values, namely $P_i = 1$ if the child participates in PROSCOL and $P_i = 0$ if he or she does not. If the ith child does not participate, then its level of schooling is S_{0i}, which stands for child i's schooling S when $P = 0$. If the child does participate then its schooling is S_{1i}. Its gain in schooling due to PROSCOL is S_{1i}–S_{0i}. The gain for the ith child who participates ($P = 1$) is then

$$G_i = S_{1i} - S_{0i} \mid P_i = 1.$$

The | stands for "given that" or "conditional on" and is needed to make it clear that the calculation is the gain for a child who actually participated. If one wants to know the average gain, this is simply the mean of all the G's, which gives the sample mean gain in schooling among all those who participated in PROSCOL. As long as this mean is calculated correctly (using the appropriate sample weights from the survey), it will provide an unbiased estimate of the true mean gain. The latter is the "expected value" of G, and it can be written as

$$G = E(S_{1i} - S_{0i} \mid P_i = 1).$$

This is another way of saying "mean." However, it need not be exactly equal to the mean calculated from the sample data, given that there will be some sampling error. In the evaluation literature, $E(S_{1i} - S_{0i} \mid P_I = 1)$ is sometimes called the "treatment effect" or the "average treatment effect on the treated." In this case PROSCOL is considered the treatment.

The statistician points out to the analyst that she has not calculated G, but rather the difference in mean schooling between children in PROSCOL families and those in non-PROSCOL families. This is the sample estimate of

$$D = E(S_{1i} \mid P = 1) - E(S_{0i} \mid P = 0).$$

There is a simple identity linking the D and G, namely:

$$D = G + B.$$

This term "B" is the bias in the estimate, and it is given by

$$B = E(S_{0i} \mid P_i = 1) - E(S_{0i} \mid P_i = 0).$$

In other words, the bias is the expected difference in schooling without PROSCOL between children who did in fact participate in the program and those who did not. This bias could be corrected if $E(S_{0i} \mid P_i = 1)$ were known, but it is not possible to even get a sample estimate of that. One cannot observe what the schooling would have been of children who actually participated in PROSCOL had they not participated; that is missing data—also called a "counterfactual" mean.

This bias presents a major concern. In the absence of the program, PROSCOL parents may well send their children to school less than do other parents. If so, then there will be a bias in the calculation. Going back to the original evaluation questions, we are interested in the extra schooling due to PROSCOL. Presumably this only affects those families who actually participate. In other words, we need to know how much less schooling could be expected without the program. If there is no bias, then the extra schooling under the program is the difference in mean schooling between those who participated and those who did not. Thus the bias arises if there is a difference in mean schooling between PROSCOL parents and non-PROSCOL parents in the absence of the program.

To eliminate this bias, the best approach would be to assign the program randomly. Then participants and nonparticipants will have the same expected schooling in the absence of the program, that is, $E(S_{0i} | P_i = 1) = E(S_{0i} | P_i = 0)$. The schooling of nonparticipating families will then correctly reveal the counterfactual, that is, the schooling that we would have observed for participants had they not had access to the program. Indeed, random assignment will equate the whole distribution, not just the means. There will still be a bias owing to sampling error, but for large enough samples one can safely assume that any statistically significant difference in the distribution of schooling between participants and nonparticipants is attributable to the program.

Within the existing design of the program, it is clear that participation is not random. Indeed, it would be a serious criticism of PROSCOL to find that it was. The very fact of its purposive targeting to poor families, which are presumably less likely to send their kids to school, would create bias.

This raises the question, if PROSCOL is working well then we should expect participants to have worse schooling in the absence of the program. Then $E(S_{0i} | P_i = 1) < E(S_{0i} | P_i = 0)$ and the analysts' original calculation will underestimate the gain from the program. We may find little or no benefit even though the program is actually working well.

The analyst now realizes that the magnitude of this bias could be huge. Suppose that poor families send their kids to work rather than school; because they are poor and cannot borrow easily, they need the extra cash now. Nonpoor families send their kids to school. The program selects poor families, who then send their kids to school. One observes negligible difference in mean schooling between PROSCOL families and non-PROSCOL families; indeed, $E(S_{1i} | P_i = 1) = E(S_{0i} | P_i = 0)$ in expectation. But the impact of the program is positive, and is given by $E(S_{0i} | P_i = 0) - E(S_{0i} | P_i = 1)$. The failure to take account of the program's purposive, pro-poor targeting could well have led to a substantial underestimation of PROSCOL's benefits from the analyst's comparison of mean schooling between PROSCOL families and non-PROSCOL families.

Learning about Forgone Income

The analyst next shows the results of her cross-tabulation of amounts received from PROSCOL against income to another colleague, an economist in the Ministry of Finance. The economist raises a main concern—that the gains to the poor from PROSCOL have been clearly overestimated because foregone income has been ignored. Children have to go to school if the family is to get the PROSCOL transfer; thus they will not be able to work, either in the family business or in the labor market. For example, children aged 15 to 18 can earn two-thirds or more of the adult wage in agriculture and construction. PROSCOL families will lose this income from their children's work. This foregone income should be taken into account when the net income gains from the program are calculated. And this net income gain should be subtracted, not the gross transfer, to work out preintervention income. This will also matter in determining how poor the family would have been in the absence of the PROSCOL transfer. The current table, therefore, might greatly overstate the program's gains to the poor.

The analyst wonders why she should factor out the forgone income from child labor, assuming that less child labor is a good thing. The economist highlights that she should look at the gains from reducing child labor, of which the main gain is the extra schooling, and hence higher future incomes, for currently poor families. The analyst has produced tables that reflect the two main ways PROSCOL reduces poverty: by increasing the current incomes of the poor and by increasing their future incomes. The impact on child labor matters to both, but in opposite directions; thus PROSCOL faces a tradeoff.

This highlights why it is important to get a good estimate of the impact on schooling; only then will it be possible to determine the forgone income. It is, for example, possible that the extra time at school comes out of nonwork time.

With regard to the second cross-tabulation, the main concern raised by the economist is that there is no allowance for all the other determinants of schooling, besides participation in PROSCOL. The economist suggests running a regression of years of schooling on a set of control variables as well as whether or not the child's family was covered by PROSCOL. For the ith child in the sample let

$$S_i = a + bP_i + cX_i + \varepsilon_i \ .$$

Here a, b, and c are parameters; X stands for the control variables, such as age of the child, mother's and father's education, the size and demographic composition of the household, and school characteristics; and ε is a residual that includes other determinants of schooling and measurement errors. The estimated value of b gives you the impact of PROSCOL on schooling.

Note that if the family of the ith child participates in PROSCOL, then $P = 1$ and so its schooling will be $a + b + cX_i + \varepsilon_i$. If it does not participate, then $P = 0$ and so its schooling will be $a + cX_i + \varepsilon_i$. The difference between the two is the gain in schooling due to the program, which is just b.

Adding Control Variables

As suggested, the analyst next runs a regression with and without the control variables. When it is run without them, the results show that the estimated value of b is not significantly different from zero (using the standard t-test given by the statistical package). These results look very similar to the first results, taking the difference in means between participants and nonparticipants—suggesting that PROSCOL is not having any impact on schooling. However, when several control variables are included in the regression, there is a positive and significant coefficient on PROSCOL participation. The calculation shows that by 18 years of age the program has added two years to schooling.

The analyst wonders why these control variables make such a difference? And are the right controls being used? She next visits her former econometrics professor and shows him her regressions. His first concern related to the regression of schooling on P and X is that it does not allow the impact of the program to vary with X; the impact is the same for everyone, which does not seem very likely. Parents with more schooling would be more likely to send their children to school, so the gains to them from PROSCOL will be lower. To allow the gains to vary with X, let mean schooling of nonparticipants be $a_0 + c_0X_i$ while that of participants is $a_1 + c_1X_i$, so the observed level of schooling is

$$S_i = (a_1 + c_1X_i + \varepsilon_{1i})P_i + (a_0 + c_0X_i + \varepsilon_{0i})(1 - P_i)$$

where ε_0 and ε_1 are random errors, each with means of zero and uncorrelated with X. To estimate this model, it is necessary to add an extra term for the interaction effects between program participation and observed characteristics to the regression already run. Thus the augmented regression is

$$S_i = a_0 + (a_1 - a_0)P_i + c_0X_i + (c_1 - c_0)P_iX_i + \varepsilon_i$$

where $\varepsilon_i = \varepsilon_{1i} P_i + \varepsilon_{0i} (1 - P_i)$. Then $(a_1 - a_0) + (c_1 - c_0)X$ is the mean program impact at any given value of X. If the mean X in the sample of participants is used, then it will give the mean gain from the program.

Understanding the Importance of Exogeneity

A second concern raised by the econometrics professor is in how the regression has been estimated. In using the regress command in the statistical package, ordinary least squares (OLS), there is concern because the OLS estimates of the parameters will be biased even in large samples unless the right-hand-side variables are exogenous. Exogeneity means that the right-hand-side variables are determined independently of schooling choices and so they are uncorrelated with the error term in the schooling regression. Because participation in the program was purposively targeted, PROSCOL's participation is not exogenous. This can affect the calculation of the program's impact as follows: The equation for years of schooling is

$$S_i = a + bP_i + cX_i + \varepsilon_i.$$

The value of $a + b + cX_i + \varepsilon_i$ was used as the estimate of the ith household's schooling when it participates in PROSCOL, while $a + cX_i + \varepsilon_i$ was used to estimate schooling if it does not participate. Thus the difference, b, is the gain from the program. However, in making this calculation the implicit assumption is that ε_i was the same either way. In other words, the assumption was that ε was independent of P, which would affect the calculation of the program's impact.

This highlights the bias due to nonrandom program placement, which may also be affecting the estimate based on the regression model suggested earlier by the economist ($S_i = a + bP_i + cX_i + \varepsilon_i$). This may not, however, mean that the results will be completely wrong.

The econometrics professor clarifies this with an explicit equation for P, namely,

$$P_i = d + eZ_i + v_i$$

where Z is several variables that include all the observed "poverty proxies" used for PROSCOL targeting. There will also be some purely random error term that influences participation; these are poverty proxies that are not in the data, and there will also have been mistakes in selecting participants that end up in this v term. This equation is linear, yet P can only take two possible values, 0 and 1. Predicted values between zero and one are acceptable, but a linear model cannot rule out the possibility of negative predicted values, or values over one. There are nonlinear models that can deal with this problem, but to simplify the discussion it will be easiest to confine attention to linear models.

There is a special case in which the above OLS regression of S on P and X will give an unbiased estimate of b. That is when X includes all the variables in Z that also influence schooling, and the error term v is uncorrelated with the error term ε in the regression for schooling. This is sometimes called "selection on observables" in the evaluation literature.

Suppose that the control variables X in the earlier regression for schooling include all the observed variables Z that influence participation P and v is uncorrelated with ε (so that the unobserved variables affecting program placement do not influence schooling conditional on X). This has then eliminated any possibility of P being correlated with ε. It will now be exogenous in the regression for schooling. In other words, the key idea of selection on observables is that there is some observable X such that the bias vanishes conditional on X.

Adding the control variables to the regression of schooling on PROSCOL participation made a big difference because the X must include variables that were among the poverty proxies used for targeting, or were correlated with them, and they are variables that also influenced schooling. This, however, only works if the assumptions are valid. There are two problems to be aware of. First, the above method breaks down if there are no unobserved determinants of participation; in other words if the error term v has zero variance, and all of the determinants of participation also affect schooling. Then there is no independent variation in program participation to allow one to identify its impact on schooling; it is possible to predict P perfectly from X, and so the regression will not estimate. This problem is unlikely to arise often, given that there are almost always unobserved determinants of program placement.

The second problem is more common, and more worrying in this case. The error term ε in the schooling regression probably contains variables that are not found in the survey but might well influence participation in the program, that is, they might be correlated with the error term $\hat\imath$ in the participation equation. If that is the case then $E(\varepsilon \mid X, P) \neq 0$, and ordinary regression methods will still be biased when regressions for schooling are estimated. Thus the key issue is the extent of the correlation between the error term in the equation for participation and that in the equation for schooling.

Exploring Better Ways to Form a Comparison Group—Propensity Score Matching

With further input from the professor, the analyst learns there are better ways to form a comparison group. The objective is to compare schooling levels conditional on observed characteristics. If the sample groups are divided into groups of families with the same or similar values of X, one compares the conditional means for PROSCOL and non-PROSCOL families. If schooling in the absence of the program is independent of participation, given X, then the comparison will give an unbiased estimate of PROSCOL's impact. This is sometimes called "conditional independence," and it is the key assumption made by all comparison-group methods.

Thus, a better way to select a comparison group, given the existing data, is to use as a control for each participant a nonparticipant with the same observed characteristics. This could, however, be very hard because the data set could have a lot of those variables. There may be nobody among the nonparticipants with exactly the same values of all the observed characteristics for any one of the PROSCOL participants.

A statistical approach, propensity score matching, provides techniques for simplifying the problem greatly. Instead of aiming to ensure that the matched control for each participant has exactly the same value of X, the same result can be achieved by matching on the predicted value of P, given X, which is called the propensity score of X. Rosenbaum and Rubin (1983) show that if (in this case) schooling without PROSCOL is independent of participation given X, then participants are also independent of participation given the propensity score of X. Since the propensity score is just one number, it is far easier to control for it than X, which could be many variables. And yet propensity score matching is sufficient to eliminate the bias provided there is conditional independence given X.

In other words, one first regresses P on X to get the predicted value of P for each possible value of X, which is then estimated for the whole sample. For each participant, one should find the nonparticipant with the closest value of this predicted probability. The difference in schooling is then the estimated gain from the program for that participant.

One can then take the mean of all those differences to estimate the impact. Or take the mean for different income groups. This, however, requires caution in how the model of participation is estimated. A linear model could give irregular predicted probabilities, above one, or negative. It is better to use the LOGIT command in the statistical package. This assumes that the error term v in the participation equation has a logistic distribution, and estimates the parameters consistent with that assumption by maximum likelihood methods. This is based on the principles of the maximum likelihood estimation of binary response models.

Another issue to be aware of is that some of the nonparticipants may have to be excluded as potential matches right from the start. In fact there are some recent results in the literature in econometrics indicating that failure to compare participants and controls at common values of matching variables is a major source of bias in evaluations (see Heckman and others 1998).

The intuition is that one wants the comparison group to be as similar as possible to the treatment group in terms of the observables, as summarized by the propensity score. We might find that some of the nonparticipant sample has a lower propensity score than any of those in the treatment sample. This is sometimes called called "lack of common support." In forming the comparison group, one should eliminate those observations from the set of nonparticipants to ensure that only gains over the same range of propensity scores are being compared. One should also exclude those nonparticipants for whom the probability of participating is zero. It is advisable to trim a small proportion of the sample, say 2 percent, from the top and bottom of the nonparticipant distribution in terms of the propensity scores. Once the participants have been identified and nonparticipants have been identified over a common matching region, it is recommended to take an average of (say) the five or so nearest neighbors in terms of the absolute difference in propensity scores (box 3.1).

Box 3.1 Steps in Propensity Score Matching

The aim of matching is to find the closest comparison group from a sample of nonparticipants to the sample of program participants. "Closest" is measured in terms of observable characteristics. If there are only one or two such characteristics then matching should be easy. But typically there are many potential characteristics. The main steps in matching based on propensity scores are as follows:

Step 1: You need a representative sample survey of eligible nonparticipants as well as one for the participants. The larger the sample of eligible nonparticipants the better, to facilitate good matching. If the two samples come from different surveys, then they should be highly comparable surveys (same questionnaire, same interviewers or interviewer training, same survey period, and so on).

Step 2: Pool the two samples and estimate a logit model of program participation as a function of all the variables in the data that are likely to determine participation.

Step 3: Create the predicted values of the probability of participation from the logit regression; these are called the "propensity scores." You will have a propensity score for every sampled participant and nonparticipant.

Step 4: Some in the nonparticipant sample may have to be excluded at the outset because they have a propensity score that is outside the range (typically too low) found for the treatment sample. The range of propensity scores estimated for the treatment group should correspond closely to that for the retained subsample of nonparticipants. You may also want to restrict potential matches in other ways, depending on the setting. For example, you may want to allow only matches within the same geographic area to help ensure that the matches come from the same economic environment.

Step 5: For each individual in the treatment sample, you now want to find the observation in the nonparticipant sample that has the closest propensity score, as measured by the absolute difference in scores. This is called the "nearest neighbor." You can find the five (say) nearest neighbors.

Step 6: Calculate the mean value of the outcome indicator (or each of the indicators if there is more than one) for the five nearest neighbors. The difference between that mean and the actual value for the treated observation is the estimate of the gain due to the program for that observation.

Step 7: Calculate the mean of these individual gains to obtain the average overall gain. This can be stratified by some variable of interest, such as income, in the nonparticipant sample.

This is the simplest form of propensity score matching. Complications can arise in practice. For example, if there is oversampling of participants, you can use choice-based sampling methods to correct for this (Manski and Lerman 1977); alternatively you can use the odds ratio ($p/(1-p)$, where p is the propensity score) for matching. Instead of relying on the nearest neighbor you can instead use all the nonparticipants as potential matches but weight them differently, according to how close they are (Heckman and others 1998).

Next, all the variables in the data set that are, or could proxy for, the poverty indicators that were used in selecting PROSCOL participants should be included. Again, X should include the variables in Z. This, however, brings out a weakness of propensity score matching. With matching, a different X will yield a different estimate of impact. With randomization, the ideal experiment, the results do not depend on what X you choose. Nor does randomization require that one specify a model for participation, whether a logit or something else. Box 3.1 summarizes the steps for doing propensity score matching.

Learning about Biases Due to Unobservables

Even after forming the comparison group, the analyst cannot be sure that this will give a much better estimate of the programs' impact. The methods described above will only eliminate the bias if there is conditional independence, such that the unobservable determinants of schooling— not included in the set of control variables X—are uncorrelated with program placement. There are two distinct sources of bias, that due to differences in observables and that due to differences in unobservables; the latter is often called "selection bias." Box 3.2 elaborates on this difference.

Going back to the professor's last equation shows that conditional independence will hold if P is exogenous, for then $E(\varepsilon_i \mid X_i, P_i) = 0$. However, endogenous program placement due to purposive targeting based on unobservables will still leave a bias. This is sometimes called selection on observables. Thus the conditions required for justifying the method raised earlier by the economist are no less restrictive than those needed to justify a version of the first method based on comparing PROSCOL families with non-PROSCOL families for households with similar values of X. Both rest on believing that these unobservables are not jointly influencing schooling and program participation, conditional on X.

Intuitively, one might think that careful matching reduces the bias, but that is not necessarily so. Matching eliminates part of the bias in the first naïve estimate of PROSCOL's impact. That leaves the bias due to any troublesome unobservables. However, these two sources of bias could be offsetting—one positive, the other negative. Heckman and others (1998) make this point. So the matching estimate could well have more bias than the naïve estimate. One cannot know on a priori grounds how much better off one is with even a well-chosen comparison group, which is an empirical question.

Reviewing What Could Have Been Done with a Baseline Survey—Double Difference Estimates

The analyst next inquires whether there would be another method besides randomization that is robust to these troublesome unobservables. This would require baseline data for both the participants and nonparticipants, collected before PROSCOL started. The idea is that data are collected on outcomes and their determinants both before and after the program is introduced, along with data for an untreated comparison group as well as the treatment group. It is then possible to just subtract the difference between the schooling of participants and the comparison group before the program is introduced from the difference after the program.

Box 3. 2 Sources of Bias in Naïve Estimates of PROSCOL's Impact

The bias described by the statistician is the expected difference in schooling without PROSCOL between families selected for the program and those not chosen. This can be broken down into two sources of bias:

- Bias due to differences in observable characteristics. This can come about in two ways. First, there may not be common support. The "support" is the set of values of the control variables for which outcomes and program participation are observed. If the support is different between the treatment sample and the comparison group then this will bias the results. In effect, one is not comparing like with like. Second, even with common support the distribution of observable characteristics may be different within the region of common support; in effect the comparison group data is misweighted. Careful selection of the comparison group can eliminate this source of bias.
- Bias due to differences in unobservables. The term selection bias is sometimes confined solely to this component (though some authors use that term for the total bias in a nonexperimental evaluation). This source of bias arises when, for given values of X, there is a systematic relationship between program participation and outcomes in the absence of the program. In other words, there are unobserved variables that jointly influence schooling and program participation conditional on the observed variables in the data.

There is nothing to guarantee that these two sources of bias will work in the same direction. So eliminating either one of them on its own does not mean that the total bias is reduced in absolute value. That is an empirical question. In one of the few studies to address this question, the true impact, as measured by a well-designed experiment, was compared with various nonexperimental estimates (Heckman and others 1998). The bias in the naïve estimate was huge, but careful matching of the comparison group based on observables greatly reduced the bias.

This is called the "double difference" estimate, or "difference in differences." This will deal with the troublesome unobserved variables provided they do not vary over time.

This can be explained by adding subscripts to the earlier equation so that the schooling after the program is introduced:

$$S_{ia} = a + bP_i + cX_{ia} + \varepsilon_{ia}.$$

Before the program, in the baseline survey, school attainment is instead

$$S_{ib} = a + cX_{ib} + \varepsilon_{ib}.$$

(Of course $P = 0$ before the program is introduced.) The error terms include an additive time invariant effect, so we can write them as

$$\varepsilon_{it} = \eta_i + \mu_{it} \text{ (for } t = a,b)$$

where η_i is the time invariant effect, which is allowed to be correlated with P_i, and μ_{it} is an innovation error, which is not correlated with P_i (or X_i).

The essential idea here is to use the baseline data to reveal those problematic unobservables. Notice that since the baseline survey is for the same households as we have now, the ith household in the equation for S_{ia} is the same household as the ith in the equation for S_{ib}. We can then take the difference between the "after" equation and the "before" equation:

$$S_{ia} - S_{ib} = bP_i + c(X_{ia} - X_{ib}) + \mu_{ia} - \mu_{ib}.$$

It is now possible to regress the change in schooling on program participation and the changes in X. OLS will give you an unbiased estimate of the program's impact. The unobservables—the ones correlated with program participation—have been eliminated.

Given this, if the program placement was based only on variables, both observed and unobserved, that were known at the time of the baseline survey, then it would be reasonable to assume that the η's do not change between the two surveys. This would hold as long as the problematic unobservables are time invariant. The changes in schooling over time for the comparison group will reveal what would have happened to the treatment group without the program.

This would require knowing the program well and being able to time the evaluation surveys so as to coordinate with the program. Otherwise there are bound to be unobserved changes after the baseline survey that influence who gets the program. This would create 0's that changed between the two surveys.

This last equation can be interpreted as meaning that the child and household characteristics in X are irrelevant to the change in schooling if those characteristics do not change over time. But the gain in schooling may depend on parents' education (and not just any change in their education), and possibly on where the household lives, because this will determine the access to schools. There can also be situations in which the changes over time in the outcome indicator are influenced by the initial conditions. Then one will also want to control for differences in initial conditions. This can be done by simply adding X_a and X_b in the regression separately so that the regression takes the form

$$S_{ia} - S_{ib} = bP_i + c_a X_{ia} + c_b X_{ib} + \mu_{ia} - \mu_{ib}.$$

Even if some (or all) variables in X do not vary over time one can still allow X to affect the changes over time in schooling.

The propensity score matching method discussed above can help ensure that the comparison group is similar to the treatment group before doing the double difference. In an interesting study of an American employment program, it was found that failure to ensure that comparisons were made in a region of common support was a major source of bias in the double-difference estimate in comparison with a randomized control group. Within the region of common support, however, the bias conditional on X did not vary much over time. Thus taking the double difference makes sense, after the matching is done (see Heckman and others (1998).

However, in practice, following up on households in surveys can be difficult. It may not be easy to find all those households that were originally included in the baseline survey. Some people in the baseline survey may not want to be interviewed again, or they may have moved to an unknown location.

If dropouts from the sample are purely random, then the follow-up survey will still be representative of the same population in the baseline survey. However, if there is some systematic tendency for people with certain characteristics to drop out of the sample, then there will be a problem. This is called "attrition bias." For example, PROSCOL might help some poor families move into better housing. And even when participant selection was solely based on information available at or about the baseline date (the time-invariant effect 0_i), selected participants may well drop out voluntarily on the basis of changes after that date. Such attrition from the treatment group will clearly bias a double-difference estimate of the program's impact. Box 3.3 outlines the steps to form a double-difference estimate.

Box 3.3 Doing a Double Difference

The double-difference method entails comparing a treatment group with a comparison group (as might ideally be determined by the matching method in box 3.2) both before and after the intervention. The main steps are as follows:

Step 1: You need a baseline survey before the intervention is in place, and the survey must cover both nonparticipants and participants. If you do not know who will participate, you have to make an informed guess. Talk to the program administrators.

Step 2: You then need one or more follow-up surveys after the program is put in place. These should be highly comparable to the baseline surveys (in terms of the questionnaire, the interviewing, and so forth). Ideally, the follow-up surveys should be of the same sampled observations as the baseline survey. If this is not possible then they should be the same geographic clusters or strata in terms of some other variable.

Step 3: Calculate the mean difference between the after and before values of the outcome indicator for each of the treatment and comparison groups.

Step 4: Calculate the difference between these two mean differences. That is your estimate of the impact of the program.

This is the simplest version of double difference. You may also want to control for differences in exogenous initial conditions or changes in exogenous variables, possibly allowing for interaction effects with the program (so that the gain from the intervention is some function of observable variables). A suitable regression model can allow these variations.

Using Instrumental Variables

Given that there is no baseline survey of the same households to do the double-difference method, the professor recommends another methodology to get an estimate that is robust to the troublesome unobservables—an "instrumental variable."

An instrumental variable is the classic solution for the problem of an endogenous regressor. An instrumental variable is an observable source of exogenous variation in program participation. In other words, it is correlated with P but is not already in the regression for schooling and is not correlated with the error term in the schooling equation, ε. So one must have to have at least one variable in Z that is not in X and is not correlated with ε. Then the instrumental variables estimate of the program's impact is obtained by replacing P with its predicted value conditional on Z. Because this predicted value depends solely on Z (which is exogenous) and Z is uncorrelated with ε, it is now reasonable to apply OLS to this new regression.

Since the predicted values depend only on the exogenous variation due to the instrumental variable and the other exogenous variables, the unobservables are no longer troublesome because they will be uncorrelated with the error term in the schooling regression. This also suggests another, more efficient, way to deal with the problem. Remember that the source of bias in the earlier estimate of the program's impact was the correlation between the error term in the schooling equation and that in the participation equation. This is what creates the correlation between participation and the error term in the schooling equation. Thus a natural way to get rid of the problem when one has an instrumental variable is to add the residuals from the first-stage equation for participation to the equation for schooling but keeping actual participation in the schooling regression. However, since we have now added to the schooling regression the estimated value of the error term from the participation equation, it is possible to treat participation as exogenous and run OLS. This only works if there is a valid instrument. If not, the regression will not estimate because the participation residual will be perfectly predictable from actual participation and X, in a linear model.

An instrumental variable can also help if there is appreciable measurement error in the program participation data, another possible source of bias. Measurement error means that there is the possibility that program participation varies more than it actually does. This overestimation in the variance of P leads naturally to an underestimation of its coefficient b. This is called attenuation bias because this bias attenuates the estimated regression coefficient.

Although an instrumental variable can be extremely useful, in practice caution is necessary. When the actual participation is just replaced with its predicted value and OLS is run, this will not give the correct standard errors because the computer will not know that previously estimated parameters to obtain the predicted values had to be used. A correction to the OLS standard errors is required, though there are statistical packages that allow one to do this easily, at least for linear models.

If there was a dependent variable, however, that could only take two possible values, at school or not at school for instance, then one should use a nonlinear binary response model, such as logit or probit. The principle of testing for exogeneity of program participation is similar in this case. There is a paper by Rivers and Vuong (1988) that discusses the problem for such models; Blundell and Smith (1993) provide a useful overview of various nonlinear models in which there is an endogenous regressor.

Testing the Methodologies

When the analyst begins to think about identifying an instrumental variable she realizes that this is not a straightforward process. Every possibility she has come up with could also be put in with the variables in X. The problem is finding a valid "exclusion restriction" that justifies putting some variable in the equation for participation but not in the equation for schooling.

The analyst decides to try the propensity score matching method. The logit model of participation looks quite sensible and suggests that PROSCOL is well targeted. Virtually all of the variables that one would expect to be associated with poverty have positive, and significant, coefficients. The analyst then does the propensity score matching. In a comparison of the mean school enrollment rates, the results show that children of the matched-comparison group had an enrollment rate of 60 percent compared with 80 percent for PROSCOL families.

To account for the issue of forgone income, the analyst draws on an existing survey of child labor that asked about earnings. (In this developing country, there is an official ban on children working before they are 16 years of age, but the government has a hard time enforcing it; nonetheless, child wages are a sensitive issue.) From this survey, the earnings that a child would have had if he or she had not gone to school can be determined.

It is then possible to subtract from PROSCOL's cash payment to participants the amount of forgone income and thus work out the net income transfer. Subtracting this net transfer from total income, it is possible to work out where the PROSCOL participants come from in the distribution of preintervention income. They are not quite as poor as first thought (ignoring forgone income) but they are still poor; for example, two-thirds of them are below country's official poverty line.

Having calculated the net income gain to all participants, it is now possible to calculate the poverty rate with and without PROSCOL. The postintervention poverty rate (with the program) is, simply stated, the proportion of the population living in households with an income per person below the poverty line, where "income" is the observed income (including the gross transfer receipts from PROSCOL). This can be calculated directly from the household survey. By subtracting the net income gain (cash transfer from PROSCOL minus forgone income from children's work) attributed to PROSCOL from all the observed incomes, the results show a new distribution of preintervention incomes. The poverty rate without the program is then the proportion of people living in poor households, based on this new distribution. The analyst finds that the observed poverty rate in the Northwest of 32 percent would have been 36 percent if PROSCOL had not existed. The program allows 4 percent of the population to escape poverty now. The schooling gains mean that there will also be both pecuniary and nonpecuniary gains to the poor in the future. In the process of measuring poverty, the analyst remembers learning that the proportion of people below the poverty line is only a basic measure because it tells you nothing about changes below the line (see Box 3.4). She then calculates both the poverty gap index and the squared poverty gap index, and the results suggest that these have also fallen as a result of PROSCOL.

Box 3.4 Poverty Measures

The simplest and most common poverty measure is the headcount index. In this case, it is the proportion of the population living in households with income per person below the poverty line. (In other countries, it is a consumption-based measure, which has some advantages; for discussion and references see Ravallion 1994.)

The headcount index does not tell us anything about income distribution below the poverty line: a poor person may be worse off but the headcount index will not change, nor will it reflect gains among the poor unless they cross the poverty line.

A widely used alternative to the headcount index is the poverty gap (PG) index. The poverty gap for each household is the difference between the poverty line and the household's income; for those above the poverty line the gap is zero. When the poverty gap is normalized by the poverty line, and one calculates its mean over all households (whether poor or not), one obtains the poverty gap index.

The poverty gap index will tell you how much impact the program has had on the depth of poverty, but it will not reflect any changes in distribution among the poor caused by the program. For example, if the program entails a small gain to a poor person who is above the mean income of the poor, at the expense of an equal loss to someone below that mean, then PG will not change.

(Box continues on the following page.)

Box 3.4 *(continued)*

There are various "distribution-sensitive" measures that will reflect such changes in distribution among the poor. One such measure is the "squared poverty gap" (Foster, Greer, and Thorbecke 1984). This is calculated the same way as PG except that the individual poverty gaps as a proportion of the poverty line are squared before taking the mean (again over both poor and nonpoor). Another example of a distribution-sensitive poverty measure is the Watts index. This is the mean of the log of the ratio of the poverty line to income, where that ratio is set to one for the nonpoor. Atkinson (1987) describes other examples in the literature.

In this calculation, the analyst also recognizes that there is some uncertainty about the country's poverty line. To test the results, she repeats the calculation over a wide range of poverty lines, finding that at a poverty line for which 50 percent of the population are poor based on the observed postintervention incomes, the proportion would have been 52 percent without PROSCOL. At a poverty line that 15 percent fail to reach with the program, the proportion would have been 19 percent without it. By repeating these calculations over the whole range of incomes, the entire "poverty incidence curves" have been traced, with and without the program. This is also called the "cumulative distribution function" (see Box 3.5).

Box 3.5 Comparing Poverty with and without the Program

Using the methods described in the main text and earlier boxes, one obtains an estimate of the gain to each household. In the simplest evaluations this is just one number. But it is better to allow it to vary with household characteristics. One can then summarize this information in the form of poverty incidence curves (PICs), with and without the program.

Step 1: The postintervention income (or other welfare indicator) for each household in the whole sample (comprising both participants and nonparticipants) should already exist; this is data. You also know how many people are in each household. And, of course, you know the total number of people in the sample (N; or this might be the estimated population size, if inverse sampling rates have been used to "expend up" each sample observation).

Step 2: You can plot this information in the form of a PIC. This gives (on the vertical axis) the percentage of the population living in households with an income less than or equal to that value on the horizontal axis. To make this graph, you can start with the poorest household, mark its income on the horizontal axis, and then count up on the vertical axis by 100 times the number of people in that household divided by N. The next point is the proportion living in the two poorest households, and so on. This gives the postintervention PIC.

Step 3: Now calculate the distribution of income preintervention. To get this you subtract the estimated gain for each household from its postintervention income. You then have a list of postintervention incomes, one for each sampled household. Then repeat Step 2. You will then have the preintervention PIC.

If we think of any given income level on the horizontal axis as a poverty line, then the difference between the two PICs at that point gives the impact on the head-count index for that poverty line (box 3.4). Alternatively, looking horizontally gives you the income gain at that percentile. If none of the gains are negative then the postintervention PIC must lie below the preintervention one. Poverty will have fallen no matter what poverty line is used. Indeed, this also holds for a very broad class of poverty measures; see Atkinson (1987). If some gains are negative, then the PICs will intersect. The poverty comparison is then ambiguous; the answer will depend on which poverty lines and which poverty measures one uses. (For further discussion see Ravallion 1994.) You might then use a priori restrictions on the range of admissible poverty lines. For example, you may be confident that the poverty line does not exceed some maximum value, and if the intersection occurs above that value then the poverty comparison is unambiguous. If the intersection point (and there may be more than one) is below the maximum admissible poverty line, then a robust poverty comparison is only possible for a restricted set of poverty measures. To check how restricted the set needs to be, you can calculate the poverty depth curves (PDCs). These are obtained by simply forming the cumulative sum up to each point on the PIC. (So the second point on the PDC is the first point on the PIC plus the second point, and so on.)

(Box continues on the following page.)

Box 3.5 *(continued)*

If the PDCs do not intersect then the program's impact on poverty is unambiguous as long as one restricts attention to the poverty gap index or any of the distribution-sensitive poverty measures described in box 3.4. If the PDCs intersect then you can calculate the "poverty severity curves" with and without the program by forming the cumulative sums under the PDCs. If these do not intersect over the range of admissible poverty lines, then the impact on any of the distribution-sensitive poverty measures in box 3.4 is unambiguous.

Incorporating Input from the Field

In the implementation of every program, there is insight from beneficiaries and program administrators that may or may not be reflected in program data. For example, in this case the perception of those working in the field is that the majority of PROSCOL families are poor and that the program indeed provides assistance. When the analyst discusses this with a sociologist working with the program, she learns of some uncertainty in the reality of forgone income and the issue of work. The sociologist discusses that in the field one observes many children from poor families who work as well as go to school, and that some of the younger children not at school do not seem to be working. The analyst realizes that this requires some checking on whether there is any difference in the amount of child labor done by PROSCOL children versus that done by a matched-comparison group. This data, however, is not available in the household survey, though it would be possible to present the results with and without the deduction for forgone income.

The sociologist also has noticed that for a poor family to get on PROSCOL it matters a lot which school-board area (SBA) the family lives in. All SBAs get a PROSCOL allocation from the center, even SBAs that have very few poor families. If one is poor but living in a well-to-do SBA, they are more likely to get help from PROSCOL than if they live in a poor SBA. What really matters then, is relative poverty—relative to others in the area in which one lives—which matters much more than the absolute level of living.

This allocation would influence participation in PROSCOL, but one would not expect it to matter to school attendance, which would depend more on one's absolute level of living, family circumstances, and characteristics of the school. Thus the PROSCOL budget allocation across SBAs can be used as instrumental variables to remove the bias in the estimates of program impact.

There is information on which SBA each household belongs to in the household survey, the rules used by the center in allocating PROSCOL funds across SBAs, and how much the center has allocated to each SBA. Allocations are based on the number of school-age children, with an "adjustment factor" for how poor the SBA is thought to be. However, the rule is somewhat vague.

The analyst attempts to take these points into account, and reruns the regression for schooling, but replacing the actual PROSCOL participation by its predicted value (the propensity score) from the regression for participation, which now includes the budget allocation to the SBA. It helps to already have as many school characteristics as possible in the regression for attendance. Although school characteristics do not appear to matter officially to how PROSCOL resources are allocated, any omitted school characteristics that jointly influence PROSCOL allocations by SBA and individual schooling outcomes will leave a bias in the analyst's instrumental variable estimates. Although there is always the possibility of bias, with plenty of geographic control variables this method should at least offer a credible comparator to the matching estimate.

From the results it is determined that the budget allocation to the SBA indeed has a significant positive coefficient in the logit regression for PROSCOL participation. Now (predicted) PROSCOL participation is significant in a regression for school enrollment, in which all the same variables from the logit regression are included except the SBA budget allocation. The coefficient implies that the enrollment rate is 15 percentage points higher for PROSCOL participants than would have otherwise been the case. A regression is also run for years of schooling, for boys and girls separately. For either boys or girls of 18 years, the results indicate that they would have dropped out of school almost two years earlier if it had not been for PROSCOL. This regression, however, raises questions—whether the right standard errors are being used and whether linear models should be used.

Planning for Future Work

Finally, the analyst is ready to report the results of the evaluations. They show that PROSCOL is doing quite well, and as a result the policymakers show interest in expanding the program. From the process the analyst has gone through in carrying out the evaluation, she has a few important observations:

- Impact evaluation can be much more difficult than first anticipated;
- It is possible to come up with a worryingly wide range of estimates, depending on the specifics of the methodology used;
- It is good to use alternative methods in the frequent situations of less-than-ideal data, though each method has pitfalls; and
- One has to be eclectic about data.

In addition to the lessons the analyst has learned, she has a few key recommendations for future evaluation work of PROSCOL. First, it would be desirable to randomly exclude some eligible PROSCOL families in the rest of the country and then do a follow-up survey of both the actual participants and those randomly excluded from participating. This would give a more precise estimate of the benefits. It would, however, be politically sensitive to exclude some. Yet if the program does not have enough resources to cover the whole country in one go, and the program will have to make choices about who gets it first, it would indeed be preferable to make that choice randomly, among eligible participants. Alternatively, it would be possible to pick the schools or the school board areas randomly, in the first wave. This would surely make the choice of school or school board area a good instrumental variable for individual program placement.

Second, if this is not feasible, it is advisable to carry out a baseline survey of areas in which there are likely to be high concentrations of PROSCOL participants before the program starts in the South. This could be done at the same time as the next round of the national survey that was used for evaluating the PROSCOL program. It would also be good to add a few questions to the survey, such as whether the children do any paid work.

And third, it would be useful to include qualitative work, to help form hypotheses to be tested and assess the plausibility of key assumptions made in the quantitative analysis.

Note

1. See Heckman, Lalonde, and Smith (1999), and Abadie, Angrist, and Imbens (1998) for discussion on quartile treatment effects.

Chapter 4
Drawing on "Good Practice" Impact Evaluations*

The previous chapters have presented the key methods, issues, and challenges that can arise in evaluating project impact. In reviewing the case studies listed in table 4.1 many illustrative examples emerge from interesting approaches in the design, use of data, choice, and application of analytical methods used, and in-country capacity building. These examples, as well as a discussion of the costs of evaluations and the political economy issues that may arise in implementation, are highlighted below.

The 15 case studies included in the review were chosen from a range of evaluations carried out by the World Bank, other donor agencies, research institutions, and private consulting firms. They were selected as a sample of "good practice" for their methodological rigor, attempting to reflect a range of examples from different sectors and regions. Although each impact evaluation has its strengths and weaknesses, the lessons learned from these experiences should help the project manager or policy analyst intending to design and implement future work.

Early and Careful Planning of the Evaluation Design

Adequate preparation during the beginning stages of project identification will ensure that the right information is collected and that the findings can be used for mid-course adjustments of project components. With early and careful planning it is possible to incorporate all the elements that contribute to a rigorous impact evaluation, such as a baseline survey with a randomized control group, and qualitative data on the processes that may affect impact.

Uganda Nutrition and Early Childhood Development Project. This evaluation, though still not yet under implementation, provides an excellent example of early and careful planning (see World Bank 1998a; Garcia, Alderman, and Rudqvist 1999). The project itself focuses on strengthening the ability of parents and communities to care for children by providing them with knowledge on better childcare practices and by enhancing

---

* This chapter draws on the best practice case studies in annex I and overview pieces prepared by Gillette Hall and Julia Lane, and Subbarao and others (1999).

opportunities to increase income. It is community-based and implemented by a network of nongovernmental organizations (NGOs). The evaluation component, which was integrated into the project cycle from day one, approaches the ideal in terms of evaluation design. First, it generates baseline and follow-up survey data, along with a randomized control group, so that the program's impact on beneficiary outcomes can be rigorously assessed. Second, it enhances this quantitative component with a participatory (qualitative) monitoring and evaluation (M&E) process.

On the quantitative side, the project was designed to allow for an experimental study design in which parishes will be randomly assigned into treatment and control groups. Health cards will then be used to record data on the child's weight in treatment and control parishes. In addition, the baseline household survey will be conducted before services are delivered to the communities, as well as a follow-up survey of the same households two years later. A rapid review of these data is expected to inform the decision to scale up some components of the intervention during the midterm review of the project. A deeper analysis of the data at the end of the project will guide the design of the second phase of the project.

Ghana Credit with Education Project. The evaluation of this project was very complex, with many intermediate steps. The project combines elements of a group lending scheme with education on the basics of health, nutrition, birth timing and spacing, and small business skills. The evaluation generally focuses on assessing the nutritional status of children, women's economic capacity to invest in food and health care, women's knowledge and adoption of breast feeding, and weaning. It begins with a very clear conceptual framework, which is illustrated below. This schematic clearly delineates the inputs, intermediate benefits, and long-term outcomes in a way that both facilitates the development of several models and their interpretation. By carefully planning the evaluation and working with a schematic at an early stage, it was possible to clarify many points in a relatively complex design (see annex 1.6).

Approaches to Evaluation When There Is No Baseline

In practice, many evaluations do not have adequate data. Evaluations are added after it is possible to do a baseline survey or in the absence of comparison groups. Some examples of this are the Bangladesh Food for Education, Mexico PROBECAT, Czech Active Labor Programs, and Argentina TRABAJAR evaluations. Without a baseline, the controls must be constructed by using the matching methods discussed in the previous chapters. This can, however, be quite tricky. The propensity score match-

(Text continues on page 71.)

Table 4.1 Summary of "Good Practice" Impact Evaluations

Project:	Country	Database type	Unit of analysis	Outcome measures	Econometric Approach						Strengths
					Randomi-zation	Matching	Reflexive compar-isons	Double differ-ence	Instru-mental variables	Quali-tative	
Education											
Radio Nicaragua	Nicaragua	Baseline and postintervention survey	Students and classrooms	Test scores	Yes	No	Yes	No	No	No	Questionnaire design
School Autonomy Reform	Nicaragua	Panel survey and qualitative assessments	Students, parents, teachers, directors	Test scores, degree of local decision-making	No	Yes	Yes	No	No	Yes	Qualitative-quantitative mx
Textbooks	Kenya	Baseline and postinterventions urvey	Students, classrooms, teachers	Test scores	Yes	No	Yes	Yes	Yes	No	Analysis of confounding factors
Dropping out	Philippines	Baseline and postintervention survey	Students, classrooms, teachers	Test scores and dropout status	Yes	No	Yes	Yes	Yes	No	Cost-benefit analysis; capacity building

(Table continues on the following page.)

Table 4.1 (continued)

Project:	Country	Database type	Unit of analysis	Outcome measures	Econometric Approach						Strengths
					Randomization	Matching	Reflexive comparisons	Double difference	Instrumental variables	Qualitative	
Labor Programs											
TRABAJAR	Argentina	Household survey, census, administrative records, social assessments	Workers, households	Income, targeting, costs	No	Yes	No	No	Yes	Yes	Judicious use of existing data sources, innovative analytic techniques
PROBECAT	Mexico	Retrospective and labor force surveys	Workers	Earnings and employment outcomes	No	Yes	No	No	No	No	Matching technique
Active Labor Programs	Czech Republic	Retrospective mail surveys	Workers	Earnings and employment outcomes	No	Yes	No	No	No	No	Matching technique
Finance											
Micro Finance	Bangladesh	Postintervention survey plus administrative records	Households	Consumption and education	Yes	Yes	No	Yes	No	No	Analysis of confounding factors

Credit with Education	Ghana	Baseline and post-intervention survey	Mother-and-child pairs	Income, health, and empowerment	Yes	Yes	No	No	Yes	Use of qualitative and quantitative information
Health Financing	Niger	Baseline and postintervention survey plus administrative records	Households and health centers	Cost recovery and access	No	Yes (on districts)	No	No	No	Use of administrative data
Food and Nutrition										
Food for Education	Bangladesh	Household expenditure survey	Households and communities	School attendance	No	No	No	Yes	No	Imaginative use of instruments to address selection problem with standard data
Health, Education, and Nutrition	Mexico	Baseline and post-intervention surveys	Households	Health, education, and nutrition outcomes	Yes	Yes	Not known	Not known	No	Clear conceptualization; analysis of confounding factors
Infrastructure										
Social Investment Fund	Bolivia	Baseline and follow-up surveys	Households, projects	Education and health indicators	Yes	Yes	Yes	Yes	No	Range of evaluation methodologies applied

(Table continues on the following page.)

69

Table 4.1 *(continued)*

Project:	Country	Database type	Unit of analysis	Outcome measures	Randomization	Econometric Approach Matching	Reflexive comparisons	Double difference	Instrumental variables	Qualitative	Strengths
Rural Roads	Vietnam	Baseline and follow-up surveys	Households, communities	Welfare indicators at household and commune levels	No	Yes	Yes	Yes	Yes	No	Measures welfare outcomes
Agriculture
National Extension Project	Kenya	Panel data, beneficiary assessments	Households, farms	Farm productivity and efficiency	No	No	Yes	No	No	No	Policy relevance of results

ing technique used in the Argentina TRABAJAR project to construct a control group with cross-sectional data on program participants and non-participants provides a good example.

The TRABAJAR II Project in Argentina. This project was focused on providing employment at low wages in small social and economic infra-structure subprojects selected by community groups. The impact evalua-tion of the program was designed to assess whether the incomes of pro-gram participants were higher than they would have been had the pro-gram not been in place. The most commonly used methods to estimate household income without the intervention were not feasible in the case of the TRABAJAR program: no randomization had taken place to con-struct a control group to use in comparing the income of project benefi-ciaries; and no baseline survey was available, ruling out the possibility of conducting a before-and-after evaluation.

The TRABAJAR evaluation instead used existing data to construct a comparison group by matching program participants to nonparticipants from the national population over a set of socioeconomic variables such as schooling, gender, housing, subjective perceptions of welfare, and membership in political parties and neighborhood associations by using a technique called propensity scoring. The study demonstrates resource-ful use of existing national household survey data—(the Encuesta de Desarrollo Social (EDS)—in generating the comparison group, combined with a smaller survey of TRABAJAR participants conducted specifically for the purposes of the evaluation. The smaller survey was carefully designed so that it used the same questionnaire as the EDS and the same interview teams and was conducted at approximately the same time in order to successfully conduct the matching exercise. This technique was possible in the TRABAJAR case because a national household survey was being canvassed and the evaluators could take advantage of this survey to oversample TRABAJAR participants. The same interview teams were used for both the national and project surveys, resulting in efficiency gains in data collection (see annex 1.1).

Czech Labor Market Programs Evaluation. This evaluation attempted to cover five active labor programs to (a) determine whether participants in the different programs were more successful in reentering the labor mar-ket than were nonparticipants and whether this varied across subgroups and with labor market conditions; and (b) determine the cost-effectiveness of each program and make suggestions for improvements. The evaluation used a matching technique because no baseline data were collected. The evaluators surveyed participants and then chose a random sample of non-participants. Since the nonparticipants were systematically older and less educated, the evaluators needed to construct a reasonable comparison group for each program. This was done by taking each participant in turn and comparing them to each individual in the nonparticipant pool on the basis of seven characteristics: age, gender, education, number of months employed prior to registration, town size, marital status, and last employment type. The closest match was then put into the comparison group. Although this approach is straightforward, there is the potential for selection bias—that the nonparticipant group is systematically different from the participant group on the basis of unobservables (annex 1.5).

Dealing with Constraints on Developing Good Controls

At times, randomization or experimental controls are possible but not politically feasible. In this case, the randomization can be carried out by taking advantage of any plans to pilot the project in certain restricted areas. Areas in which the project will be piloted can initially be randomly selected, with future potential project areas as controls. Over time, additional communities can be randomly included in the project. Three examples illustrate how to handle a situation in which randomization was politically or otherwise infeasible. In Vietnam, a rural transport project will be evaluated with limited information and no randomization. The Honduras Social Investment Fund provides an example of how to construct a control group in demand-driven projects, using an ex post matched comparison based on a single cross-section of data. Evaluating demand-driven projects can be particularly difficult given that it is not known which projects or communities will participate in the project ahead of time. And third, the evaluation of the Bolivian Social Investment Fund in the Chaco Region provides a good example of how to incorporate randomization in demand-driven projects in a way that allows targeting.

The Vietnam Rural Roads Project. This project aims at reducing poverty in rural areas by improving access to rural communities and linking them to the district and provincial road networks. The design of the impact evaluation centers on baseline and follow-up survey data collected for a sample of project and comparison-group communities identified through matched-comparison techniques. Baseline and postintervention information on indicators such as commune-level agricultural production yields, income source diversification, employment opportunities, availability of goods, services and facilities, and asset wealth and distribution will be collected from a random sample of project (treatment) and nonproject (comparison) communes. These data will be used to compare the change in outcomes before and after the intervention between project and nonproject communes using "double differencing."

Ideally, treatment and comparison communes should be equivalent in all their observed and unobserved characteristics, the only difference between them being that treatment communes benefit from the intervention whereas comparison communes do not. Since random assignment to treatment and comparison groups had not taken place, and the requisite data to make informed choices on appropriate controls were not available at the time of sample selection, random samples of project communes and nonproject communes were drawn. Specifically, project communes were selected from a list of all communes with proposed projects in each province. Next, comparison communes were selected from a list of all remaining communes without proposed projects but in the same districts as treatment communes. Using information collected for the evaluation, propensity score matching techniques will then be used to ensure that selected nonproject communes are appropriate comparison groups. Any controls with unusual attributes relative to the treatment communes will be removed from the sample (annex 1.15).

Honduran Social Investment Fund. The Honduran Social Investment Fund (FHIS) (see World Bank 1998b) aims to improve the living conditions for marginal social groups by financing small-scale social and economic infrastructure subprojects. The FHIS is a demand-driven institution that responds to initiatives from municipalities, government ministries, NGOs, and community groups by providing financing for investments in infrastructure, equipment, and training. The impact evaluation of the FHIS uses matched-comparison techniques, drawing the treatment group sample randomly from a list of communities in which FHIS projects have been in operation for at least one year. The comparison group, by contrast, was selected from a list of "pipeline" projects—those that have been requested and approved but for which the FHIS investment has not yet taken place. In theory, comparison-group communities are automatically matched to project communities according to the self-selection process and FHIS project approval criteria. A household survey was then conducted in both treatment and comparison-group communities, complemented by a qualitative evaluation component (focus groups and interviews with key informants) conducted in a subset of treatment communities. This initial evaluation is a first step toward establishing an ongoing M&E system that will be eventually integrated into FHIS operations. In particular, the data collected from communities with pipeline projects will become a useful baseline from which to track future changes in impact indicators, after FHIS investment takes place.

Educational Investments in the Chaco Region of Bolivia. Education projects financed by the Bolivian Social Investment Fund (SIF) are aimed at upgrading physical facilities and training teachers in rural public school. Delays in the implementation of the project in the Chaco Region and limited funds for school upgrading provided an opportunity to use an experimental evaluation design while also ensuring that the neediest schools benefit from the project. Schools in the Chaco Region were ranked according to a school quality index based on the sum of five school infrastructure and equipment indicators: electric lights, sewerage, water source, desks per student, and square meters of space per student. Only schools below a particular cutoff value were eligible for a SIF intervention. Among eligible facilities, the worst-off schools were automatically selected to benefit from investments financed by SIF. The next highest priority group contained 120 schools, but funds were available to upgrade only less than half of them. Thus, eligible schools in this second priority group were randomly assigned to treatment or comparison groups, providing the conditions for an experimental evaluation design (Annex 1.4).

Combining Methods

For most evaluations, more than one technique is required to achieve robust results that address several evaluation questions. Each question may necessitate different techniques, even within one project design. Three examples illustrate how several techniques were combined in one evaluation; the Bolivia Social Fund, the TRABAJAR Evaluation in Argentina, and the Nicaragua School Reform.

The Bolivia Social Fund. Social funds generally include several different types of subprojects, and thus designing an evaluation can involve several approaches. In the Bolivia Social fund, the pattern of project implementation dictated evaluation methods. In the case of education, schools that were to receive the intervention had already been identified; therefore randomization could not be used. Instead, matching methods were adopted. In the case of health projects, reflexive methods were used because the intervention was to be implemented in all health centers in the region (see Annex 1.4).

Using a Broad Mix of Evaluation Components—Argentina TRABAJAR II. The TRABAJAR evaluation includes an array of components designed to assess how well the program is achieving its policy objectives. The first component draws on household survey data to assess the income gains to TRABAJAR participants. The second component monitors the program's funding allocation (targeting), tracking changes over time as a result of reform. This component generates twice-yearly feedback used to refine program targeting. Additional evaluation components include a cost-benefit analysis of infrastructure projects, and social assessments designed to provide community feedback on project implementation. Each of these components has been conducted twice. Three future components are planned. The matched-comparison research technique will be applied again to assess the impact of TRABAJAR program participation on labor market activity. Infrastructure project quality will be reassessed, this time for projects that have been completed for at least one year to evaluate durability, maintenance, and utilization rates. Finally, a qualitative research component will investigate program operations and procedures by interviewing staff members in agencies that sponsor projects as well as program beneficiaries.

The evaluation results provide clear direction to policy reform. The first evaluation component reveals that the TRABAJAR program is highly successful at targeting the poor—self-selection of participants by offering low wages is a strategy that works in Argentina, and participants do experience income gains as a result of participation. The second component finds that the geographic allocation of program funding has improved over time—the program is now more successful at directing funds to poor areas; however, the ongoing evaluation process indicates that performance varies and is persistently weak in a few provinces, findings to which further policy attention is currently being directed. Disappointing evaluation results on infrastructure project quality have generated tremendous efforts by the project team at improving performance in this area through policy reform—insisting on more site visits for evaluation and supervision, penalizing agencies with poor performance at project completion, and strengthening the evaluation manual. And finally, the social assessments uncovered a need for better technical assistance to NGOs and rural municipalities during project preparation and implementation, as well as greater publicity and transparency of information about the TRABAJAR program (Annex 1.1).

Nicaragua's School Autonomy Reform. In 1993, the Nicaraguan Government took decisive steps to implement a major decentralization initiative in the education sector granting management and budgetary autonomy to selected primary and secondary schools. The goal of the reforms is to enhance student learning: as school management becomes more democratic and participatory, local school management and spending patterns can be allocated toward efforts that directly improve pedagogy and boost student achievement. The impact of this reform has been evaluated by using a combination of quantitative and qualitative techniques to asses the outcome as well as the process of decentralization. The purpose of the qualitative component is to illuminate whether or not the intended management and financing reforms are actually taking place in schools, and why or why not. The quantitative component fleshes out these results by answering the question, "Do changes in school management and financing actually produce better learning outcomes for children?" The qualitative results show that successful implementation of the reforms depends largely on school context and environment (that is, poverty level of the community), whereas the quantitative results indicate that increased decisionmaking by schools is in fact significantly associated with improved student performance.

Different but complementary methodologies and data sources were used to combine both approaches. On the one hand, the quantitative evaluation followed a quasi-experimental design in which test scores from a sample of students in autonomous schools (treatment group) are compared with results from a matched sample of nonautonomous public schools and private schools (comparison group). Data for this component of the evaluation were collected from a panel of two matched school-household surveys and student achievement test scores. The qualitative evaluation design, on the other hand, consisted of a series of key informant interviews and focus group discussions with different school-based staff and parents in a subsample of the autonomous and traditional schools included in the quantitative study.

Using both qualitative and quantitative research techniques generated a valuable combination of useful, policy-relevant results. The quantitative work provided a broad, statistically valid overview of school conditions and outcomes; the qualitative work enhanced these results with insight into why some expected outcomes of the reform program had been successful while others had failed and hence helped guide policy adjustments. Furthermore, because it is more intuitive, the qualitative work was more accessible and therefore interesting to Ministry staff, which in turn facilitated rapid capacity building and credibility for the evaluation process within the ministry (Annex 1.11).

Exploiting Existing Data Sources

Existing data sources such as a national household survey, census, program administrative record, or municipal data can often provide valuable input to evaluation efforts. Drawing on existing sources reduces the need for costly data collection for the sole purpose of evaluation, as illustrated in the case of the Vietnam Rural Roads evaluation. Furthermore, although existing data may not contain all of the information one would ideally collect for purposes of the evaluation, innovative evaluation techniques can often compensate for missing data, as shown in the Kenya National Agricultural Extension Project.

The Vietnam Rural Roads Project. The data used in this evaluation draw on an effective mix of existing national and local data sources with surveys conducted specifically for the purposes of the evaluation. The evaluation household survey is efficiently designed to replicate a number of questions in the Vietnam Living Standards Survey so that, drawing on information common to both surveys, regression techniques can be used to estimate each household's position in the national distribution of welfare.

The evaluation draws extensively on commune-level data collected annually by the communes covering demographics, land use, and production activities. This data source is augmented with a commune-level survey conducted for the purposes of the evaluation. Two additional databases were set up using existing information. An extensive province-level database was established to help understand the selection of the provinces into the project. This database covers all of Vietnam's provinces and has data on a wide number of socioeconomic variables. Finally, a project-level database for each of the project areas surveyed was also constructed in order to control for the magnitude of the project and the method of implementation in assessing project impact (Annex 1.15).

The Kenya National Extension Project (NEP). The performance of the Kenya National Extension Project (NEP) has been controversial and is part of the larger debate on the cost-effectiveness of the training and visit (T&V) approach to agricultural extension services. In the Kenyan context, the debate has been elevated by, on the one hand, very high estimated returns to T&V reported in one study (Bindlish, Evenson, and Gbetibouo 1993, 1997) and, on the other, the lack of convincing visible results, including the poor performance of Kenyan agriculture in recent years.

The disagreement over the performance of NEP has persisted pending the results of this evaluation, which was designed to take a rigorous, empirical approach to assessing the program's institutional development and impact on agricultural performance. The evaluation uses a mix of qualitative and quantitative methods to ask highly policy-relevant questions and reveals serious weaknesses in the program: (a) The institutional development of NEP has been limited, and after 15 years there is little improvement in the effectiveness of its services; (b) the quality and quantity of service provision are poor; and (c) extension services have only a small positive impact on farm efficiency and none on farm productivity.

The evaluation is able to draw an array of concrete policy conclusions from these results, many of which are relevant to the design of future agricultural extension projects. First, the evaluation reveals a need to enhance T&V targeting, focusing on areas and groups where the impact is likely to be greatest. Furthermore, advice needs to be carefully tailored to meet farmer demands, taking into account variations in local technological and economic conditions. Successfully achieving this level of service targeting calls for appropriate flows of timely and reliable information—hence a program M&E system generating a constant flow of feedback from beneficiaries on service content. In order to raise program efficiency, a leaner and less intense T&V presence with wider coverage is likely to be more cost-effective. The program's blanket approach to service delivery, using a single methodology (farm visits) to deliver standard messages, also limits program efficiency. Institutional reform is likely to enhance the effectiveness of service delivery. Decentralization of program design, including participatory mechanisms that give voice to the farmer (such as cost sharing and farmer organizations) should become an integral part of the delivery mechanism. Finally, cost recovery, even if only partial, would provide appropriate incentives, address issues of accountability and quality control, make the service more demand-driven and responsive, and provide some budgetary improvement (Annex 1.8).

Costs and Financing

There are no doubt many costs involved in carrying out an impact evaluation, which explains why some countries are reluctant to finance such studies. These costs include data collection and the value of staff time for all the members of the evaluation team. Financing for an impact evaluation can come from within a project, other government resources, a research grant, or an outside donor. Information for a sample of World Bank evaluations shows that although many countries assumed the majority of the evaluation costs, the successful implementation of an impact evaluation required substantial outside resources beyond those provided for in a project's loan or credit. These resources came from a combination of the following sources: (a) a World Bank loan or credit financing for the data collection and processing; (b) the government, through the salaries paid to local staff assigned to the evaluation effort (as explained in table 4.1, these staff costs have not been included in the calculation of the evaluation costs conducted for the cases reviewed here because of data limitations); (c) World Bank research grants and bilateral donor grants that financed technical assistance from consultants with specific expertise required for the evaluation; and (d) the World Bank overhead budget through the staff time provided to guide the impact evaluation and often actively participate in the analytical work.

Although few impact evaluations document the cost of carrying out the work, table 4.2 provides cost estimates for a sample of impact evaluations with World Bank involvement. These cost estimates do not, however, include the value of the staff time contributed by client country

Table 4.2 Summary of Estimated Costs from Several World Bank Impact Evaluations

Project	Estimated cost of evaluation ($)[a]	Cost as % of total project cost[b]	Cost as % of IBRD loan or IDA credit[b]	Breakdown of Evaluation Costs (%)			
				Travel[c]	World Bank staff	Consultants	Data collection
Nicaragua School-Based Management	495,000	1.26	1.5	8.1	18.1	39.0	34.8
El Salvador School-Based Management	443,000	0.60	1.3	7.7	7.4	25.8	59.2
Colombia Voucher Program	266,000	0.20	0.3	9.4	9.8	21.8	59.0
Honduras Social Fund	263,000	0.23	0.9	3.0	11.5	53.2	32.3
Nicaragua Social Fund	449,000	0.30	0.8	4.9	33.0	7.8	55.7
Bolivia Social Fund	878,000	0.50	1.4	3.4	14.6	12.9	69.1
Trinidad and Tobago Youth Training	238,000	0.80	1.2	7.6	11.5	17.9	63.1
Average	433,000	0.56	1.0	6.3	15.1	25.5	53.3

a. This cost does not include the cost of local counterpart teams not financed from the loan or credit. The figures refer to the time period under which the projects in the evaluation sample were selected, not total financing ever provided by the Bank and others to those institutions.
b. These costs as a percentage of the loan or credit or of the project are presented as a reference only. In many cases the actual financing for the evaluation was obtained from sources outside of the project financing.
c. The travel cost estimates include mission travel for World Bank staff and international consultants to the client countries, as well as travel from client country counterparts, particularly to participate in strategy sessions and analytical workshops with international consultants and World Bank staff.
Source: World Bank Project Files.

counterparts (which can be significant) because this information was unavailable. As a benchmark, in the 8 cases above it was not unusual to have up to five staff assigned to the evaluation effort for several years, a level of effort sufficient to substantially raise the cost of the evaluation in many of the cases.

The average estimated cost for the impact evaluation was $433,000. This reflects a range from $263,000 for the evaluation of a vocational skills training program for unemployed youth in Trinidad and Tobago to $878,000 for the evaluation of the Bolivian Social Investment Fund. Spending on the impact evaluations for the projects below reflects, on average, 0.6 percent of the total cost of the project (which sometimes included financing from several donors), or 1.3 percent of the cost of the International Bank for Reconstruction and Development (IBRD) loan or the International Development Association (IDA) credit. The most expensive components of the evaluations listed below were data collection and consultants, both local and international. In many of the cases travel costs included local staff travel to meet with World Bank staff and researchers for strategy sessions and training because capacity building for client country staff was a key objective. The two examples below for the impact evaluations of projects in Trinidad and Tobago and Bolivia illustrate some of the variation that can arise in program costs.

The vocational skills training program evaluation in Trinidad and Tobago took advantage of a national income and employment survey to oversample program graduates and create a comparison group from a subset of the national sample. In addition, the evaluation team helped design and use available administrative data from records of program applicants, so preintervention data were available and no enumeration was required to locate program graduates. The total sample size for each of the three tracer studies was approximately 2,500 young people, counting both the treatment and comparison groups. There was only one short questionnaire administered in the survey, and the questionnaire was given only to the program graduates. Trinidad and Tobago is a small country, communities are relatively easy to access by road, and English is the common language in the country and among program graduates.

The Bolivia Social Fund (SIF) evaluation used its own baseline and follow-up surveys of treatment and comparison groups to evaluate interventions in health, education, water, and sanitation. There were no national surveys available from which to conduct analyses or carry out oversampling, which placed the entire burden of data collection on the evaluation. The sample of treatment and comparison groups consisted of close to 7,000 households and 300 facilities interviewed in both the 1993 baseline survey and 1998 follow-up survey.

In Bolivia, the data collection instruments for the impact evaluation consisted of portable laboratories for conducting laboratory-based water quality tests, achievement tests, and eight questionnaires for informants from households and facilities. The eight questionnaires consisted of two household questionnaires (one for the principal informant and one for women of childbearing age), a community questionnaire, four different health center questionnaires for the different types of health centers (ranging from small community clinics to hospitals), and a school questionnaire for the school director. To assess targeting, the evaluation included a consumption-based measure of poverty, which required the collection of detailed consumption data from households as well as regional price data from communities. The fieldwork was conducted in rural areas where the majority of the SIF projects are located and included a random sample of rural households that were often accessible only by foot or on horseback. Finally, the questionnaires had to be developed and administered in Spanish, Quechua, and Aymara.

Political Economy Issues

There are several issues of political economy that affect not only whether an evaluation is carried out but also how it is implemented. The decision to proceed with an evaluation is very much contingent on strong political support. Many governments do not see the value of evaluating projects and thus do not want to invest resources in this. Additionally, there may be reluctance to allow an independent evaluation that may find results contrary to government policy, particularly in authoritarian or closed regimes. More open governments may, however, view evaluations and the dissemination of the findings as an important part of the democratic process.

Evaluations are also sensitive to political change. Three of the eight impact studies listed in table 4.2 were canceled because of political economy issues. Turnover in regimes or key posts within a counterpart government office and shifts in policy strategies can affect not only the evaluation effort, but more fundamentally the implementation of the program being evaluated. One example of this type of risk comes from the experience of a team working on the design and impact evaluation of a school-based management pilot in Peru as part of a World Bank financed primary education project. The team composed of Ministry of Education officials, World Bank staff, and international and local consultants had worked for over a year developing the school-based management models to be piloted, establishing an experimental design, designing survey instruments and achievement tests, and collecting baseline data on school characteristics and student achievement. Just prior to the pilot's introduction in the randomly selected schools, high level government officials canceled the school-based management experiment in a reaction to perceived political fallout from the pilot. A similar reform was introduced several years later, but without the benefit of a pilot test or an evaluation.

In Venezuela, an evaluation of a maternal and infant health and nutrition program was redesigned three times with three different client counterparts as the government shifted responsibility for the evaluation from one agency to another. Each change was accompanied by a contract rene- gotiation with the private sector firm that had been identified to carry out the data collection and the majority of the analysis for the evaluation. When the legitimacy of the third government counterpart began to be questioned, the firm nullified the contract and the evaluation was aban- doned. These incidents occurred during a period of political flux charac- terized by numerous cabinet reshufflings that ended with the collapse of the elected government serving as a counterpart for the project, so the evaluation was hardly alone in suffering from the repercussions of polit- ical instability. Nonetheless, in both the Peruvian and Venezuelan cases, it is sobering to reflect upon the amount of resources devoted to an effort that was never brought to fruition. A less dramatic example of the effect of political change on evaluation strategies comes from El Salvador, where the recognized success of a reform introduced in rural schools prompted the government to introduce a similar education reform in all of the urban schools at once, instead of randomly phasing in schools over time as originally planned. This decision eliminated the possibility of using an experimental design and left using a less-robust reflexive com- parison as the only viable evaluation design option.

Bibliography

The word *processed* describes informally reproduced works that may not be commonly available through libraries.

Abadie, A., J. Angrist, and G. Imbens. 1998. "Instrumental Variables Estimation of Quartile Treatment Effects." National Bureau of Economic Research Working Paper Series, No. 229:1–28.

Atkinson, Anthony. 1987. "On the Measurement of Poverty." *Econometrica* 55: 749–64.

Bamberger, Michael. 2000. *Integrating Quantitative and Qualitative Methods in Development Research.* Washington, D.C.: World Bank.

Barnes, Carolyn. 1966. "Assets and the Impact of Microenterprise Finance Programs." USAID AIMS Project Brief 6. Washington, D.C.: USAID.

Barnes, Carolyn, and Erica Keogh. 1999. "An Assessment of the Impact of Zambuko's Microenterprise Program in Zimbabwe: Baseline Findings." USAID AIMS Project Brief 23. Washington, D.C.: USAID.

Benus, Jacob, Neelima Grover, and Recep Varcin. 1998. *Turkey: Impact of Active Labor Programs.* Bethesda, Md.: Abt Associates.

Benus, Jacob, Neelima Grover, Jiri Berkovsky, and Jan Rehak. 1998. *Czech Republic: Impact of Active Labor Programs.* Bethesda, Md.: Abt Associates.

Besharov, Douglas J., Peter Germanis, and Peter H. Rossi. 1997. *Evaluating Welfare Reform: A Guide for Scholars and Practitioners.* College Park, Md.: University of Maryland.

Bindlish, V., R. Evenson, and Mathurin Gbetibouo. 1993. *Evaluation of T & V-Based Extension in Burkina Faso.* Washington, D.C.: World Bank.

Bloom, Howard S., Larry L. Orr, George Cave, Stephen H. Bell, Fred Doolittle, and Winston Lin. 1994. *The National JTPA Study: Overview, Impacts, Benefits, and Costs of Title II-A.* Bethesda, Md.: Abt Associates.

Blundell, Richard W., and R. J. Smith. 1993. "Simultaneous Microeconometric Models with Censoring or Qualitative Dependent Variables." In G. S. Maddala, C. R. Rao, and H. D. Vinod, eds., *Handbook of Statistics*. Vol. 11. Amsterdam: North Holland.

Bourguignon, Francois, Jaime de Melo, and Akiko Suwa. 1991. "Distributional Effects of Adjustment Policies: Simulations for Archetype Economies in Africa and Latin America." *World Bank Economic Review* 5 (2): 339–66.

Burtless, Gary. 1995. "The Case for Randomized Field Trials in Economic and Policy Research." *Journal of Economic Perspectives* 9 (Spring): 63–84.

Card, David, and Philip K. Robins. 1996. "Do Financial Incentives Encourage Welfare Recipients to Work? Evidence from a Randomized Evaluation of the Self-Sufficiency Project." National Bureau of Economic Research Paper 5701, August. Cambridge, Mass.: NBER.

Carvalho, Soniya, and Howard White. 1994. "Indicators for Monitoring Poverty Reduction." World Bank Discussion Papers 254. Washington, D.C.: World Bank.

Chen, Martha Alter, and Donald Snodgrass. 1999. "An Assessment of the Impact of Sewa Bank in India: Baseline Findings." USAID AIMS Project, Processed. Washington, D.C.: USAID.

Cohen, Monique, and Gary Gaile. 1997. "Highlights and Recommendations of the Virtual Meeting of the CGAP Working Group on Impact Assessment Methodologies." USAID AIMS Project. Washington, D.C.: Management Systems International.

———. 1998. "Highlights and Recommendations of the Second Virtual Meeting of the CGAP Working Group on Impact Assessment Methodologies." USAID AIMS Project. Washington, D.C.: Management Systems International.

Dar, Amit, and Indermit S. Gill. 1998. "Evaluating Retraining Programs in OECD Countries: Lessons Learned." *The World Bank Research Observer* 13 (February): 79–101.

Dar, Amit, and Zafiris Tzannatos. 1999. "Active Labor Market Programs: A Review of Evidence from Evaluations." World Bank Social Protection Discussion Paper 9901. Washington, D.C.: World Bank.

Dehejia, Rajeev H,. and Sadek Wahba. 1998. "Causal Effects in Non-Experimental Studies: Re-Evaluating the Evaluation of Training Programs." NBER Working Paper Series 6586. Cambridge, Mass.: NBER   http://www.nber.org/papers/w6586.

Dennis, Michael L., and Robert F. Boruch. 1989. "Randomized Experiments for Planning and Testing Projects in Developing Countries: Threshold Conditions." *Evaluation Review* 13 (June): 292–309.

Diagne, Aliou, and Manfred Zeller. 1998. "Determinants of Access to Credit and Its Impact on Income and Food Security in Malawi." Manuscript submitted to the International Food Policy Research Institute (IFPRI) Publication Review Committee for consideration as an IFPRI Research Report.

Diop, F., A. Yazbeck, and R. Bitran. 1995. "The Impact of Alternative Cost Recovery Schemes on Access and Equity in Niger." *Health Policy and Planning* 10 (3): 223–40.

Donecker, Jane, and Michael Green. 1998. *Impact Assessment in Multilateral Development Institutions.* London: Department for International Development.

Dunn, Elizabeth. 1999. "Microfinance Clients in Lima, Peru: Baseline Report for AIMS Core Impact Assessment." USAID AIMS Project, Processed. Washington, D.C.: USAID.

Edgecomb, Elaine L., and Carter Garber. 1998. "Practitioner-Led Impact Assessment: A Test in Honduras." USAID AIMS. Washington, D.C.: USAID.

Ezemenari, Kene, Anders Ruqvist, and K. Subbarao. 1999. "Impact Evaluation: A Note on Concepts and Methods." World Bank Poverty Reduction and Economic Management Network, Processed. Washington, D.C.: World Bank.

Foster, James, J. Greer, and Erik Thorbecke. 1984. "A Class of Decomposable Poverty Measures." *Econometrica* 52: 761–65.

Friedlander, Daniel, and Gayle Hamilton. 1993. *The Saturation Work Initiative Model in San Diego: A Five-Year Follow-Up Study.* New York: Manpower Demonstration Research Corporation.

Friedlander, Daniel, and Philip K. Robins. 1995. "Evaluating Program Evaluations: New Evidence on Commonly Used Nonexperimental Methods." *American Economic Review* 85 (September): 923–37.

Friedlander, Daniel, David H. Greenberg, and Philip K. Robins. 1997. "Evaluating Government Training Programs for the Economically Disadvantaged." *Journal of Economic Literature* 35 (December): 1809–55.

Fuller, Bruce, and Magdalena Rivarola. 1998. *Nicaragua's Experiment to Decentralize Schools: Views of Parents, Teachers and Directors.* Working Paper Series on Impact Evaluation of Education Reforms, paper no. 5. Washington, D.C.: World Bank.

Gaile, Gary L., and Jenifer Foster. 1996. "Review of Methodological Approaches to the Study of the Impact of MicroEnterprise Credit Programs." USAID AIMS Brief 2. Washington, D.C.: USAID

Glewwe, Paul, Michael Kremer, and Sylvie Moulin. 1998. "Textbooks and Test Scores: Evidence from a Prospective Evaluation in Kenya." Development Research Group, World Bank, October 28.

Goodman, Margaret, Samuel Morley, Gabriel Siri, and Elaine Zuckerman. 1997. *Social Investment Funds in Latin America: Past Performance and Future Role.* Washington D.C.: Inter American Development Bank. March.

Government of Denmark. 1995. *Methods for Evaluation of Poverty Oriented Aid Interventions.* Copenhagen: Ministry of Foreign Affairs.

Greene, W. H. 1997. *Econometric Analysis.* Hemel Hempstead, New Jersey: Prentice Hall Press.

Greenberg, David, and Mark Shroder. 1997. *The Digest of Social Experiments*, 2nd ed. Washington, D.C.: The Urban Institute Press.

Grosh, Margaret E., and Juan Muñoz. 1996. "A Manual for Planning and Implementing the Living Standards Measurement Study Survey." LSMS Working Paper #126. World Bank, Washington, D.C.

Grossman, Jean Baldwin. 1994. "Evaluating Social Policies: Principles and U.S. Experience." *The World Bank Research Observer* 9 (July): 159–80.

Habicht, J. P., C. G. Victoria, and J. P. Vaughan. 1999. "Evaluation Designs for Adequacy, Plausibility and Probability of Public Health Programme Performance and Impact." *International Journal of Epidemiology* 28: 10–18.

Harrell, Adele, Martha Burt, Harry Hatry, Shelli Rossman, Jeffrey Roth, and William Sabol. 1996. *Evaluation Strategies for Human Service Programs: A Guide for Policymakers and Providers.* Washington, D.C.: Urban Institute.

Heckman, James. 1997. "Instrumental Variables. A Study of Implicit Behavioral Assumptions Used in Making Program Evaluations." *Journal of Human Resources* 32 (3): 441–61.

Heckman, James, R. Lalonde, and J. Smith. 1999. "The Economics and Econometrics of Active Labor Market Programs." In O. Ashenfelter and D. Card, eds., *Handbook of Labor Economics,* vol. III. New York: Elsevier Science Publishing Co.

Heckman, James, and Richard Robb. 1985. "Alternative Methods of Evaluating the Impact of Interventions: An Overview." *Journal of Econometrics* 30: 239–67.

Heckman, James J., and Jeffrey A. Smith. 1995. "Assessing the Case for Social Experiments." *Journal of Economic Perspectives* 9 (2): 85–110.

Heckman, J., H. Ichimura, J. Smith, and P. Todd. 1998. "Characterizing Selection Bias Using Experimental Data." *Econometrica* 66: 1017–99.

Hicks, Norman. 1998. *Measuring the Poverty Impact of Projects in LAC.* World Bank Latin America and the Caribbean Region, Processed. Washington, D.C.: World Bank.

Holder, Harold D., Andrew J. Treno, Robert F. Saltz, and Joel W. Grube. 1997. "Summing Up: Recommendations and Experiences for Evaluation of Community-Level Prevention Programs." *Evaluation Review* 21 (April): 268–78.

Hollister, Robinson G., and Jennifer Hill. 1995. *Problems in the Evaluation of Community-Wide Initiatives.* New York: Russell Sage Foundation.

Hulme, David. 1997. "Impact Assessment Methodologies for Microfinance: Theory, Experience and Better Practice." Manchester,

U.K.: Institute for Development Policy and Management, University of Manchester.

International Food Policy Research Institute. 1998. *Programa Nacional de Educación, Salud, y Alimentación (PROGRESA): A Proposal for Evaluation* (with technical appendix). Washington, D.C.: IFPRI.

Jalan, Jyotsna, and Martin Ravallion. 1998a. "Income Gains from Workfare: Estimates for Argentina's TRABAJAR Program Using Matching Methods." Washington D.C.: Development Research Group, World Bank.

————. 1998b. "Transfer Benefits from Workfare: A Matching Estimate for Argentina." Washington, D.C.: Development Research Group, World Bank.

Jamison, Dean T., Barbara Serle, Klaus Galda, and Stephen P. Heyneman. 1981. "Improving Elementary Mathematics Education in Nicaragua: An Experimental Study of the Impact of Textbooks and Radio on Achievement." *Journal of Educational Psychology* 73 (4): 556–67.

Karoly, Lynn A., Peter W. Greenwood, Susan S. Everingham, Jill Houbé, M. Rebecca Kilburn, C. Peter Rydell, Matthew Sanders, and James Chiesa. 1998. *Investing in Our Children: What We Know and Don't Know about the Costs and Benefits of Early Childhood Interventions.* Santa Monica, Calif.: Rand.

Kemple, James J., Fred Doolittle, and John W. Wallace. 1993. *The National JTPA Study: Site Characteristics and Participation Patterns.* New York: Manpower Demonstration Research Corporation.

Khandker, Shahidur R. 1998. *Fighting Poverty with Microcredit: Experience in Bangladesh.* New York: Oxford University Press for the World Bank.

Killick, Tony. 1995. *IMF Programmes in Developing Countries, Design and Impact.* London: England.

King, Elizabeth, and Berk Ozler. 1998. *What's Decentralization Got to Do with Learning? The Case of Nicaragua's School Autonomy Reform.* Working Paper Series on Impact Evaluation of Education Reforms, paper no. 9. Washington, D.C.: World Bank.

King, Elizabeth, Berk Ozler, and Laura Rawlings. 1999. *Nicaragua's School Autonomy Reform: Fact or Fiction?* Washington, D.C.: World Bank.

Kish, Leslie. 1965. *Survey Sampling.* New York: John Wiley and Sons.

Levinson, James F., Beatrice Lorge Rogers, Kristin M. Hicks, Thomas Schaetzel, Lisa Troy, and Collette Young. 1998. *Monitoring and Evaluation: A Guidebook for Nutrition Project Managers in Developing Countries.* Medford, Mass.: International Food and Nutrition Center, Tufts University School of Nutrition Science and Policy, March.

Manski, Charles, and Irwin Garfinkel, eds. 1992. *Evaluating Welfare and Training Programs.* Cambridge, Mass.: Harvard University Press.

Manski, Charles, and Steven Lerman. 1977. "The Estimation of Choice Probabilities from Choice-Based Samples." *Econometrica* 45: 1977–88.

McKay, H., A. McKay, L. Siniestra, H. Gomez, and P. Lloreda. 1978. "Improving Cognitive Ability in Chronically Deprived Children" *Science 2000*(21): 270–78.

Meyer, Bruce D. 1995. "Natural and Quasi-Experiments in Economics." *Journal of Business and Economic Statistics*, 13 (April): 151–161.

Miles, Matthew B., and A. Michael Huberman. 1994. *Qualitative Data Analysis.* London: Sage Publications.

MkNelly, Barbara, and Karen Lippold. 1998. "Practitioner-Led Impact Assessment: A Test in Mali." USAID AIMS Brief 21. Washington, D.C.: USAID

MkNelly, Barbara, and Christopher Dunford (in collaboration with the Program in International Nutrition, University of California, Davis). 1998. "Impact of Credit with Education on Mothers' and Their Young Children's Nutrition: Lower Pra Rural Bank Credit with Education Program in Ghana." Freedom from Hunger Research Paper No. 4, March.

Moffitt, Robert. 1991. "Program Evaluation with Nonexperimental Data." *Evaluation Review* 15 (3): 291–314.

90 EVALUATING THE IMPACT OF DEVELOPMENT PROJECTS ON POVERTY

Mohr, Lawrence B. 1995. *Impact Analysis for Program Evaluation*, 2nd ed. Thousand Oaks, Calif.: Sage Publications.

———. 1999. "The Qualitative Method of Impact Analysis." Processed.

Morduch, Jonathan. 1998a. "The Microfinance Schism." Harvard Institute for International Development, Development Discussion Paper 626, February.

———. 1998b. "Does Microfinance Really Help the Poor? New Evidence from Flagship Programs in Bangladesh." Harvard University Institute for International Development, Processed, June.

———. 1999. "The Microfinance Promise." *Journal of Economic Literature* 37(4): 1569–1614.

Newman, John, Menno Pradhan, Laura Rawlings, Ramiro Coa, and Jose Luis Evia. 2000. "An Impact Evaluation of Education, Health, and Water Supply Investments of the Bolivia Social Investment Fund." Processed.

Newman, John, Laura Rawlings, and Paul Gertler. 1994. "Using Randomized Control Designs in Evaluating Social Sector Programs in Developing Countries." *The World Bank Research Observer* 9 (July): 181–202.

Operations Evaluation Department, World Bank. 1994. "An Overview of Monitoring and Evaluation in the World Bank." June 30.

Poppele, J. S. Summarto, and L. Pritchett. 1999. "Social Impacts of the Indonesia Crisis: New Data and Policy Implications." Social Monitoring Early Response Unit, World Bank, Washington, D.C. Processed.

Pradhan, Menno, Laura Rawlings, and Geert Ridder. 1998. "The Bolivian Social Investment Fund: An Analysis of Baseline Data for Impact Evaluation." *World Bank Economic Review* 12 (3): 457–82.

Ravallion, Martin. 1994. *Poverty Comparisons, Fundamentals in Pure and Applied Economics*, vol. 56. Harwood Academic Publishers.

———. 1999. *Monitoring Targeting Performance When Decentralized Allocations to the Poor Are Unobserved*. World Bank, Washington, D.C. Processed.

Ravallion, Martin, and Quentin Wodon. 1998. *Evaluating a Targeted Social Program When Placement Is Decentralized.* World Bank Policy Research Working Paper 1945. Washington, D.C.: World Bank.

Ravallion, Martin, Dominique van de Walle, and Madhur Gautam. 1995. "Testing a Social Safety Net." *Journal of Public Economics* 57: 175–99.

Rawlings, Laura. 2000. "Assessing Educational Management and Quality in Nicaragua." In Bamberger: *Integrating Quantitative and Qualitative Methods in Development Research.* Washington, D.C.: World Bank.

Rebien, Claus C. 1997. "Development Assistance Evaluation and the Foundations of Program Evaluation." *Evaluation Review* 21 (August): 438–60.

Revenga, Ana, Michelle Riboud, and Hong Tan. 1994. "The Impact of Mexico's Retraining Program on Employment and Wages." *World Bank Economic Review* 8 (2): 247–77.

Rivers, Douglas, and Quang H. Vuong. 1988. "Limited Information Estimators and Exogeneity Tests for Simultaneous Probit Models." *Journal of Econometrics* 39: 347–66.

Robinson, Sherman. 1991. "Macroeconomics, Financial Variables, and Computable General Equilibrium Models." *World Development,* 19(11): 1509–25.

Rosenbaum, P., and D. Rubin. 1983. "The Central Role of the Propensity Score in Observational Studies for Causal Effects." *Biometrika* 70: 41–55.

————. 1985. "Constructing a Control Group Using Multivariate Matched Sampling Methods that Incorporate the Propensity Score." *American Statistician* 39: 35–39.

Rossman, Gretchen B., and Bruce L. Wilson. 1985. "Numbers and Words: Combining Quantitative and Qualitative Methods in a Single Large-Scale Evaluation Study. *Evaluation Review* 9 (3): 627–43.

Sahn, David, Paul Dorosh, and Stephen Younger. 1996. "Exchange Rate, Fiscal and Agricultural Policies in Africa: Does Adjustment Hurt the Poor?" *World Development,* 24(4): 719–47.

Sebstad, Jennifer, and Gregory Chen. 1996. "Overview of Studies on the Impact of MicroEnterprise Credit." USAID AIMS, June. Washington, D.C.: USAID

Sharma, Manohar, and Gertrud Schrieder. 1998. "Impact of Finance on Food Security and Poverty Alleviation—A Review and Synthesis of Empirical Evidence." Paper presented to Workshop on Innovations in Micro-Finance for the Rural Poor: Exchange of Knowledge and Implications for Policy, Ghana, November.

Smith, William. 1998. *Group Based Assessment of Change: Method and Results.* Hanoi, Vietnam: ActionAid.

Subbarao, K., Kene Ezemenari, John Randa, and Gloria Rubio. 1999. *Impact Evaluation in FY98 Bank Projects: A Review.* World Bank Poverty Reduction and Economic Management Network, Processed, January.

Tan, J.P, J. Lane, and G. Lassibille. 1999. "Schooling Outcomes in Philippine Elementary Schools: Evaluation of the Impact of Four Experiments." *World Bank Economic Review*, September.

Taschereau, Suzanne. 1998. *Evaluating the Impact of Training and Institutional Development Programs, a Collaborative Approach.* Economic Development Institute of the World Bank, January.

USAID. 1984. "Study of Low Cost Housing." New Delhi: USAID. June.

———. 1995. "Assessing the Impacts of MicroEnterprise Interventions: A Framework for Analysis." MicroEnterprise Development Brief, June.

Valadez, J., and M. Bamberger, ed. 1994. "Monitoring and Evaluating Social Programs in Developing Countries." Economic Development Institute of the World Bank Series, World Bank, Washington, D.C.

van de Walle, Dominique. 1999. "Assessing the Poverty Impact of Rural Road Projects." World Bank. Processed.

Walker, Ian, Rafael del Cid, Fidel Ordoñez, and Florencia Rodriguez. 1999. "Evaluación Ex-Post del Fondo Hondureño de Inversión Social (FHIS 2)." ESA Consultores, Tegucigalpa, Honduras.

Weiss, Carol H. 1998. *Evaluation.* Upper Saddle River, New Jersey: Prentice Hall.

Wilson, Sandra Jo. 1998. "A Multi-Method Proposal to Evaluate the Impact of CGIAR-Instigated Activities on Poverty Reduction." Paper presented to the Annual Conference of the American Evaluation Association, November.

World Bank, Poverty and Human Resources Division, Policy Research Department. 1994a. *Impact Evaluation of Education Projects Involving Decentralization and Privatization.* Working Paper. Washington, D.C.: World Bank.

———, Learning and Leadership Center and Operations Policy Department. 1996. *Handbook on Economic Analysis of Investment Operations.* Washington, D.C.: World Bank.

———, Operations and Evaluation Department. 1998a. *1998 Annual Review of Development Effectiveness.* Washington, D.C.: World Bank.

———, Poverty Reduction and Economic Management, Latin America and Caribbean Region. 1998b. *Measuring the Poverty Impact of Projects in LAC.* Washington, D.C.: World Bank.

———, Operations and Evaluation Department. 1999. *World Bank Agricultural Extension Projects in Kenya: An Impact Evaluation.* Report No. 19523. Washington, D.C.: World Bank.

———, Poverty Reduction and Economic Management Unit, 1999. *Strategy for Impact Evaluation.* Washington, D.C.: World Bank.

Wouters, A. 1995. "Improving Quality through Cost Recovery in Niger." *Health Policy and Planning* 10 (3): 257–70.

Zeller, Manfred, Akhter Ahmed, Suresh Babu, Sumiter Broca, Aliou Diagne, and Manohar Sharma. 1996. "Security of the Poor: Methodologies for a Multicountry Research Project." IFPRI Discussion Paper 11.

Annex 1
Case Studies

Annex 1.1: Evaluating the Gains to the Poor from Workfare: Argentina's TRABAJAR Program

I. Introduction

Project Description. Argentina's TRABAJAR program aims to reduce poverty by simultaneously generating employment opportunities for the poor and improving social infrastructure in poor communities. TRABAJAR I, a pilot program, was introduced in 1996 in response to a prevailing economic crisis and unemployment rates of over 17 percent. TRABAJAR II was launched in 1997 as an expanded and reformed version of the pilot program, and TRABAJAR III began approving projects in 1998. The program offers relatively low wages in order to attract ("self-select") only poor, unemployed workers as participants. The infrastructure projects that participants are hired to work on are proposed by local government and nongovernmental organizations (NGOs), which must cover the non-wage costs of the project. Projects are approved at the regional level according to central government guidelines.

The program has undergone changes in design and operating procedures informed by the evaluation process. TRABAJAR II included a number of reforms designed to improve project targeting. The central government's budget allocation system is now more heavily influenced by provincial poverty and unemployment indicators, and a higher weight is given to project proposals from poor areas under the project approval guidelines. At the local level, efforts have been made in both TRABAJAR II and III to strengthen the capability of provincial offices for helping poor areas mount projects and to raise standards of infrastructure quality.

Impact Evaluation. The evaluation effort began during project preparation for TRABAJAR II and is ongoing. The aim of the evaluation is to determine whether or not the program is achieving its policy goals and to indicate areas in which the program requires reform in order to maximize its effectiveness. The evaluation consists of a number of separate studies that assess (a) the net income gains that accrue to program participants, (b) the allocation of program resources across regions (targeting), (c) the quality of the infrastructure projects financed, and (d) the role of the community and NGOs in project outcome.

94

Two of the evaluation components stand out technically in demonstrating best practice empirical techniques. First, the study of net income gains illustrates best-practice techniques in matched comparison as well as resourceful use of existing national household survey data in conducting the matching exercise. Second, the study of targeting outcomes presents a new technique for evaluating targeting when the incidence of public spending at the local level is unobserved. The overall evaluation design also presents a best-practice mix of components and research techniques—from quantitative analysis to engineering site visits to social assessment—which provide an integrated stream of results in a timely manner.

II. Evaluation Design

The TRABAJAR evaluation includes an array of components designed to assess how well the program is achieving its policy objectives. The first component draws on household survey data to assess the income gains to TRABAJAR participants. This study improves upon conventional assessments of workfare programs, which typically measure participants' income gains as simply their *gross* wages earned, by estimating net income gains. Using recent advances in matched-comparison techniques, the study accounts for forgone income (income given up by participants in joining the TRABAJAR program), which results in a more accurate, lower estimate of the net income gains to participants. The second component monitors the program's funding allocation (targeting), tracking changes over time as a result of reform. Through judicious use of commonly available data (program funding allocations across provinces and a national census), the design of this component presents a new methodology for assessing poverty targeting when there is no actual data on program incidence. This analysis began with the first supervisory mission (November 1997) and has been updated twice yearly since then.

Additional evaluation components include a cost-benefit analysis conducted for a subsample of infrastructure projects, along with social assessments designed to provide feedback on project implementation. Each of these activities has been conducted twice, for both TRABAJAR II and TRABAJAR III. Three future evaluation activities are planned. The matched-comparison research technique will be applied again to assess the impact of TRABAJAR program participation on labor market activity. Infrastructure project quality will be reassessed, this time for projects that have been completed for at least one year to evaluate durability, maintenance, and utilization rates. Finally, a qualitative research component will investigate program operations and procedures by interviewing staff members in agencies that sponsor projects as well as program beneficiaries.

III. Data Collection and Analysis Techniques

The assessment of net income gains to program participants draws on two data sources, a national living standards survey (Encuesta de Desarrollo Social—EDS) and a survey of TRABAJAR participants conducted specifically for the purposes of evaluation. (The EDS survey was financed under another World Bank project. It was designed to improve the quality of information on household welfare in Argentina, particularly in the area of access to social services and government social programs.) These surveys were conducted in August (EDS) and September (TRABAJAR participant survey) of 1997 by the national statistical office, using the same questionnaire and same interview teams. The sample for the EDS survey covers 85 percent of the national population, omitting some rural areas and very small communities. The sample for the TRABAJAR participant survey is drawn from a random sample of TRABAJAR II projects located within the EDS sample frame and generates data for 2,802 current program participants (total TRABAJAR II participants between May 1997 and January 1998 numbered 65,321). The reliability of the matching technique is enhanced by the ability to apply the same questionnaire to both participants and the control group at the same time and to ensure that both groups are from the same economic environment.

To generate the matching control group from the EDS survey, the study uses a technique called propensity scoring. (The fact that the EDS questionnaire is very comprehensive, collecting detailed data on household characteristics that help predict program participation, facilitates the use of the propensity scoring technique.) An ideal match would be two individuals, one in the participant sample and one in the control group, for whom all of these variables (x) predicting program participation are identical. The standard problem in matching is that this is impractical given the large number of variables contained in x. However, matches can be calculated on each individual's propensity score, which is simply the probability of participating conditional on (x). (The propensity score is calculated for each observation in the participant and control group sample by using standard logit models.) Data on incomes in the matching control group of nonparticipants allows the income forgone by actual TRABAJAR II participants to be estimated. Net income arising from program participation is then calculated as total program wages minus forgone income.

The targeting analysis is remarkable in that no special data collection was necessary. Empirical work draws on data from the ministry's project office on funding allocations by geographic department for TRABAJAR I (March 1996 to April 1997) and the first six months of TRABAJAR II (May to October 1997). It also draws on a poverty index for each department (of which there are 510), calculated from the 1991 census as the proportion of households with "unmet basic needs." This is a composite index representing residential crowding, sanitation facilities, housing quality, educational attainment of adults, school enrollment of children, employment, and dependency (ratio of working to nonworking family members). The index is somewhat dated, although this has the advantage of the departmental poverty measure being exogenous to (not influenced by) TRABAJAR interventions. To analyze targeting incidence, data on public spending by geographic area—in this case, department—are regressed on corresponding geographic poverty rates. The resulting coefficient consistently estimates a "targeting differential" given by the difference between the program's average allocations to the poor and nonpoor. This national targeting differential can then be decomposed to assess the contribution of the central government's targeting mechanism (funding allocations across departments) versus targeting at the provincial level of local government.

The cost-benefit analysis was conducted by a civil engineer, who conducted a two-stage study of TRABAJAR infrastructure projects. In the first stage she visited a sample of 50 completed TRABAJAR I projects and rated them based on indicators in six categories: technical, institutional, environmental, socioeconomic, supervision, and operations and maintenance. Projects were then given an overall quality rating according to a point system, and cost-benefit analyses were performed where appropriate (not for schools or health centers). A similar follow-up study of 120 TRABAJAR II projects was conducted a year later, tracking the impact of reforms on infrastructure quality.

The social assessments were conducted during project preparation for both TRABAJAR I and TRABAJAR II. They provide feedback on project implementation issues such as the role of NGOs, the availability of technical assistance in project preparation and construction, and the selection of beneficiaries. Both social assessments were carried out by sociologists by means of focus groups and interviews.

IV. Results

Taking account of forgone income is important to gaining an accurate portrayal of workfare program benefits. Descriptive statistics for TRABAJAR II participants suggest that without access to the program (per capita family income minus program wages) about 85 percent of program participants would fall in the bottom 20 percent of the national income distribution—and would therefore be classified as poor in Argentina. However, matching-method estimates of forgone income are sizable, so that average net income gained through program participation is about half of the TRABAJAR wage. Program participants could not afford to be unemployed in the absence of the program; hence some income is forgone through program participation. It is this forgone income that is estimated by observing the incomes of nonparticipants "matched" to those of program participants. However, even allowing for forgone income, the distribution of gains is decidedly pro-poor, with 80 percent of program participants falling in the bottom 20 percent of the income distribution. Female participation in the program is low (15 percent), but net income gains are virtually identical for male and female TRABAJAR participants; younger participants do obtain significantly lower income gains.

Targeting performance improved markedly as a result of TRABAJAR II reforms. There was a sevenfold increase in the implicit allocation of resources to poor households between TRABAJAR I and TRABAJAR II. One-third of this improvement results from better targeting at the central level, and two-thirds results from improved targeting at the provincial level. There are, however, significant differences in targeting outcomes between provinces. A department with 40 percent of people classified as poor can expect to receive anywhere from zero to five times the mean departmental allocation, depending upon the province to which it belongs. Furthermore, those targeting performance tended to be worse in the poorest provinces.

Infrastructure project quality was found to be adequate, but TRABAJAR II reforms, disappointingly, did not result in significant improvements. Part of the reason was the sharp expansion of the program, which made it difficult for the program to meet some of the operational standards that had been specified ex ante. However, projects were better at meeting the priority needs of the community. The social assessment uncovered a need for better technical assistance to NGOs and rural municipalities as well as greater publicity and transparency of information about the TRABAJAR program.

V. Policy Application

The evaluation results provide clear evidence that the TRABAJAR program participants do come largely from among the poor. Self-selection of participants by offering low wages is a strategy that works in Argentina, and participants do experience income gains as a result of participation (although these net gains are lower than the gross wage, owing to income forgone). The program does not seem to discriminate against female participation. TRABAJAR II reforms have successfully enhanced geographic targeting outcomes—the program is now more successful at directing funds to poor areas; however, performance varies and is persistently weak in a few provinces that merit further policy attention. Finally, disappointing results on infrastructure project quality have generated tremendous efforts by the project team to improve performance in this area by enhancing operating procedures—insisting on more site visits for evaluation and supervision, penalizing agencies with poor performance in project completion, and strengthening the evaluation manual.

VI. Evaluation Costs and Administration

Costs. The cost for carrying out the TRABAJAR survey (for the study of net income gains) and data processing was approximately $350,000. The two evaluations of subproject quality (cost-benefit analysis) cost roughly $10,000 each, as did the social assessments, bringing total expenditures on the evaluation to an estimated $390,000.

Administration. The evaluation was designed by World Bank staff member Martin Ravallion and implemented jointly with the World Bank and the Argentinean project team. Throughout its different stages, the evaluation effort also required coordination with several local government agencies, including the statistical agency, the Ministry of Labor (including field offices), and the policy analysis division of the Ministry for Social Development.

VII. Lessons Learned

Importance of Accounting for Forgone Income in Assessing the Gains to Workfare. Forgone income represents a sizable proportion (about half) of the gross wage earned by workfare program participants in Argentina. The result suggests that conventional assessment methods (using only the gross wage) substantially overestimate income gains and hence also overestimate how poor participants would be in absence of the program.

Propensity-Score Matching Method. When the matched-comparison evaluation technique is used, propensity scores allow reliable matches to be drawn between a participant and nonparticipant (control group) sample.

Judicious Use of Existing National Data Sources. Often, existing data sources such as the national census or household survey can provide valuable input to evaluation efforts. Drawing on existing sources reduces the need for costly data collection for the sole purpose of evaluation. Innovative evaluation techniques can compensate for missing data, as the assessment of TRABAJAR's geographic targeting outcomes aptly illustrates.

Broad Range of Evaluation Components. The TRABAJAR evaluation design illustrates an effective mix of evaluation tools and techniques. Survey data analysis, site visits, and social assessments are all used to generate a wide range of results that provide valuable input to the project's effectiveness and pinpoint areas for reform.

Timeliness of Results. Many of the evaluation components were designed explicitly with the project cycle in mind, timed to generate results during project preparation stages so that results could effectively be used to inform policy. Several components now generate data regularly in a continuous process of project monitoring.

VIII. Sources

Jalan, Jyotsna, and Martin Ravallion. 1999. "Income Gains from Workfare and Their Distribution." World Bank, Washington, D.C. Processed.

Ravallion, Martin. 1999. Monitoring Targeting Performance When Decentralized Allocations to the Poor Are Unobserved." World Bank, Washington, D.C. Processed.

Annex 1.2: Does Microfinance Really Help the Poor? New Evidence from Flagship Programs in Bangladesh

I. Introduction

Project Description. The microfinance programs of the Grameen Bank, the Bangladesh Rural Advancement Committee, and the Bangladesh Rural Development Board are flagship programs for those instituted in many other countries. These programs provide small loans to poor households who own less than one-half acre of land. Loans are accompanied by innovative contracts and loan schedules. The programs have served over 4 million poor clients in Bangladesh and have apparently been quite successful. For example, the top quartile of borrowers from the Grameen Bank consume 15 percent more and have almost twice as high a proportion of sons in school and a substantially increased proportion of daughters in school compared with the bottom quartile.

Highlights of Evaluation. The evaluation investigates the impact of the programs on 1,800 households in Bangladesh and compares them with a control group of households in areas without any microcredit financing. The major contribution of the study is to demonstrate that simple estimates of the impact of programs can be substantially overstated: correction for selection bias nullifies apparently impressive gains. The evaluation shows that much of the perceived gains is driven by differences in who gets the loans: they tend to be wealthier and work more than control groups. Once appropriate techniques are used, there is no impact of borrowing on consumption, and children in program areas actually do worse than children in control areas. The key determining factor is the fact that program lending has not followed eligibility guidelines—in fact, many of the borrowers had landholdings in excess of the half-acre maximum.

The evaluation both uses an interesting survey technique and makes imaginative use of econometric techniques. Another interesting angle is that the evaluation also looks at the effect of the impact on the variance as well as the mean outcome and finds that the main gain from the programs is risk reduction rather than increasing mean outcomes.

II. Research Questions and Evaluation Design

The researchers are interested in identifying the impact of microfinance programs on log consumption per capita, variance of log consumption, log labor per adult in previous month, variance of per adult log labor, adult male labor hours in past month, adult female labor hours in past month, percentage of male school enrollment (ages 5 to 17), and percentage of female school enrollment (ages 5 to 17).

The evaluation is survey-based and covers 87 villages surveyed three times during 1991 and 1992. Villages were chosen randomly from a census and administrative lists, from 5 subdistricts that served as controls and 24 subdistricts where the programs were implemented. Twenty households were surveyed per village.

This enabled the researchers to split the households into five different types, depending on the eligibility criterion of holding one-half acre of land. It is worth reproducing the schematic, which illustrates how to create dummy variables that characterize the typology and how to think about selection bias.

Village 1: With program			Village 2: Control
A Not eligible [b=1;e=0;c=0]		Households with more than 1/2 acre	B would not be eligible [b=0;e=0;c=0]
C eligible but does not participate [b=1;e=1;c=0]	D Participants [b=1;e=1;c=1]	Households with 1/2 acre and below	E Would be eligible [b=0;e=1;c=0]

Comparing outcomes for group D with those for group C is fraught with selection problems: evidence suggests that group C households do not participate because they are afraid of not being able to pay back. If landholding is exogenous, groups C and D can be compared with group E, however, because outcome difference depends on program placement rather than self-selection. This is not true, of course, if there are differences across villages. If there are differences (due, possibly, to nonrandom placement), then it is better to take a difference-in-difference approach. Thus, an evaluator can calculate mean outcomes for C and D, mean outcomes for A, and then calculate the difference. Similarly, the difference between mean outcomes for E and mean outcomes for B can be calculated, and then the within-village differences can be compared.

III. Data

The researchers collected data on 1,798 households; 1,538 of these were eligible to participate and 905 actually participated. The surveys were collected in 1991 and 1992 after the harvests of the three main rice seasons. The key variables of interest were consumption per capita in the previous week, the amount of credit received, amount of land held, labor supply in the past month, and demographic characteristics. A secondary data source on land transactions is also used to check on market activity in land.

IV. Econometric Techniques

There are three interesting components to the techniques used. The first is the use of administrative data to check the key assumptions necessary to use a regression discontinuity design strategy: the exogeneity of land-holding. The second is a very nice use of nonparametric graphing techniques to describe both the probability of being found eligible and the probability of getting a loan as a function of landholdings. This is combined with a very good discussion of when it is appropriate to use a regression discontinuity design—since the graphical analysis suggests that there is no clear breaking point at 0.5 acre. Finally, the study primarily uses difference and difference-in-differences techniques.

V. Who Carried It Out

The data were collected by the Bangladesh Institute for Development Studies on behalf of the World Bank. The analysis was performed by researcher Jonathan Morduch.

VI. Results

The results suggest that almost all the apparent gains from the program are due to selection bias resulting from loan mistargeting. In particular, the authors find that 20 to 30 percent of the borrowers own more land than the half-acre maximum requirement for the program, which suggests that program officers are likely to bend the rules in unobservable ways. When the comparisons are restricted to only those borrowers who meet the land restriction, the authors find that average consumption in the villages with access to microfinancing is less than the controls with both the difference and difference-in-differences methods. This suggests that there was substantial mistargeting of program funds, and as a result regression discontinuity approaches cannot be used to analyze program effects.

The evaluation is also useful in the comparison of results from different econometric techniques: results differ markedly when fixed effects and difference-in-differences or simple difference approaches are used.

The evaluation makes a convincing case that the former is less appropriate when unobservable target group differences are used in making the location decision. However, there are conflicting results in the two approaches about whether the programs reduced variation in consumption and income, highlighting the need for longitudinal data. The impact on education is actually reverse after correction for selection bias.

It is also worth noting that although this analysis shows little impact of the treatment relative to the control group, the control group may not, in fact, have lacked access to financing because this may be supplied by NGOs. The expenditure of millions of dollars to subsidize microfinance programs is, however, called into question.

VII. Lessons Learned

There are several very important lessons from this study. The first is the importance of checking whether the program functions as prescribed. The second is the consideration of the appropriateness of regression discontinuity design versus difference in differences or simple difference techniques. The third is considering the impact of an intervention on the second as well as on the first moment of the distribution, since the reduction in risk may, in itself, be a useful outcome. There is a more fundamental lesson that is not directly addressed but is clearly learned from the study. That lesson is one of political economy: if there is a strong incentive to bend the rules, those rules will be bent.

VIII. Sources

Morduch, Jonathan. 1998. "Does Microfinance Really Help the Poor? New Evidence from Flagship Programs in Bangladesh." Processed, June 17.

Also see:

Khandker, Shahidur R. 1998. *Fighting Poverty with Microcredit: Experience in Bangladesh.* New York: Oxford University Press for the World Bank.

Annex 1.3: Bangladesh Food for Education: Evaluating a Targeted Social Program When Placement Is Decentralized

I. Introduction

Project Description. The Food for Education (FFE) program in Bangladesh was designed to increase primary school attendance by providing rice or wheat to selected households as an incentive to parents. This began as a pilot program but has grown in size and importance: its share of the Primary and Mass Education Division's budget grew from 11 percent in 1993–94 to 26 percent in 1995–96 and reached 2.2 million children, or 13 percent of total enrollment. The design is quite interesting: the program was hierarchically targeted in that FFE was given to all schools in selected economically backward geographic units with low schooling levels. Then households were chosen to receive the food by community groups within the geographic units, based on set, albeit somewhat discretionary, criteria (landless households, female-headed households, and low-income households). Children in these households must attend at least 85 percent of the classes each month.

Highlights of Evaluation. This evaluation is extremely useful because it illustrates what can be done when the intervention design is not at all conducive to standard evaluation techniques and when the evaluation has to be done using existing data sources. In fact, the approach in the FFE was almost the polar opposite to a completely random assignment: not only were the geographic areas chosen because they had certain characteristics but the individuals within them were chosen because they needed help. Thus, since the program was targeted at the poorest of the poor, simple analysis will understate the impact.

This intervention design creates a major problem with creating a counterfactual because clearly selection into the program is determined by the household's need for the program. The evaluation provides an innovative—and readily generalizable— approach to addressing the resulting bias by relying on the decentralization of the decisionmaking process. In brief, because the central government allocates expenditures across geographic areas, but local agents make the within-area allocation, the evaluation uses instrumental variable techniques based on geography to reduce the bias inherent in the endogenous selection procedure. The application of the method results in much higher estimated impacts of FFE than ordinary least squares approaches.

II. Research Questions and Evaluation Design

The research question is to quantify the impact of the FFE on school attendance, measured as the attendance rate for each household. There is little in the way of prospective evaluation design: the evaluation is performed with already existing data— in particular, using both a nationally representative household expenditure survey and a detailed community survey. The retrospective evaluation was in fact designed to obviate the need for a baseline survey; the evaluation simply needed surveys that included household characteristics and specific geographic characteristics of the household area. The subsequent sections provide more detail on how these can be structured so that they reliably infer the impact of the intervention.

III. Data

The data are from the 1995–96 Household Expenditure Survey (HES), a nationally representative survey conducted by the Bangladesh Bureau of Statistics that both includes questions on FFE participation and has a local level survey component. The authors use responses on demographic household characteristics, land ownership, school, and program variables from 3,625 rural households to identify the impact on school attendance. School attendance for each child is actually directly measured in the HES: both the days that are missed and the days that the school is closed are counted. The dependent variable was constructed to be the household average number of days school was attended as a proportion of the feasible number of days. Both parts of this survey are critical. On the one hand, information on the household helps to capture the impact of demographic characteristics on school attendance. On the other hand, information on the characteristics of geographic location helps to model the decisionmaking strategy of the centralized government and reduce the selection bias noted above.

IV. Econometric Techniques

The evaluation addresses two very important problems faced by field researchers. One is that program placement is decentralized, and hence the allocation decision is conditioned on variables that are unobservable to the econometrician but observable to the people making the decision. This means that the evaluation requires a measure that determines program placement at the individual level but is not correlated with the error term (and hence program outcomes). The second is that there is only a single cross-section survey to work with, with no baseline survey of the participants, so it is difficult to estimate the pure impact of the intervention.

The evaluation is extremely innovative in that it uses the two-step allocation process itself as an instrument. The key feature that is necessary in order to do this is that the cross-sectional data include both household characteristics and geographic characteristics. In this particular case, the model is as follows:

$$W_i = \alpha IP_i + \beta'X_i + \eta'Z_i + \mu_i. \tag{1}$$

Here W is the individual's welfare outcome, X and Z include household and geographic characteristics, and IP, which is the individual's placement in the program, is correlated with the error term. Clearly, and of fundamental importance in the evaluation literature, least squares estimates of $\forall$ will be biased.

The evaluation uses the geographic differences in placement as instruments for individual placement, because this is not correlated with the error term, as well as household characteristics. This then characterizes this relationship as

$$IP_i = \gamma GP_i + \pi'X_i + v_i. \tag{2}$$

It is important to note here that it is critical that Z contains all the information that is used in making the geographic placement decision. In this case, the two sets of geographic variables are used. One set of geographic variables is fairly standard and actually directly affects attendance decisions in their own right: distance to school, type of school, and school quality variables. The second set has to do with the placement decision itself and, although long, is worth noting for illustrative purposes. The variables include land distribution; irrigation intensity; road quality; electrification; distance and time to local administration headquarters and to the capital; distance to health care and financial facilities; incidence of natural disasters; attitudes to women's employment, education, and family planning; average schooling levels of the head and spouse; majority religion of the village; and the population size of the village. These are calculated at the village level and appear to predict selection fairly well: a probit regression on a total of 166 villages resulted in a relatively good fit (a pseudo-R^2 of 0.55). This suggests that these variables do in fact capture overall placement.

This set of equations can then be modeled by using three-stage least squares and compared with the results from ordinary least squares regression.

V. Who Carried It Out

The evaluation was carried out by Martin Ravallion and Quentin Wodon of the World Bank as part of a long-term collaborative effort between the Bangladesh Bureau of Statistics and the Poverty Reduction and Economic Management Unit of the World Bank's South Asia Region.

VI. Results

There are clear differences in the two approaches: the estimated impact of FFE using the three-stage least squares approach was 66 percent higher than the ordinary least squares estimates without geographic controls and 49 percent higher than with the controls. In other words, simple estimates that only control for variation across households (ordinary least squares without geographic controls) will substantially *understate* the effectiveness of the program. Even including geographic controls to apparently control for geographic placement does not erase the attendant bias. In substantive terms, the average amount of grain in the program appeared to increase attendance by 24 percent when the method outlined above was used.

It is worth noting that the key factor to make this a valid approach is that enough variables are available to model the targeting decision and that these variables are close to those used by administrators. If there are still omitted variables, the results continue to be biased.

VII. Lessons Learned

Many evaluations do not have the luxury of designing a data collection strategy from the ground up, either because the evaluation was not an integral part of the project from the beginning, or simply for cost reasons. This is an important evaluation to study for two reasons. First, it documents the degree of bias that can occur if the wrong econometric approach is used. Second, it describes an econometrically valid way of estimating the impact of the intervention without the cost and time lag involved in a prospective evaluation.

VIII. Source

Ravallion and Wodon. 1998. *Evaluating a Targeted Social Program When Placement Is Decentralized.* Policy Research Working Paper 1945, World Bank, Washington, D.C.

Annex 1.4: Evaluating Bolivia's Social Investment Fund

I. Introduction

Project Description. The Bolivian Social Investment Fund (SIF) was established in 1991 as a financial institution promoting sustainable investment in the social sectors, notably health, education, and sanitation. The policy goal is to direct investments to areas that have been historically neglected by public service networks, notably poor communities. SIF funds are therefore allocated according to a municipal poverty index, but within municipalities the program is demand-driven, responding to community requests for projects at the local level. SIF operations were further decentralized in 1994, enhancing the role of sector ministries and municipal governments in project design and approval. The Bolivian SIF was the first institution of its kind in the world and has served as a prototype for similar funds that have since been introduced in Latin America, Africa, and Asia.

Impact Evaluation. Despite the widespread implementation of social funds in the 1990s, there have been few rigorous attempts to assess their impact on poverty reduction. The Bolivian SIF evaluation, carried out jointly by the World Bank and SIF, began in 1991 and is ongoing. The study features baseline (1993) and follow-up (1997) survey data that combine to allow a before-and-after impact assessment. It includes separate evaluations of education, health, and water projects and is unique in that it applies a range of evaluation techniques and examines the benefits and drawbacks of these alternative methodologies. The initial evaluation results are complete and are currently being presented to donors and government agencies for feedback. Final results and methodological issues will be explored in greater depth in conjunction with the Social Investment Funds 2000 report, along with an analysis of cost-effectiveness.

II. Evaluation Design

The Bolivian SIF evaluation process began in 1991, and is ongoing. The design includes separate evaluations of education, health, and water projects that assess the effectiveness of the program's targeting to the poor as well as the impact of its social service investments on desired community outcomes such as improved school enrollment rates, health conditions, and water availability. It illustrates best-practice techniques in evaluation using baseline data in impact analysis. The evaluation is also innovative in that it applies two alternative evaluation methodologies—randomization and matched comparison—to the analysis of education projects and contrasts the results obtained according to each method. This is an important contribution because randomization (random selection of program beneficiaries within an eligible group) is widely viewed as the more statistically robust method, and yet matched comparison (using a nonrandom process to select a control group that most closely "matches" the characteristics of program beneficiaries) is more widely used in practice.

III. Data Collection and Analysis Techniques

Data collection efforts for the Bolivian SIF evaluation are extensive and include a pre-SIF II investment ("baseline") survey conducted in 1993 and a follow-up survey in 1997. The surveys were applied to both the institutions that received SIF funding and the households and communities that benefit from the investments. Similar data were also collected from comparison (control group) institutions and households. The household survey gathers data on a range of characteristics, including consumption, access to basic services, and each household member's health and education status. There are separate samples for health projects (4,155 households, 190 health centers), education projects (1,894 households, 156 schools), water projects (1,071 households, 18 water projects) and latrine projects (231 households, 15 projects).

The household survey consists of three subsamples: (a) a random sample of all households in rural Bolivia plus the Chaco region (one province); (b) a sample of households that live near the schools in the treatment or control group for education projects; and (c) a sample of households that will benefit from water or latrine projects.

To analyze how well SIF investments are actually targeted to the poor, the study uses the baseline (pre-SIF investment) data and information on where SIF investments were later placed to calculate the probability that individuals will be SIF beneficiaries conditional on their income level. The study then combines the baseline and follow-up survey data to estimate the average impact of SIF in those communities that received a SIF investment, using regression techniques. In addition to average impact, it explores whether the characteristics of communities, schools, or health centers associated with significantly greater than average impacts can be identified.

In education, for which SIF investments were randomly assigned among a larger pool of equally eligible communities, the study applies the "ideal" randomized experiment design (in which the counterfactual can be directly observed). In health and sanitation projects, in which projects were not assigned randomly, the study uses the "instrumental variable" method to compensate for the lack of a direct counterfactual. Instrumental variables are correlated with the intervention but do not have a direct correlation with the outcome.

IV. Results

SIF II investments in education and health do result in a clear improvement in infrastructure and equipment. Education projects have little impact on school dropout rates, but school achievement test scores among sixth graders are significantly higher in SIF schools. In health, SIF investments raise health service utilization rates and reduce mortality. SIF water projects are associated with little improvement in water quality but do improve water access and quantity and also reduce mortality rates.

A comparison of the randomized versus matched-comparison results in education shows that the matched-comparison approach yields less comparable treatment and comparison groups and therefore less robust results in discerning program impact. In illustration of this finding, evidence of improvements in school infrastructure (which one would clearly expect to be present in SIF schools) is picked up in the randomized evaluation design but not in the matched-comparison design.

Finally, the results show that SIF II investments are generally not well targeted to the poor. Health and sanitation projects benefit households that are relatively better off in terms of per capita income, and there is no relationship between per capita income and SIF education benefits.

V. Policy Application

The results on targeting reveal an inherent conflict between the goal of targeting the poor and the demand-driven nature of SIF. With the introduction of the popular participation law in 1994, subprojects had to be submitted through municipal governments. The targeting results suggest that even in a highly decentralized system it is important to monitor targeting processes. In the Bolivian case, it appears that better-off, more organized communities, rather than the poorest, are those most likely to obtain SIF investments. In the case of SIF sanitation projects in particular, the bias against poorest communities may be hard to correct. Investment in basic sanitation is most efficient in populated areas that already have access to a water system so that the project can take advantage of economies of scale.

The fact that SIF investments have had no perceptible impact on school attendance has prompted a restructuring of SIF interventions in this sector. Rather than focusing solely on providing infrastructure, projects will provide a combination of inputs designed to enhance school quality. Similarly, disappointing results on water quality (which shows no improvement resulting from SIF projects compared with the preexisting source) have generated much attention, and project design in this sector is being rethought.

VI. Lessons Learned

Effectiveness of the Randomization Technique. The randomized research design, in which a control group is selected at random from among potential program beneficiaries, is far more effective at detecting program impact than the matched-comparison method of generating a control group. Randomization must be built into program design from the outset in determining the process through which program beneficiaries will be selected, and random selection is not always feasible. However, when program funds are insufficient to cover all beneficiaries, an argument can be made for random selection from among a larger pool of qualified beneficiaries.

Importance of Institutionalizing the Evaluation Process. Evaluations can be extremely complex and time consuming. The Bolivia evaluation was carried out over the course of seven years in an attempt to rigorously capture project impact, and achieved important results in this regard. However, the evaluation was difficult to manage over this length of time and given the range of different actors involved (government agencies and financing institutions). Management and implementation of an evaluation effort can be streamlined by incorporating these processes into the normal course of local ministerial activities from the beginning. Further, extensive evaluation efforts may be best limited to only a few programs—for example, large programs in which there is extensive uncertainty regarding results—in which payoffs of the evaluation effort are likely to be greatest.

VII. Evaluation Costs and Administration

Costs. The total estimated cost of the Bolivia SIF evaluation to date is $878,000, which represents 0.5 percent of total project cost. Data collection represents a relatively high proportion of these costs (69 percent), with the rest being spent on travel, World Bank staff time, and consultants.

Administration. The evaluation was designed by World Bank staff and financed jointly by the World Bank, KfW, and the Dutch, Swedish, and Danish governments. Survey work was conducted by the Bolivian

National Statistical Institute and managed by SIF counterparts for the first round and later the Ministry of Finance for the second round.

VIII. Source

Pradhan, Menno, Laura Rawlings, and Geert Ridder. 1998. "The Bolivian Social Investment Fund: An Analysis of Baseline Data for Impact Evaluation." *World Bank Economic Review* 12 (3): 457–82.

Annex 1.5: Impact of Active Labor Programs: Czech Republic

I. Introduction

Project Description. Many developing countries face the problem of retraining workers when state-owned enterprises are downsized. This is particularly complicated in transition economies that are also characterized by high unemployment and stagnant or declining wages. However, all retraining programs are not created equal. Some are simply disguised severance pay for displaced workers; others are disguised unemployment programs. This makes the case for evaluation of such programs particularly compelling.

Training programs are particularly difficult to evaluate, however, and the Czech evaluation is no exception. Typically, several different programs are instituted to serve different constituencies. There are also many ways of measuring outcomes, including employment, self-employment, monthly earnings, and hourly earnings. More than with other types of evaluations, the magnitude of the impact can be quite time-dependent: very different results can be obtained depending on whether the evaluation is one month, six months, one year, or five years after the intervention.

Highlights of Evaluation. This evaluation quantified the impact of four active labor market programs (ALP) in the Czech Republic using quasi-experimental design methods—matching ALP participants with a similar group of nonparticipants. Both administrative and follow-up survey data were used in an ex post evaluation of a variety of different outcomes: duration of unemployment, likelihood of employment, self-employment, and earnings. Regression analysis is used to estimate the impact of each of the five programs on these outcomes, controlling for baseline demographic characteristics.

Several important lessons were learned from this evaluation. One set of lessons is practical: how to design quite a complex evaluation, how to use administrative data, how to address the problems associated with administering the survey, and the mechanics of creating the matched sample. The second is how to structure an analysis to provide policy-relevant information—made possible by a detailed evaluation of the impact by subgroup. This led to a policy recommendation to target ALP programs to particular types of clients and concluded that one type of ALP is not at all effective in changing either employment or earnings.

II. Research Questions and Evaluation Design

This is part of a broader evaluation of four countries: the Czech Republic, Poland, Hungary, and Turkey. The common context is that each country had high unemployment, partially caused by the downsizing of state-owned enterprises, which had been addressed with passive income support programs, such as unemployment benefits and social assistance. This was combined with the ALPs that are the subject of this evaluation. The five ALPs are Socially Purposeful Jobs (new job creation), Publicly Useful Jobs (short-term public employment), Programs for School Leavers (subsidies for the hiring of recent graduates), Retraining (occupation-specific training lasting a few weeks to several months), and Programs for the Disabled and Disadvantaged. The last is rather small and not included in the evaluation.

There are two research questions. One is to examine whether participants in different ALPs are more successful at reentering the labor market than are nonparticipants and whether this varies across subgroups and with labor market conditions. The second is to determine the cost-effectiveness of each ALP and make suggestions for improvement.

The evaluation is an ex post, quasi-experimental design—essentially a matched cohort. The participant group is matched with a constructed non-participant group (with information drawn from administrative records) on people who registered with the state employment service but were not selected for the ALP. The fundamental notion is that an individual is selected at random from the ALP participant group. This individual's outcomes are then compared with those for individuals in the nonparticipant group (based on age, gender, education, number of months unemployed, town size, marital status, and last employment type). The evaluation is particularly strong in its detailed analysis of the comparison versus the participant group.

There are inevitably some problems with this approach, and they have been extensively addressed elsewhere (Burtless 1995, and Heckman and Smith 1995). One obvious concern that is endemic to any nonrandomized trial is that participants may have been "creamed" by the training program on the basis of characteristics unobservable to or unmeasured by the researchers. The second major concern is that nonparticipants may have substituted other types of training for public training in the case of the retraining program. The third concern is that subsidies to employ workers may have simply led to the substitution of one set of workers by another.

III. Data

One very interesting component of this evaluation was the use of government administrative data to create the sample frame for the survey.

The team thus visited the Ministry of Labor and Social Affairs (MOLSA) in Prague and three local labor market offices to develop an understanding of both the administration and implementation of ALPs and of the administrative data on ALP participants. From this, 20 districts were chosen for survey, based on criteria of geographic dispersion and variation in industrial characteristics. There was also a broad range of unemployment rates across districts. The survey contained both quantitative questions about the key program outcomes and qualitative questions about the participants' rating of the program.

Another valuable component was the implementation of a pilot survey in four districts. This approach, which is always important, identified not only technical problems but also a legal problem that can often arise with the use of administrative records. This issue is the interpretation of privacy law: in this case, MOLSA did not permit a direct mailing but required that potential respondents give permission to the labor office to allow their addresses to be given out. This delayed the evaluation schedule, increased costs, and dramatically lowered the response rate.

The survey was conducted in early 1997 on a random sample of 24,973 labor office registrants who were contacted. Of these, 9,477 participated in ALP during 1994–95. The response rate for nonparticipants was 14 percent; for participants it was 24.7 percent, resulting in a total number of 4,537 respondents. The dismal response rate was directly attributable to the legal ruling: most people did not respond to the initial request, but among those who did allow their address to be given, the response rate was high. Worse, the resulting bias is unknown.

IV. Econometric Techniques

The difficulty of measuring both the temporal nature and the complexity of labor market outcomes is illustrated by the use of seven different outcome measures: percent currently employed, percent currently self-employed, percent ever employed, length of unemployment, length of receiving unemployment payments, total unemployment payments, and current monthly earnings

The evaluation approach, however, was fairly straightforward in its use of both simple differences across groups and ordinary least squares with group-specific dummies to gauge the impact of the interventions. The overall impact was calculated, followed by estimated impacts by each of the subgroup categories (age, sex, education, and, for earnings outcomes, size of firm). This last analysis was particularly useful because it identified subgroups of individuals for whom, in fact, the impact of the interventions was different, leading to quite different policy implications. Indeed, a major recommendation of the evaluation was that the ALPs be more tightly targeted.

V. Who Carried It Out

The evaluation was part of a four-country cross-country evaluation of active labor programs, with the express motivation of understanding the impact of ALPs under different economic conditions. The evaluation was supervised by a project steering committee, which had representatives from the World Bank, from each of the four countries, from the external financing agencies, and from the technical assistance contractors (Abt Associates and the Upjohn Institute).

The team contracted with a private survey firm to carry out the survey itself—for data quality reasons as well as to reduce the possibility of intimidation if the local labor office were to carry out the survey. It is worth making the point that the credibility of the study could be contaminated if the employment service were responsible for conducting the survey. Indeed, this moral hazard problem is generally an important one if the agency responsible for training is also responsible for collecting information on the outcomes of that training.

VI. Results

The results are typical of evaluations for training programs. Some interventions appear to have some (albeit relatively weak) impacts for some types of workers in some situations. A strong point of the evaluation is that it does identify one program that appears to have wasted money—no impact was shown either overall or for any subgroup. Another strong point is the presentation of the evaluation itself, which is particularly important if the evaluation is to be read by policymakers. Here, tables are provided for each program summarizing the combined benefits in terms of wages and employment, both in aggregate and for each subgroup.

A very negative point is that, despite the initial promise, no cost-benefit analysis was performed. It would have been extremely useful to have the summary benefit information contrasted with the combined explicit and implicit cost of the program. Thus, although, for example, the evaluators found that one program increased the probability of employment across the board, it should be noted that this came at a cost of a nine-month training program. A full calculation of the rate of return of investment would have combined the explicit cost of the program with the opportunity cost of participant time and compared this with the increase in earnings and employment.

VII. Lessons Learned

Several important lessons were learned from this study. First among these are the pragmatic components discussed in the introduction, particularly the importance of taking the political environment into consideration in designing an evaluation scheme. The inability to convince the employment service of the importance of the evaluation project meant that the survey instrument was severely compromised. Second, the study provides a useful demonstration of the construction of a matched sample. Finally, the evaluation provides a good illustration of the importance of conducting analysis not just in aggregate but also on subgroups, with the resultant possibility of fruitful targeted interventions.

VIII. Sources

Benus, Jacob, Grover Neelima, Jiri Berkovsky, and Jan Rehak. 1998. *Czech Republic: Impact of Active Labor Market Programs.* Cambridge, Mass., and Bethesda, Md.: Abt Associates, May.

Burtless, Gary. 1995. "The Case for Randomized Field Trials in Economic and Policy Research." *Journal of Economic Perspectives* 9 (2): 63–84.

Heckman, James J., and Jeffrey A. Smith. 1995. "Assessing the Case for Social Experiments." *Journal of Economic Perspectives* 9 (2) : 85–110.

Schematic Used for Designing the Czech Active Labor Programs Evaluation

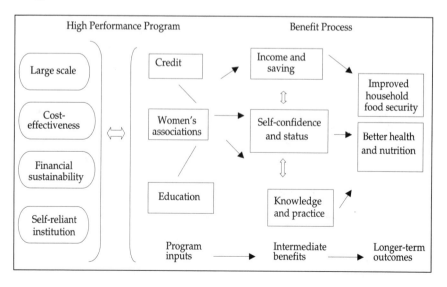

Annex 1.6: Impact of Credit with Education on Mothers' and Their Young Children's Nutrition: Lower Pra Rural Bank Program in Ghana

I. Introduction

Project Description. The Credit with Education program combines elements of the Grameen Bank program with education on the basics of health, nutrition, birth timing and spacing, and small business skills. The aim is to improve the nutritional status and food security of poor households in Ghana. Freedom from Hunger, together with the Program in International Nutrition at the University of California Davis, provided Credit with Education services to poor rural women in the Shama Ahanta East District of the Western Region of Ghana. A partnership was formed with five rural banks to deliver such services—more than 9,000 loans, totaling $600,000, were made by March 1997 with a repayment rate never below 92 percent.

Highlights of Evaluation. The evaluation is interesting for three reasons. First, the sample design was quite appropriate: the program was administered to 19 communities and data were collected on three different sample groups of women: those who participated at least one year, those who did not participate but were in the program communities, and those in control communities. Second, the study had a clear description of its underlying approach: it identified and evaluated both intermediate and longer-term outcomes. Finally, it provided a nice blend of both qualitative and quantitative results, often highlighting the quantitative outcomes with an anecdotal illustrative example.

II. Research Questions and Evaluation Design

The research questions focused on the program's effects on (a) the nutritional status of children; (b) women's economic capacity (income, savings, time) to invest in food and health care; (c) women's knowledge and adoption of breastfeeding, weaning, and diarrhea management and prevention practices; and (d) women's ability to offer a healthy diet to their children.

In doing this, the evaluation separated out the ultimate goals of improved household food security and nutritional status from the intermediate benefits of changing behavior, reducing poverty, and female empowerment.

A quasi-experimental design was used in fielding two surveys (in 1993 and 1996) to evaluate the impact of the strategy on children's nutritional status; mothers' economic capacity, women's empowerment, and mothers' adoption of child health and nutrition practices. A total of 299 mother-and-child pairs were surveyed in the first period and 290 different pairs in the second period. Both qualitative and quantitative information was gathered.

The evaluation design was quite complex. The Lower Pra Rural Bank identified 19 communities that had not yet had Credit with Education services, and the consultants divided communities into large and small (greater or less than 800) and then again by whether they were close to a main road. Within each stratification, the 13 of the 19 communities were assigned either to a treatment or to a control group. Three were given the treatment for political reasons and three communities were selected as matched controls to the politically selected three based on their proximity, commercial development, size, and access to main roads. Two communities dropped out because of lack of interest and the small number of communities in the classification. Thus, in the follow-up study only 17 communities were surveyed.

Ten mother-and-child pairs, with children aged 12 to 23 months, were chosen for the baseline surveys from small communities, and 30 from the large communities. Two important problems arose as a result. The first is that this construction did not allow the surveys to follow the same women over time because few women in the baseline survey also had infants in the 1996 survey. The second problem was that the age restriction cut the second sample so much that it was extended to women with children under three years of age in 1996. A major advantage of this complex evaluation design was that it was possible to classify women in the baseline samples as future participants and future nonparticipants.

Three types of women were surveyed: participants, nonparticipants in the program communities, and residents in control communities. All participants were included; the latter two types were randomly selected from women with children under three. It is worth noting that the total sample size (of 360) was calculated based on the standard deviations found in previous studies, a requirement that the sample be able to detect a 0.4 difference in the z-score values of the control and target groups and with a target significance level of 0.05 and a power of 0.8.

III. Data

Both quantitative and qualitative data were collected on the household, mother and child, focusing on both intermediate and long-term measures—and particularly the multidimensional nature of the outcomes.

For the intermediate outcomes, this led to a set of questions attempting to measure women's economic capacity (incomes, profit, contribution to total household income, savings, entrepreneurial skill, and expenditures on food and households). Similarly, another set of measures addressed the woman's knowledge of health and nutrition (breastfeeding, child feeding, diarrhea treatment and prevention, and immunization). Yet another set captured women's empowerment (self-confidence and hope about the future, status and decisionmaking in the household, and status and social networks in the community). For the ultimate outcomes, such as nutritional status and food security, more direct measures were used (anthropometric measures for the former, questions about hunger in the latter case).

Although a total sample size of 360 mother-and-child pairs was planned, only 299 pairs were interviewed in the first survey (primarily because two communities were dropped) and 290 in the second. Mother and household characteristics were compared across each of the three groups and no significant differences were found.

IV. Econometric Techniques

The econometric techniques used are fairly straightforward and exploited the strength of the survey design. The group mean is calculated for each of the varied outcome measures used, and then t-tests are performed to examine whether differences between controls and participants are significant. This is essentially a simple-difference approach. These are well supplemented with graphics.

A series of major questions were not addressed, however. First, the sample design was clustered—and because, almost by construction, the outcomes of each individual mother-and-child pair will be correlated with the others in the community, the standard errors will be biased down and the t-statistics spuriously will be biased up. In the extreme case, in which all the individual outcomes are perfectly correlated with each other, the sample size is actually 17 rather than 300. This will lend significance to results that may, in fact, not be significant. Second, although the design was explicitly stratified, the impact of that stratification was not addressed: either whether large or small communities benefited more or whether communities close to a road were better off than those a long way away from a road. This is particularly surprising, since presumably the reason to have such a sample design is to examine the policy implications. Third, although selection bias problems are discussed, there is no formal analysis of or correction for this fundamental problem. Finally, although there were significant differences in item nonresponse rates, which suggests the potential for selection bias even within the survey, this was neither addressed nor discussed.

V. Who Carried It Out

An international not-for-profit institute, Freedom from Hunger, developed the Credit with Education program and collaborated with the Program in International Nutrition at the University of California Davis, in evaluating it. The institute partnered with the Lower Pra Rural Bank (an autonomous bank, regulated by the Bank of Ghana), and subsequently four other rural banks in Ghana, to deliver the program. The Lower Pra Rural Bank played a role in identifying and selecting the communities to be surveyed.

VI. Results

The intermediate goals were generally achieved: although women's incomes and expenditures did not increase, women's entrepreneurial skills and savings were significantly higher. Women's health and nutrition knowledge was generally improved. Women were also more likely to feel empowered. In terms of the ultimate goals the evaluation suggested that the program did improve household food security and child nutritional status but not maternal nutritional status.

VII. Lessons Learned

A key contribution of the evaluation is the very interesting sample design: the stratification and the choice of participant and nonparticipant groups with respect to their future participation is a very useful approach. Another lesson is the productive use of many outcome dimensions—sometimes on quite nonquantitative factors such as women's empowerment. The other key lesson is the value of nonquantitative data to illustrate the validity of quantitative inferences.

VIII. Source

MkNelly, Barbara, and Christopher Dunford (in collaboration with the Program in International Nutrition, University of California Davis). 1998. "Impact of Credit with Education on Mothers' and their Young Children's Nutrition: Lower Pra Rural Bank Credit with Education Program in Ghana." Freedom from Hunger Research Paper No. 4, March.

Annex 1.7: Textbooks and Test Scores: Evidence from a Prospective Evaluation in Kenya

I. Introduction

Project Description. Evaluating the effect of different types of education expenditure on student outcomes is particularly important in developing countries. Prior studies have suggested that the provision of textbooks is a cost-effective way of increasing test scores, and Kenya, with the extraordinarily scarce resources available to educators, makes a good case study. The evaluators note that only one in six children in grades 3, 4, and 5 has textbooks; this rises to one in four in later grades. In addition, physical facilities are extremely poor with many children sitting on the floor to learn.

The evaluation assessed the impact on learning outcomes of a 1996 program in which all grades in a randomly selected subset of 25 out of 100 rural Kenyan primary schools were provided with textbooks. English textbooks were given to grades 3 through 7, with a ratio of 6 textbooks to every 10 children; mathematics textbooks to grades 3, 5, and 7, with a 50 percent ratio; and science textbooks to grade 8, with a 60 percent ratio. In addition, each class was provided with a teacher's guide. Achievement tests were given to the students before textbooks were distributed and then again 10 months later. The same tests were also given to the control schools. This approach combines a randomized design with reflexive comparisons.

Highlights of Evaluation. This evaluation is an excellent illustration of developing and implementing a good survey design and then following that up with appropriate econometric techniques. It is particularly strong in showing how to draw inferences on level outcomes with stacked data, the use of difference-in-difference estimators, how to address selection and attrition bias, as well as measurement error and crowding-out issues. Another very interesting component of the evaluation is the focus on the intervention's impact on students in all parts of the distribution. Finally, the recognition and analysis of potential secondary effects is a very good example of looking at all dimensions of an intervention.

II. Research Questions and Evaluation Design

The main focus of the research is to evaluate the effect of textbooks on learning outcomes. Because this is a complex concept, the outcomes are measured as the difference between textbook and comparison schools in several dimensions: posttest scores, test score gains, differences between subject-grade combinations that did and did not receive textbooks, and child and teacher activity. The evaluation also considered other (often ignored) secondary effects, particularly the possibility that the provision of such a subsidy would reduce parental involvement, particularly in terms of crowding out other fundraising.

The evaluation design is quite complex. The Ministry of Education chose 100 needy schools for the intervention in 1995. These were divided into four groups—first on the basis of geography, then on an alphabetical basis within the geography. There was then an ordered assignment, on the basis of the alphabet, of each school to each of the four groups. Textbook assistance was staggered to go to the first group in 1996, the second group in 1997, and so on. Mathematics, English, and science textbooks were provided to different grades—primarily grades 3 through 7.

III. Data

Math, English, and science exams were given to children in all these grades in each of the 100 schools before textbooks were distributed. The evaluation itself, however, makes use of pretests that were administered in grades 3 through 7 in October 1996 and posttests in October 1997. There are therefore data on some 8,800 students (in all grades) for each subject in the 100 schools and a total of over 26,000 observations. Because 25 schools received the textbooks in this period, students in these schools become the "textbook" group; the other 75 are the comparison group. In addition to test scores, data were also collected on school finances and on pedagogical methods.

Information on classroom utilization of textbooks was gathered by trained observers who visited each school and took minute-by-minute notes on eight possible classroom activities (ranging from general teacher and pupil activity to the use of textbooks by teachers and pupils). These notes covered 15 minutes and were then used to construct percentages of time spent by teachers and students in each different activity for a total of 551 class periods. Four to five students in each class were interviewed by field staff, who filled out a questionnaire on the basis of their responses.

Finally, data were gathered on school finances from a 1997 school and school committee questionnaire, which asked about fund-raising activities.

IV. Econometric Techniques

It is worth noting the interesting issues generated by this sampling technique. Test scores within a school are likely to be correlated with each other, as are within-class scores. Similarly, test scores for different subjects taken by the same child will be correlated. The intervention can also be evaluated in terms of the impact on outcomes on student learning levels or on student learning gains. In general, the effect of an intervention should be robust to different econometric techniques and different ways of looking at the data, and this was certainly the case here.

The evaluation proceeds by first providing estimates from a simple dummy-variable-level regression, with treatment dummies for each grade-subject combination with school, grade, and subject random effects (the dependent variable is the change in test scores from the pre- to the posttest). One attractive feature of this is that the dummies can be combined in very useful ways:

- Pooling several grades to estimate the impact of textbooks for a subject
- Pooling all test scores to estimate the average impact of textbooks for a grade; and
- Pooling all grades and subjects to estimate the weighted average impact of textbooks for all grades and subjects.

Clearly, the structure of the random effects varies with each approach, and the evaluation is very clear in this component.

The evaluation then proceeds with a difference-in-difference approach, which is relatively straightforward in that it simply compares post- and pretest scores between control and treatment schools.

The third approach, which is a little more complicated because it exploits within-school variation, deserves discussion. The regression applied here involves regressing test scores on dummies that capture whether the students were (a) in a textbook school and (b) in a subject-grade combination that received a textbook. This reduces problems introduced by school heterogeneity as well as sample selection problems—in the latter case because it captures the effect on test scores for the same student depending on whether or not the student received a textbook. It does assume, however, that test scores in different grade-subject combinations can be added and subtracted, and this very strong assumption may be the reason for very different results from this approach.

A recurring theme in evaluations is the desire to capture not just the average effect of the intervention but also the effect on subgroups of recipients. This evaluation provides a very useful illustration of the use of interaction terms and quantile regression. The former approach involves interaction between initial test scores and textbook dummies to capture the effect of textbooks on better versus poorer students, using both actual and instrumented values (initial test scores are correlated with the error term, causing a bias). The second approach, which involves using quantile regression, is also useful and increasingly popular. More specifically, since least squares regression only captures the average impact of the textbook program, quintile regressions allow the effect of the treatment to vary depending on where the student is in the distribution.

The evaluation is also particularly strong in providing an application of how to look for selection and attrition bias. The major potential source of problems in this intervention is differential promotion and repetition rates between textbook and comparison schools. For example, children might be differentially promoted from grade 2 (a nontextbook grade) to grade 3 (a textbook grade) in textbook schools. Differential promotion biases down the results in the classes that the worst students are added to, and possibly biases up the results in the classes they came from. These two effects were captured in the evaluation by reestimating the model in two ways: dropping all repeaters from both sets of schools and dropping the worst students in each grade. The robustness of the results under both approaches confirmed the impact of the intervention.

Finally, in an illustration of considering the importance of secondary effects, the evaluation quantified the impact of textbook provision on parent fundraising. They found that the intervention did crowd out parent contributions—the amount of non-ICS aid received by comparison schools was $465 and for textbook schools $267 (the average value of ICS textbooks was $485). They used simple regression analysis and also investigated, and confirmed, the hypothesis that smaller schools had more crowding out than larger schools.

Who Carried It Out. A Dutch nonprofit organization, International Christelijk Steunfonds, funded the project. The evaluation was performed by a Massachusetts Institute of Technology professor (Kremer) and two World Bank economists (Paul Glewwe and Sylvie Moulin). Some of the costs were covered by the National Science Foundation and the World Bank research committee.

V. Results

The result of this evaluation was in marked contrast to the results of other evaluations of textbook interventions. The basic result was that there was no significant impact of textbooks on learning outcomes on average, but that there was a significant effect for better students. This was robust to different estimation techniques and cuts of the data.

VI. Lessons Learned

The most useful lesson learned from this evaluation was the importance of using different econometric techniques to check for the robustness of the empirical results. Even though the data collection was close to ideal, it is important that the estimated impact of the intervention remain roughly the same with different econometric assumptions and model specifications. The application of quantile regression and interaction terms was also a very useful way to analyze the impact on different sub-groups of the population. Finally, it is important to look for and identify secondary effects—in this case, the potential for crowding out.

VIII. Source

Glewwe, Paul, Michael Kremer, and Sylvie Moulin. 1998. "Textbooks and Test Scores: Evidence from a Prospective Evaluation in Kenya." Development Resrach Group (DECRG), World Bank, Washington, D.C. Processed.

Annex 1.8: Evaluating Kenya's Agricultural Extension Project

I. Introduction

Project Description. The first National Extension Project (NEP-I) in Kenya introduced the Training and Visit (T&V) system of management for agricultural extension services in 1983. The project had the dual objectives of institutional development and delivering extension services to farmers with the goal of raising agricultural productivity. NEP-II followed in 1991 and aimed to consolidate the gains made under NEP-I by increasing direct contact with farmers, improving the relevance of extension information and technologies, upgrading skills of staff and farmers, and enhancing institutional development.

Impact Evaluation. The performance of the Kenyan extension system has been controversial and is part of the larger debate on the cost-effectiveness of the T&V approach to extension. Despite the intensity of the debate, the important role of agricultural extension services in the World Bank's development strategy for Africa, and the large volume of investments made, very few rigorous attempts have been made to measure the impact of T&V extension. In the Kenyan case, the debate has been elevated by very high estimated returns to T&V reported in an earlier study, and the lack of convincingly visible results, including the poor performance of Kenyan agriculture in recent years.

The disagreement (between the Operations Evaluation Department and the Africa Region of the World Bank) over the performance of NEP-I has persisted pending this evaluation, which takes a rigorous empirical approach to assess the program's impact on agricultural performance. Using the results-based management framework, the evaluation examines the impact of project services on farm productivity and efficiency. It also develops measures of program outcomes (that is, farmer awareness and adoption of new techniques) and outputs (for example, frequency and quality of contact) to assess the performance of the extension system and to confirm the actual, or the potential, impact.

II. Evaluation Design

The evaluation strategy illustrates best-practice techniques in using a broad array of evaluation methods in order to assess program implementation, output, and its impact on farm productivity and efficiency.

(No attempt is made to study the impact on household welfare, which is likely to be affected by a number of factors far beyond the scope of T&V activities.) It draws on both quantitative and qualitative methods so that rigorous empirical findings on program impact could be complemented with beneficiary assessments and staff interviews that highlight practical issues in the implementation process. The study also applied the contingent valuation method to elicit farmers' willingness to pay for extension services. [The contingent valuation method elicits individuals' use and nonuse values for a variety of public and private goods and services. Interviewees are asked to state their willingness to pay (accept) to avoid (accept) a hypothetical change in the provision of the goods or services— that is, the "contingent" outcome. In this case, farmers were asked how much they would be willing to pay for continued agricultural extension services should the government cease to provide them.]

The quantitative assessment is complicated by the fact that the T&V system was introduced on a national scale, preventing a with-program and without-program (control group) comparison. The evaluation methodology therefore sought to exploit the available preproject household agricultural production data for limited before-and-after comparisons using panel data methods. For this, existing household data were complemented by a fresh survey to form a panel. Beneficiary assessments designed for this study could not be conducted, but the evaluation draws on the relevant findings of two recent beneficiary assessments in Kenya. The study is noteworthy in that it draws on a range of preexisting data sources in Kenya (household surveys, participatory assessments, and so forth), complemented by a more comprehensive data collection effort for the purpose of the evaluation.

III. Data Collection and Analysis Techniques

The evaluation approach draws on several existing qualitative and quantitative data sources. The quantitative evaluation is based largely on a 1998 household survey conducted by the World Bank's Operations Evaluation Department. This survey generates panel data by revisiting as many households as could be located from a 1990 household survey conducted by the Africa Technical Department, which in turn drew from a subsample of the 1982 Rural Household Budget Survey. (These three surveys generate a panel data set for approximately 300 households. The surveys cover household demographics, farm characteristics, and input-output data on agricultural production; the 1990 and 1998 surveys also collect information on contact with extension services, including awareness and adoption of extension messages.) These data are supplemented by a survey of the extension staff, several recent reviews of the extension service conducted or commissioned by the Ministry of Agriculture, and individual and focus group discussions with extension staff. The study also draws on two recent beneficiary assessments: a 1997 study by ActionAid Kenya, which elicited the views of users and potential users of Kenya's extension services; and a 1994 Participatory Poverty Assessment, which inquired about public services, including extension, and was carried out jointly by the World Bank, British Overseas Development Administration, African Medical and Research Foundation, UNICEF, and the government of Kenya.

The analysis evaluates both the implementation process and the outcome of the Kenyan T&V program. The study evaluates institutional development by drawing on secondary and qualitative data—staff surveys, interviews, and the ministry's own reviews of the extension service. Quality and quantity of services delivered are assessed by using a combination of the findings of participatory (beneficiary) assessments, staff surveys, and through measures of outreach and the nature and frequency of contact between extension agents and farmers drawn from the 1998 OED survey. The survey data are also used to measure program outcomes, measured in terms of farmer awareness and adoption of extension recommendations.

The program's results—its actual impact on agricultural production in Kenya—are evaluated by relating the supply of extension services to changes in productivity and efficiency at the farm level. Drawing on the household panel data, these impacts are estimated by using the data envelopment analysis , a nonparametric technique, to measure changes in farmer efficiency and productivity over time, along with econometric analysis measuring the impact of the supply of extension services on farm production. Contingent valuation methods are used to directly elicit the farmers' willingness to pay for extension services.

IV. Results

The institutional development of NEP-I and NEP-II has been limited. After 15 years, the effectiveness of extension services has improved little. Although there has been healthy rethinking of extension approaches recently, overall the extension program has lacked the strategic vision for future development. Management of the system continues to be weak, and information systems are virtually nonexistent. The quality and quantity of service provision are poor. Beneficiaries and extension service staff alike report that visits are infrequent and ineffective. Although there continues to be unmet demand for technically useful services, the focus of the public extension service has remained on simple and basic agronomic messages. Yet the approach taken—a high intensity of contact with a limited number of farmers—is suited to deliver more technical information. The result has been a costly and inefficient service delivery system. Extension activities have had little influence on the evolution of patterns of awareness and adoption of recommendations, which indicates limited potential for impact. In terms of the actual impact on agricultural production and efficiency, the data indicate a small positive impact of extension services on technical efficiency but no effect on allocative or overall economic efficiency. Furthermore, no significant impact of the supply of extension services on productivity at the farm level could be established by using the data in hand. The data do show, however, that the impact has been relatively greater in the previously less productive areas, where the knowledge gap is likely to have been the greatest. These findings are consistent with the contingent valuation findings. A vast majority of farmers, among both the current recipients and nonrecipients, are willing to pay for advice, indicating an unmet demand. However, the perceived value of the service, in terms of the amount offered, is well below what the government is currently spending on delivering it.

V. Policy Implications

The Kenya Extension Service Evaluation stands out in terms of the array of practical policy conclusions that can be derived from its results, many of which are relevant to the design of future agricultural extension projects. First, the evaluation reveals a need to enhance targeting of extension services, focusing on areas and groups in which the difference between the average and best practice is the greatest and hence the impact is likely to be greatest. Furthermore, advice needs to be carefully tailored to meet farmer demands, taking into account variations in local technological and economic conditions. Successfully achieving this level of service targeting calls for regular and timely flows of appropriate and reliable information, and the need for a monitoring and evaluation system to provide regular feedback from beneficiaries on service content.

To raise program efficiency, a leaner and less-intense presence of extension agents with wider coverage is likely to be more cost-effective. There are not enough technical innovations to warrant a high frequency of visits, and those currently without access demand extension services. The program's blanket approach to service delivery, relying predominantly on a single methodology (farm visits) to deliver standard simple messages, also limits program efficiency. Radio programs are now popular, younger farmers are more educated, and alternative providers (nongovernmental organizations) are beginning to emerge in rural Kenya. A flexible pluralistic approach to service delivery, particularly one that uses lower-cost means of communication, is likely to enhance the program's cost-effectiveness.

Finally, the main findings point to the need for institutional reform. As with other services, greater effectiveness in the delivery of extension services could be achieved with more appropriate institutional arrangements. The central focus of the institution should be the client (farmer). Decentralization of program design, including participatory mechanisms that give voice to the farmer (such as cost sharing and farmer organizations) should become an integral part of the delivery mechanism. Financial sustainability is critical. The size and intensity of the service should be based on existing technological and knowledge gaps and the pace of flow of new technology. Cost recovery, even if only partial, offers several advantages: it provides appropriate incentives, addresses issues of accountability and quality control, makes the service more demand-driven and responsive, and provides some budgetary respite. Such decentralized institutional arrangements remain unexplored in Kenya and in many extension programs in Africa and around the world.

VI. Evaluation Costs and Administration

Costs. The total budget allocated for the evaluation was $250,000, which covered household survey data collection and processing ($65,000—though this probably is an underestimate of actual costs); extension staff survey, data, and consultant report ($12,500); other data collection costs ($12,500); and a research analyst ($8,000). Approximately $100,000 (not reflected in the official costs) of staff costs for data processing, analysis, and report writing should be added to fully reflect the study's cost.

Administration. To maintain objectivity and dissociate survey work from both the government extension service and the World Bank, the household survey was implemented by the Tegemeo Institute of Egerton University, an independent research institute in Kenya. The analysis was carried out by Madhur Gautam of the World Bank.

VII. Lessons Learned

- The combination of theory-based evaluation and a results-based framework can provide a sound basis for evaluating the impact of project interventions, especially when many factors are likely to affect intended outcomes. The design of this evaluation provided for the measurement of key indicators at critical stages of the project cycle, linking project inputs to the expected results to gather sufficient evidence of impact.

- An empirical evaluation demands constant and intense supervision. An evaluation can be significantly simplified with a well-functioning and high quality monitoring and evaluation system, especially with good baseline data. Adequate resources for these activities are rarely made available. This evaluation also benefited tremendously from having access to some, albeit limited, data for the preproject stage and also independent sources of data for comparative purposes.
- Cross-validation of conclusions using different analytical approaches and data sources is important to gather a credible body of evidence. Imperfect data and implementation problems place limits on the degree of confidence that individual methods can provide answers to key evaluative questions. Qualitative and quantitative assessments strongly complement each other. The experience from this evaluation indicates that even in the absence of participatory beneficiary assessments, appropriately designed questions can be included in a survey to collect qualitative as well as quantitative information. Such information can provide useful insights to complement quantitative assessments.
- If properly applied, contingent valuation can be a useful tool, especially in evaluating the value of an existing public service. The results of the application in this evaluation are encouraging, and the responses appear to be rational and reasonable.

VIII. Sources

World Bank. 1999. *World Bank Agricultural Extension Projects in Kenya: An Impact Evaluation.* Operations Evaluation Department, Report no. 19523. Washington, D.C.

In addition, the following working papers are also available from the World Bank Operations Evaluation Department:

The Efficacy of the T&V system of Agricultural Extension in Kenya: Results from a Household Survey

Awareness and Adoption of Extension Messages

Reconsidering the Evidence on Returns to T&V Extension in Kenya

Farmer Efficiency and Productivity Change in Kenya: An Application of the Data Envelopment Analysis

The Willingness to Pay for Extension Services in Kenya: An Application of the Contingent Valuation Method

Annex 1.9: The Impact of Mexico's Retraining Program on Employment and Wages (PROBECAT)

I. Introduction

This case is somewhat unusual in that three evaluations of the program have been carried out—first, by the World Bank using data from 1992 (Revenga, Riboud, and Tan 1994); second, by the Mexican Ministry of labor using data from 1994 (STPS 1995); and third, an update by the World Bank (Wodon and Minowa 1999). The methodologies used for the first two evaluations were quite similar, and they gave similar results. Methodological enhancements in the third evaluation led to fairly different findings and policy conclusions. The fact that the results differ substantially between the first two evaluations and the third highlights the importance of the methodology and data used, and caution in interpreting results when carrying out program evaluations.

Project Description. PROBECAT (Programa de Becas de Capacitacion para Trabajadores) is a Mexican short-term training program targeted at increasing earnings and employment for unemployed and displaced workers. PROBECAT is administered through the state employment offices. Trainees receive minimum wage during the training period, which lasts from one to six months, and the local employment office provides placement. Originally, the program was small (50,000 or so participants), but in recent years it has grown dramatically, to cover more than 500,000 persons per year.

Highlights of the Evaluations. The highlights are as follows:

- The 1994 evaluation is interesting for four reasons: the imaginative use of existing data; the construction of a matched-comparison group; the explicit recognition of the multifaceted nature of the intervention outcomes, particularly for heterogeneous groups of workers; and the explicit cost-benefit analysis. The findings of the evaluation were quite positive in terms of the impact of the program on beneficiaries.
- The 1995 evaluation is a replication of the methodology of the 1994 evaluation on a more recent data set. The findings are also favorable for the impact of the program. Because the design and findings of the 1995 evaluation match those of the 1994 evaluation, the 1995 evaluation will not be discussed below.

- The 1999 evaluation was carried out as part of the Mexico poverty assessment with the data set used for the 1995 evaluation but with a different econometric methodology. The controls used for the endogeneity of program participation showed a vanishing of the impact of the program on the probability of working and on wages after training. Although this does not imply that the program has no benefit, it suggests that it works more as a temporary safety net for the unemployed than as a job training program.

II. Research Questions and Evaluation Design

In the 1994 evaluation, the authors estimate the impact of training on (a) the probability of employment after 3, 6, and 12 months; (b) the time to exit unemployment; (c) the effect on monthly earnings, work hours per week, and hourly wages; and (d) the return on investment.

The 1999 evaluation looks at the same questions except work hours per week and hourly wages. Given that there is no impact in that evaluation on employment and monthly earnings, the return is zero, but again the program may work as a safety net.

The design of both evaluations is innovative in constructing the comparison group. In both cases, the evaluations combine an existing panel labor force survey, Encuesta Nacional de Empleo (ENEU), with a panel of trainees for the same period. That is, the program's selection criteria are used to define the control group from the ENEU. Although there is no alternative to this combination of surveys because of data limitations, the construction of the joint sample (control and treatment groups) can be critiqued, as discussed in the 1999 evaluation:

- In using the unemployed individuals in the ENEU to form the control group, it is assumed that none of the ENEU individuals have benefited from the program. This is not the case because every individual in the ENEU has some probability of having participated in PROBECAT. Fortunately, given that the program was small until 1993, only a very small minority of the individuals in the control group are likely to have participated in the program (the data for the 1999 evaluation are for 1993–94);
- The combination of two random samples (PROBECAT trainees and ENEU unemployed individuals) is not a random sample, so that in the absence of the standard properties for the residuals, the results of regressions may not yield consistent parameter estimates, especially because the models used are sensitive to the assumption of bivariate normality. In the absence of better data, not much can be done on this.

The main differences between the 1994 and 1999 evaluations are as follows;

- In the 1994 evaluation, the authors attempt to address the selection bias problems resulting from PROBECAT's nonrandom selection of trainees by estimating a probit model of the probability of participation. The comparison group is then limited to those individuals who are highly likely to participate. In the 1999 evaluation, the authors argue that this method does not eliminate the problem of endogeneity. Instead, they use an instrumental variable to control for the endogeneity of program participation.
- In the estimation of earnings in the 1994 evaluation, while participation in PROBECAT is controlled for, the sample selection bias resulting from the decision to work is not accounted for. In the 1999 study, both sample selection problems are accounted for.

III. Data

In the 1994 evaluation, data on trainees are gathered from a 1992 retrospective survey administered to 881 men and 845 women who were trained in 1990. This is supplemented with panel data on 371 men and 189 women derived from a household survey of the 16 main urban areas in Mexico. This survey was part of a regular quarterly labor force survey, ENEU, undertaken by the Mexican statistical agency. The authors exploited the rotation group structure of the survey to take workers who were unemployed in the third quarter of 1990 and then tracked those workers for a year. This was supplemented by a cohort that became unemployed in the fourth quarter of 1990 and was tracked for nine months. The same method was used in the 1999 evaluation, but for more recent data.

IV. Econometric Techniques

The key econometric techniques used are survival analysis (duration models) for the probability of working and Heckman regressions for wages. What follows is based on the 1999 evaluation. Differences with the 1994 evaluation are highlighted.

Impact of PROBECAT on the Length of Employment Search. In the survival analysis, the survivor function S(t) represents the length of unemployment after training (measured in months). Given S(t), the hazard function $\lambda(t)$ denoting the chance of becoming employed (or the risk of remaining unemployed) at time t among the individuals who are not yet employed at that time is $\lambda(t) = -d(\log S(t))/dt$. The survivor curve can be specified as a function of program participation P, individual characteristics X, and state characteristics Z, so that $\lambda = \lambda(t; X, Z, P)$. In Cox's proportional hazard model, if i denotes a household and j denotes the area in which the household lives, we have

$$\lambda(t; X, Z, P1, P2) = \lambda_0(t) \exp(\gamma'X_{ij} + \delta'Z_j + \mu P_{ij}). \tag{1}$$

Cox proposed a partial maximum likelihood estimation of this model in which the baseline function $\lambda_0(t)$ does not need to be specified. If μ is positive and statistically significant, the program has a positive effect on employment. In a stylized way, the difference between the 1994 and 1996 evaluations can be described as follows:

- In the 1994 evaluation, the authors run a probit on program participation and delete from the control group those individuals with a low probability of participating in the program. They then run equation (1) without further control for endogeneity.
- In the 1999 evaluation, the authors also run a probit on program participation, but they use program availability at the local level (obtained from administrative data) as an additional determinant of participation (but not of outcome conditional on individual participation.) Then they run equation (1), not with the actual value of the participation variable but with the predicted (index) value obtained from the first stage probit. This is an instrumental variable procedure. The idea follows work on program evaluation using decentralization properties by Ravallion and Wodon (2000) and Cord and Wodon (1999). The authors compare their results with other methods, showing that other methods exhibit a bias in the value of the parameter estimates owing to insufficient control for endogeneity.

Impact of PROBECAT on Monthly Earnings. To carry out this analysis, a model with controls for sample selection in labor force and program participation is used in the 1999 evaluation (the 1994 evaluation controls only for program participation). Denote by log w the logarithm of the expected wage for an individual. This wage is nonzero if and only if it is larger than the individual's reservation wage (otherwise, the individual would choose not to work). Denote the unobserved difference between the individual's expected wage and his or her reservation wage by Δ^*. The individual's expected wage is determined by a number of individual (vector E, consisting essentially of the individual's education and past experience) and geographic variables Z, plus program participation P. The difference between the individual's expected wage and his or her reservation wage is determined by the same variables, plus the number of children, the fact of being a household head, and the fact of being married, captured by D. The model is thus

$$\Delta_{ij}^* = \phi_\Delta' E_{ij} + \pi_\Delta' D_{ij} + \eta_\Delta' Z_j + \alpha_\Delta P_{ij} + v_{ij} \text{ with } \Delta_{ij} = 1 \text{ if } \Delta_{ij}^* > 0, \text{ and } 0 \text{ if } \Delta_{ij}^* < 0 \tag{2}$$

$$\text{Log } w_{ij}^* = \phi_w' E_{ij} + \eta_w' Z_j + \alpha_w P + \kappa_{ij} \text{ with Log } w = \log w^* \text{ if } \Delta = 1 \text{ and } 0 \text{ if } \Delta = 0. \tag{3}$$

As for the survival model, in order to control for endogeneity of program participation, in the 1999 evaluation a probit for program participation is first estimated by using program availability at the local level as a determinant of individual participation. Then the above equations are estimated by using the predicted (index) value of program participation instead of its true value. In the 1994 evaluation, the model does not control for the decision to participate in the labor market given in equation (2) above. This equation is replaced by the program participation probit estimated without local availability of the program as an independant variable. Again, comparisons of various models show that bias is present when the instrumental variable technique is not used.

V. Who Carried It Out

The 1994 evaluation was conducted by Ana Revenga in the Latin America and Caribbean Country Department II of the World Bank, Michelle Riboud in the Europe and Central Asia Country Department IV of the World Bank, and Hong Tan in the Private Sector Development Department of the World Bank. The 1999 evaluation was carried out by Quentin Wodon and Mari Minowa, also at the World Bank (Latin America region).

VI. Results

The results obtained in the various evaluations are very different. The 1994 and 1995 evaluations find positive impacts of the program on employment and wages. No positive impact was found in the 1999 evaluation, which is based on the same data used for the 1995 evaluation. In terms of cost-benefit analysis, the first two evaluations are favorable but the last evaluation is not. The disappointing results in the last evaluation are not surprising. Most retraining programs in Organisation for Economic Co-operation and Development countries have been found to have limited impacts, and when programs have been found to have some impact, this impact tends to vanish after a few years (Dar and Gill 1998).

The fact that PROBECAT may not be beneficial in the medium to long run for participants according to the last evaluation does not mean that it should be suppressed. The program could be viewed as providing temporary safety nets (through the minimum wage stipend) rather than training. Or it could be improved so as to provide training with longer-lasting effects.

VII. Lessons Learned

Apart from some of the innovative features of these evaluations and their limits, the key lesson is that one should be very careful in doing program evaluations and using the results to recommend policy options. The fact that a subsequent evaluation may contradict a previous one with the use of different econometric techniques should always be kept in mind. There have been many such cases in the literature.

VIII. Sources

Revenga, Ana, Michelle Riboud, and Hong Tan. 1994. "The Impact of Mexico's Retraining Program on Employment and Wages." *World Bank Economic Review* 8 (2): 247–77.

Wodon, Quentin, and Mari Minowa. "Training for the Urban Unemployed: A Reevaluation of Mexico's PROBECAT." World Bank, Government Programs and Poverty in Mexico, Report No. 19214-ME, Vol. II.

Annex 1.10: Mexico, National Program for Education, Health, and Nutrition (PROGRESA): A Proposal for Evaluation

I. Introduction

Project Description. PROGRESA is a multisectoral program aimed at fighting extreme poverty in Mexico by providing an integrated package of health, nutrition, and educational services to poor families. The Mexican government will provide monetary assistance, nutritional supplements, educational grants, and a basic health package for at least three consecutive years. It plans to expand PROGRESA from its current size of 400,000 families to 1 to 1.5 million families at the end of 1998, with an expenditure of $500 million.

Highlights of Evaluation. The evaluation is particularly complex because three dimensions of the program are evaluated: operation, targeting effectiveness, and impact. Adding to the complexity, outcomes are themselves multidimensional. There are thus many different evaluation components: beneficiary selection, evaluation methods, nonexperimental analytical framework, data requirements, impacts on education, impacts on health, impacts on food consumption and nutrition, impacts on consumption expenditures and intrahousehold allocation, potential second-round impacts of the program, simulations of changes in program benefits, and cost-effectiveness and cost-benefit issues.

Although the evaluation is an outline of ideas rather than the results of an implementation, a major lesson learned from it is how to think about and structure an evaluation before actually implementing it. In particular, there is a very useful outline of the conceptual and empirical issues to be addressed in an evaluation and the ways in which the issues can be addressed. Another useful component of the evaluation is its breadth: rather than simply evaluating the impact of an intervention, it will help pinpoint whether the outcome is due to successes or failures in the intervention operation and targeting.

II. Research Questions and Evaluation Design

The core research questions are to evaluate the three dimensions of PROGRESA's performance—operational aspects, targeting, and impact. The operational aspect of an intervention is often ignored, despite the fact that interventions could be turned from failures into successes if corrective measures were taken. A similar argument could be made for targeting: a program may seem to have failed simply because of poor targeting rather than because the intervention itself was flawed. The evaluation of the impact is more standard, although even this goal is quite ambitious in that both the magnitude of the impact and the pathways by which it is achieved are analyzed.

The monitoring of the program operation is a two-step procedure. The team develops a schematic of the sequence of steps for the intervention. The team then uses observations, interviews, focus groups, and workshops with stakeholders to assess, analyze, and potentially change program processes.

A two-step approach is also used to target households for PROGRESA. The first is to identify which localities in a region are eligible to receive PROGRESA by means of a poverty-based index. The second is to identify the eligibility of a family within the locality, based on the interaction between PROGRESA officials and local leaders. The study will address the validity of this targeting by (a) comparing the distribution of household consumption levels in participant and nonparticipant households in treatment localities, (b) deriving an eligibility cutoff for household consumption that is consistent with the total number of households that PROGRESA can serve, (c) conducting sensitivity and specificity analysis of PROGRESA and non-PROGRESA households versus the households selected and not selected under this cutoff, (d) exploring the ability of current criteria to predict consumption, (e) identifying alternative criteria from other data sources, and (f) simulating models that could improve targeting with alternative criteria (International Food Policy Research Institute 1998, p. 6).

For the impact evaluation, the same system was followed, with the result that localities were randomly allocated to 296 treatment and 173 nontreatment groups, with 14,382 families in the former category and 9,202 families in the latter category. Eligible families in the control category will receive treatment after at least one year has passed.

The consultants plan to test for possible nonrandomization by comparing the characteristics of treatment and control groups. If they are systematically different, then three nonexperimental methods will be used: control function methods, matching methods, and regression methods.

III. Data

The operational data component is obtained from observation and interviews, focus groups, and workshops with stakeholders. The main focus is on identifying what and why things are happening, the level of satisfaction with the process, and improvement suggestions. These data are collected across localities and will also rely heavily on PROGRESA's internal administrative records.

Two surveys have been implemented: December 1997 census surveys and March 1998 baseline surveys. The central variable for the targeting criterion is clearly household consumption, and while this was not collected in the census, it was collected in the March survey. This variable, however, lacks information on self-consumption, and although it will be collected later, it will be contaminated by the implementation of PROGRESA. The consultants plan to work exclusively with eligible and noneligible households in the control localities.

The evaluation of the impact hinges on the choice of impact indicators. PROGRESA should affect both the quality and quantity of services provided and investment in health, nutrition, and education. A host of evaluation indicators are proposed based on a number of impact outcomes, and each has an associated data source. Household welfare, as measured by household consumption, savings, accumulation of durable goods, will be measured by baseline and follow-up surveys; the nutritional and health status of children will be measured by a nutrition subsample baseline and follow-up surveys; child educational achievement will be measured by standardized national tests; food consumption will be captured by the baseline and follow-up surveys; school use will be addressed by both a school-level survey and by the baseline and follow-up surveys; health facility use can be monitored by health clinic records and the surveys; and women's status can also be measured by surveys and by the stakeholder investigations.

One very attractive feature of the proposed evaluation is the analytical approach taken to examine current outcome measures and the extensive discussion of more appropriate outcome and control measures for education, health, and consumption.

A cost-benefit analysis is planned. A set of benefits is developed, despite the inherent difficulty of monetizing quality of life and empowerment improvements. Two different types of cost are also identified: administrative program costs and program costs. The former consist of screening, targeted delivery mechanisms, and monitoring costs; the latter include forgone income generation.

IV. Econometric Techniques

The econometric techniques applied depend on the relationships to be estimated. The consultants discuss the appropriateness of the production function relationship (for example, for academic achievement), demand relationships (for example, for health or education services), and conditional demand relationships (in which some variables are determined by the family rather than the individual).

The most interesting econometric technique used is applied to the estimation of a Working-Leser expenditure function of the form

$$W_j = \alpha_T + \beta_{1j} \text{ lpcexp} + \beta_{2j} \text{ lsiz} + \Sigma_k \delta_{kj} \text{ dem}_k + \Sigma_s \Theta_{sj} z_s + \beta_{3j} P + e_j$$

where w_j is the budget share of the jth good; lpcexp is the log of per capita total expenditures; lsiz is the log of household size; dem_k is the proportion of demographic group k in the household; z_s is a vector of dummy variables affecting household location; P captures Progresa participation; and e_j is the error term.

This approach has many advantages: it permits the inclusion of control factors; it satisfies the adding-up constraint; and it is widely used, permitting comparisons with other studies. Finally, the model can be used to identify three different paths in which PROGRESA can affect expenditures: through changing household resources (β_{1j} times the marginal propensity to consume, estimated separately), through changing the income distribution (by modifying it to include the proportion of adult women in the household), and through a greater participation effect. The baseline and follow-up surveys allow difference-in-difference methodologies to be used.

They also identify key econometric issues that are likely to be faced: collinearity, measurement error, omitted variables, simultaneity, and identifying the time period within which it is reasonable to expect an impact to be observable.

V. Who Will Carry It Out

The International Food Policy Research Institute staff include Gaurav Datt, Lawrence Haddad, John Hoddinott, Agnes Quisumbing, and Marie Ruel. The team includes Jere Behrman, Paul Gertler, and Paul Schultz.

VI. Lessons Learned

The primary lesson learned here is the value of identifying evaluation issues, methodology, and data sources—and critically evaluating the evaluation—before the evaluation takes place. This evaluation outline provides a very valuable service in developing a thoughtful illustration of all the possible issues and pitfalls an evaluator is likely to encounter. In particular, some common-sense issues with evaluating an impact are identified: (a) policy changes may be hard to predict because of cross-substitution and behavior adjustment; (b) marginal benefits and marginal costs depend on a number of things: externalities (putting a wedge between social and private valuation), the actors (parents versus children); (c) the importance of unobserved characteristics; (d) the importance of controlling for individual, family, and community characteristics; and (e) the empirical estimates depend on a given macroeconomic, market, policy, and regulatory environment.

VII. Source

International Food Policy Research Institute. 1998. *Programa Nacional de Educación, Salud, y Alimentación (PROGRESA): A Proposal for Evaluation* (with technical appendix). Washington, D.C.: IFPRI.

Annex 1.11: Evaluating Nicaragua's School Reform: A Combined Quantitative-Qualitative Approach

I. Introduction

Project Description. In 1991, the Nicaraguan government introduced a sweeping reform of its public education system. The reform process has decentralized school management (decisions on personnel, budgets, curriculum, and pedagogy) and transferred financing responsibilities to the local level.

Reforms have been phased in over time, beginning with a 1991 decree that established community-parent councils in all public schools. Then a 1993 pilot program in 20 hand-picked secondary schools transformed these councils into school management boards with greater responsibility for personnel, budgets, curriculum, and pedagogy. By 1995, school management boards were operational in 100 secondary schools and over 300 primary schools, which entered the program through a self-selection process involving a petition from teachers and school directors. School autonomy was expected to be almost universal by the end of 1999.

The goal of the Nicaraguan reforms is to enhance student learning by altering organizational processes within public schools so that decision-making benefits students as a first priority. As school management becomes more democratic and participatory and locally generated revenues increase, spending patterns are to become more rational and allocated to efforts that directly improve pedagogy and boost student achievement.

Impact Evaluation. The evaluation of the Nicaraguan School Autonomy Reform represents one of the first systematic efforts to evaluate the impact of school decentralization on student outcomes. The evaluation, carried out jointly by the World Bank and the Ministry of Education, began in 1995 and was to be complete by the end of 1999. The design is innovative in that it combines both qualitative and quantitative assessment methods, and the quantitative component is unique in that it includes a separate module assessing school decisionmaking processes. The evaluation also illustrates "best-practice" techniques when there is no baseline data and when selective (nonrandom) application of reforms rules out an experimental evaluation design.

The purpose of the qualitative component of the evaluation is to illuminate whether or not the intended management and financing reforms are actually observed in schools and to assess how various stakeholders viewed the reform process. The quantitative component fleshes out these results by answering the following question: "Do changes in school management and financing actually produce better learning outcomes for children?" The qualitative results show that successful implementation of the reforms depends largely on school context and environment (i.e., poverty level of the community), whereas the quantitative results suggest that increased decisionmaking by schools is in fact significantly associated with improved student performance.

II. Evaluation Design

The design of the Nicaraguan School Autonomy Reform evaluation is based on the "matched comparison technique," in which data for a representative sample of schools participating in the reform process are compared with data from a sample of nonparticipating schools. The sample of nonparticipating schools is chosen to match, as closely as possible, the characteristics of the participating schools and hence provides the counterfactual. This design was chosen because the lack of baseline data ruled out a before-and-after evaluation technique and because reforms were not applied randomly to schools, which ruled out an experimental evaluation design (in which the sample of schools studied in the evaluation would be random and therefore nationally representative).

III. Data Collection and Analysis Techniques

The qualitative study draws on data for a sample of 12 schools, 9 reformers and 3 nonreformers, which represent the control group. (Data were actually gathered for 18 schools, but only 12 of these schools were included in the qualitative study because of delays in getting the transcripts prepared and a decision to concentrate the bulk of the analysis on reform schools, which provided more relevant material for the analysis.) The sample of 12 schools was picked to represent both primary and secondary schools, rural and urban schools, and, based on data from the 1995 quantitative survey, schools with differing degrees of actual autonomy in decisionmaking. A total of 82 interview and focus-group sessions were conducted, focusing on discovering how school directors, council members, parents, and teachers understood and viewed the decentralization process. All interviews were conducted by native Nicaraguans, trained through interview simulation and pilot tests to use a series of guided questions without cueing responses. Interviews were audiorecorded, transcribed, and then distilled into a two- to four-page transcript, which was then analyzed to identify discrete sets of evidence and fundamental themes that emerged across schools and actors and between reform schools and the control group.

Quantitative data collection consisted of two components, a panel survey of schools that was conducted in two rounds (November–December 1995 and April–August 1997) and student achievement tests for students in these schools that were conducted in November 1996. The school survey collected data on school enrollment, repetition and dropout rates, physical and human resources, school decisionmaking, and characteristics of school directors, teachers, students, and their families. The school decisionmaking module is unique and presents a series of 25 questions designed to gauge whether and how the reform has actually increased decisionmaking by schools. The survey covered 116 secondary schools (73 reformers and 43 nonreformers representing the control group) and 126 primary schools (80 reformers and 46 nonreformers). Again, the control groups were selected to match the characteristics of the reform schools. The survey also gathered data for 400 teachers, 182 council members, and 3,000 students and their parents, and 10–15 students were chosen at random from each school. Those students who remained in school and could be traced were given achievement tests at the end of the 1996 school year and again in the second round of survey data collection in 1997.

Quantitative data analysis draws on regression techniques to estimate an education production function. This technique examines the impact of the school's management regime (how decentralized it is) on student achievement levels, controlling for school inputs, and household and student characteristics. The analysis measures the effect of both de jure and de facto decentralization; de jure decentralization simply indicates whether or not the school has legally joined the reform, whereas de facto decentralization measures the degree of actual autonomy achieved by the school. De facto decentralization is measured as the percentage of 25 key decisions made by the school itself and is expected to vary across schools because reforms were phased in (so schools in the sample will be at different stages in the reform process) and because the capacity to successfully implement reforms varies according to school context (a result identified in the qualitative study).

IV. Results

The qualitative study points out that policy changes at the central level do not always result in tidy causal flows to the local level. In general, reforms are associated with increased parental participation as well as management and leadership improvements. But the degree of success with which reforms are implemented varies with school context. Of particular importance are the degree of impoverishment of the surrounding community (in poor communities, increasing local school financing is difficult) and the degree of cohesion among school staff (when key actors such as teachers do not feel integrated into the reform process, success at decentralization has been limited). Policymakers often ignore the highly variable local contexts into which new programs are introduced. The qualitative results point out that in the Nicaraguan context the goal of increased local financing for schools is likely to be derailed in practice, particularly in poor communities, and therefore merits rethinking.

The quantitative study reinforces the finding that reform schools are indeed making more of their own decisions, particularly with regard to pedagogical and personnel matters. De jure autonomy—whether a school has signed the reform contract—does not necessarily translate into greater school-level decisionmaking, or affect schools equally. The degree of autonomy achieved depends on the poverty level of the community and how long the school has been participating in the reform process. The regression results show that de jure autonomy has little bearing on student achievement outcomes; but de facto autonomy—the degree of actual decentralization achieved by the school—is significantly associated with improved student achievement. (This result is preliminary pending further exploration of the panel data, which have recently become available.) Furthermore, simulations indicate that increased school decentralization has a stronger bearing on student achievement than improvements in other indicators of typical policy focus, such as teacher training, lowering class size, and increasing the number of textbooks.

V. Policy Application

The evaluation results provide concrete evidence that Nicaragua's School Autonomy Reform has produced tangible results. Reform schools are indeed making more decisions locally—decentralization is happening in practice, not just on the books—and enhanced local decisionmaking does result in improved student achievement.

The results also point out areas in which policy can be improved, and, as a result, the Ministry of Education has introduced a number of changes in the school reform program. The program now places greater emphasis on the role of teachers and on promoting the pedagogical aspects of the reform. Teacher training is now included as part of the program, and the establishment of a pedagogical council is being considered. Further, in response to the financing problems of poor communities, the ministry has developed a poverty map–driven subsidy scheme. Finally, the tangible benefits from this evaluation have prompted the ministry to incorporate a permanent evaluation component into the reform program.

VI. Evaluation Costs and Administration

Costs. The total cost of the evaluation was approximately $495,000, representing less than 1.5 percent of the World Bank credit. (This total does not include the cost of local counterpart teams in the Nicaraguan Ministry of Eduation.) Of this total evaluation cost, 39 percent was spent on technical support provided by outside consultants, 35 percent on data collection, 18 percent on World Bank staff time, and 8 percent on travel.

Administration. The evaluation was carried out jointly by the Nicaraguan Ministry of Education and the World Bank. In Nicaragua the evaluation team was led by Patricia Callejas, Nora Gordon, and Nora Mayorga de Caldera in the Ministry of Education. At the World Bank the evaluation was carried out as part of the research project, "Impact Evaluation of Education Projects Involving Decentralization and Privatization" under the guidance of Elizabeth King, with Laura Rawlings and Berk Ozler. Coordinated by the World Bank team, Bruce Fuller and Madgalena Rivarola from the Harvard School of Education worked with Liliam Lopez from the Nicaraguan Ministry of Education to conduct the qualitative evaluation.

VII. Lessons Learned

Value of the Mixed-Method Approach. Using both qualitative and quantitative research techniques generated a valuable combination of useful, policy relevant results. The quantitative work provided a broad, statistically valid overview of school conditions and outcomes; the qualitative work enhanced these results with insight into why some expected outcomes of the reform program had been successful whereas others had failed and hence helped guide policy adjustments. Furthermore, because it is more intuitive, the qualitative work was more accessible and therefore interesting to ministry staff, which in turn facilitated rapid capacity building and credibility for the evaluation process within the ministry.

Importance of Local Capacity Building. Local capacity building was costly and required frequent contact and coordination with World Bank counterparts and outside consultants. However, the benefit was the rapid development of local ownership and responsibility for the evaluation process, which in turn fostered a high degree of acceptance of the evaluation results, whether or not these reflected positively or negatively on the program. These evaluation results provided direct input to the reform as it was evolving. The policy impact of the evaluation was also enhanced by a cohesive local team in which evaluators and policymakers worked collaboratively, and because the minister of education was brought on board as an integral supporter of the evaluation process.

VIII. Sources

The following documents provide detailed information on the Nicaraguan School Autonomy Reform Evaluation:

Fuller, Bruce, and Magdalena Rivarola. 1998. *Nicaragua's Experiment to Decentralize Schools: Views of Parents, Teachers and Directors.* Working Paper Series on Impact Evaluation of Education Reforms, paper no. 5. World Bank, Washington, D.C.

King, Elizabeth, and Berk Ozler. 1998. *What's Decentralization Got to Do with Learning? The Case of Nicaragua's School Autonomy Reform.* Working Paper Series on Impact Evaluation of Education Reforms, paper no. 9. World Bank, Washington, D.C.

King, Elizabeth, Berk Ozler, and Laura Rawlings. 1999. *Nicaragua's School Autonomy Reform: Fact or Fiction?* Washington, D.C.: World Bank.

Nicaragua Reform Evaluation Team. 1996. *Nicaragua's School Autonomy Reform: A First Look.* Working Paper Series on Impact Evaluation of Education Reforms, paper no. 1. World Bank, Washington, D.C.

Nicaragua Reform Evaluation Team. 1996. *1995 and 1997 Questionnaires, Nicaragua School Autonomy Reform.* Working Paper Series on Impact Evaluation of Education Reforms, paper no. 7. World Bank, Washington, D.C.

Rawlings, Laura. 2000. "Assessing Educational Management and Quality in Nicaragua." In Bamberger, *Integrating Quantitative and Qualitative Methods in Development Research.* Washington, D.C.: World Bank.

Annex 1.12: Improving Elementary Mathematics Education in Nicaragua: An Experimental Study of the Impact of Textbooks and Radio on Achievement

I. Summary of Evaluation

Most poor countries have extremely limited resources for education, which makes it important to allocate those resources effectively. Of the three common policy options available—smaller class sizes, longer teacher training programs, and textbook provision—only the last has frequently been found to have a significantly positive effect on student learning. This evaluation quantified the impact of textbook availability on mathematics learning for Nicaraguan first grade students.

The design of the evaluation was to provide textbooks to all students in a subset of classes that were originally designated to be controls in an ongoing study of the effectiveness of radio instructional programs. Half of the classes received textbooks; half did not. All classes received both a pretest at the beginning of the year and a posttest at the end. The study then used simple regression techniques to compare the mean classroom posttest scores as a function of pretest scores and the intervention.

A major lesson learned is how to carefully design an evaluation: the randomization was particularly well-constructed and cleverly combined with a test that maximized cross-class comparability. Another lesson learned was one of pragmatism: the evaluation was designed to forestall potentially quite serious political economy issues. Finally, the evaluation provides a series of practical examples of the types of decisions that must be made in fieldwork.

II. Research Questions and Evaluation Design

There are two very interesting components of the evaluation design: the piggy-backing on a preexisting evaluation and the up-front understanding of the political environment within which the evaluation was to take place. The key research question was straightforward: to assess the impact of increased textbook availability on first grade student learning—particularly focusing on whether the textbooks were actually used in the classroom. Because there was already a radio instructional program intervention (Radio Mathematics) in place, the question was broadened to compare the impact of textbook availability with radio instruction as well as with a control group.

It is worth discussing the decision to monitor the actual use of text-books, which makes the evaluation more difficult. Many educational interventions provide materials to classrooms, but clearly the impact of the provision depends on use. However, as the evaluators point out, this decision means that the evaluation "does not assess the potential that textbooks or radio lessons have for improving student achievement under optimal outcomes. Rather, it attempts to assess their impact as they might be adopted in the typical developing country" (Jamison, 1981 p. 559). Thus simple textbook provision may not in itself suffice without also designing a method to ensure that teachers use the textbooks as intended.

The evaluation used a randomized design that was piggybacked on a preexisting project evaluation. In the existing Radio Nicaragua Project, an entire mechanism had already put random assignment and testing procedures in place in order to evaluate the effectiveness of a radio-based instructional program. The existing project had already classified all primary schools in three provinces in Nicaragua as radio or control using a random sampling process stratified by urbanization (about 30 percent of students are in rural schools, but equal numbers of classes were chosen in each stratum).

The textbook evaluation exploited this preexisting design by selecting treatment and control schools in the following fashion. First, the evaluators acquired a list of all schools with eligible classrooms for each of the six categories (three provinces, rural and urban). They then randomly assigned schools to treatment or control from these master lists for each category, and then schools were used in the order that they appeared (one school, which refused to participate, was replaced by the next one on the list). Requests to participate from classes in control groups were denied, and all use of the experimental material was controlled by the authors. It is useful to note that the evaluation design had addressed this potential political difficulty up front. The evaluation team announced their intentions from the outset; the team obtained official approval and support of the policy, and the team also established clear and consistent procedures for the program.

The study thus randomly selected 88 classrooms: 48 radio and 40 control schools. Twenty of the control schools received textbooks for each child, and teachers received both written and oral instruction and the teachers' editions of the tests. The radio component consisted of 150 daily mathematics lessons, combined with student worksheets and written and oral teacher instructions.

An interesting decision that was made was the deliberate lack of supervision of treatment groups. This was clearly difficult because the absence of supervision made it hard to assess program utilization.

However, the cost in terms of influencing behavior was judged to be too high. Surprise visits, which were the accepted compromise solution, could not be used because of political turmoil during the assessment year and so had to be conducted the following year.

A second decision was to have tests administered by project staff rather than classroom teachers. This clearly increased administrative costs but reduced potential bias in test taking. The students were given a pretest of mathematical readiness during the first three weeks of school. The posttest, which measured achievement, was intended to be given in the last three weeks of school but was administered two weeks early because of political problems. The students had, as much as possible, identical conditions for both tests when they took them because they had the same length of time for the tests and because instructions were taped.

III. Data

There are two main lessons to be drawn from the data collection component. The first is that logistical difficulties are often inevitable. Despite the careful design there were a series of problems with developing a perfect set of pretest-posttest comparisons. Although there were a total of 20 control classes, 20 textbook classes, and 47 radio classes, the numbers of pretest and posttest scores were different in each group because of late registration, dropping out, absence, and failure to be tested because of overcrowding. Individual information on the students does not appear to have been collected.

The second lesson is the imaginative way in which the evaluators designed the posttest to minimize burden and yet obtain the necessary information. A series of issues were faced:

- There were no standardized tests in use in Nicaragua.
- The test had to assess the achievement of the curriculum objectives.
- The test had to capture achievement on each topic to facilitate an evaluation of the effectiveness of the intervention on each topic as well as in total.

The evaluators used a multiple matrix-sampling design to address these issues. The test had two types of questions: those given to all the students in the class (40 G items) and those given to subsets of students (44 I items). All I items were tested in every classroom; one-quarter of all G items were tested in each classroom. This enables the researchers to randomly assign units across two dimensions: schools and test forms. The mean posttest scores for treatment and control groups are derived by adding average scores for each test, and the standard errors are calculated by using the residual variance after removing the main effects of items and students.

Information on textbook usage was also collected the year after the intervention from 19 of the 20 textbook-using schools.

IV. Econometric Techniques

The structure of the evaluation meant that a simple comparison of means between treatment and control groups would be appropriate, and this was in fact used. The approach can be very cumbersome if there are multiple strata and multiple interventions, which was the case with this evaluation. Thus the evaluators also used a simple regression approach. Here the class was the unit of analysis, and the class mean posttest score was regressed against the mean pretest score as well as dummies for the radio and textbook interventions, an urban-rural dummy, and the average class pretest score as independent variables.

An important component of any evaluation is whether different groups are affected differently by the same treatment. This can often be achieved, as was done in this evaluation, by imaginative use of interactive variables. Differences between urban and rural areas were captured by interacting the urban-rural dummy with the intervention; difference in the effect of the intervention based on initial test scores was captured by interacting initial test scores with the intervention.

V. Who Carried It Out

The World Bank supported the research project, but it was imbedded in the joint United States Agency for International Development–Nicaragua Ministry of Education Radio Mathematics Project.

VI. Results

The authors found that both textbook and radio treatments had important effects on student outcomes: textbook availability increased student posttest scores by 3.5 items correct, radio lessons by 14.9 items—quite substantial given that the classroom standard deviation is 8.3 and that of individual items is 11.8. Radio lessons and textbooks were both more effective in rural schools and could potentially play a large part in reducing the gap between urban and rural quality. These results appear to be independent of the initial skill level of the class, as measured by pretest scores.

The authors attribute the difference in outcomes for the radio and the textbook interventions to differences in textbook usage, particularly given poorly educated teachers.

VII. Lessons Learned

Three main lessons were learned: the importance of politics in design decisions, the usefulness of imaginative test designs, and the difficulties associated with fieldwork. First, the political economy of randomized design was highlighted in this study: there are clearly quite strong political pressures that can be brought to bear and that need to be addressed early on and with the support of the government. Second, the authors were able to measure many facets of learning outcomes without having unrealistically long tests, by imaginative application of a test design. Finally, the evaluators clearly addressed a number of fieldwork questions: whether and how to monitor the actual adoption of textbooks and who should administer the tests.

VIII. Source

Jamison, Dean T., Barbara Serle, Klaus Galda, and Stephen P. Heyneman. 1981. "Improving Elementary Mathematics Education in Nicaragua: An Experimental Study of the Impact of Textbooks and Radio on Achievement." *Journal of Educational Psychology* 73 (4): 556–67.

Annex 1.13: The Impact of Alternative Cost-Recovery Schemes on Access and Equity in Niger

I. Introduction

Project Description. The ability to recover some portion of health care costs is critical to the provision of health care. Little is known, however, about the effect of different strategies on quality and welfare outcomes. The evaluation estimates the impact on the demand for health care of two pilot cost-recovery schemes in the primary care (nonhospital) sector in Niger. Niger is a poor, rural economy; public health costs are 5 to 6 percent of the government budget; and much of this financing is mistargeted toward hospitals and personnel. The government wanted to evaluate the consequences of different payment mechanisms and considered two: a pure fee-for-service and a tax plus fee-for-service financing mechanism, both of which were combined with quality and management improvements. The government was particularly interested in finding out how the demand for health care changed, particularly among vulnerable groups, and in examining whether such quality improvements were sustainable.

Highlights of Evaluation. The different payment mechanisms were implemented in three districts, one for each treatment and one control. The evaluation used a quasi-experimental design based on household surveys combined with administrative data on utilization and operating costs. The evaluation is particularly attractive in that it directly addresses political economy issues with a survey instrument that asks respondents about their willingness to pay for the improved service. This explicit recognition that significant outcomes are not, by themselves, enough to guarantee a sustainable project is an extremely valuable contribution. Another useful aspect is the explicit evaluation of the impact of the intervention on different target groups (children, women, villages without a public health facility, and the poorest citizens).

II. Research Questions and Evaluation Design

The main questions were the impact of the treatment on (a) the demand for and utilization of public health care facilities, (b) specific target groups (poor, women, and children), (c) financial and geographic access, (d) the use of alternative services, and (e) the sustainability of improvements under cost recovery (patient and drug costs as well as revenues and willingness to pay).

Three health districts were selected in different provinces from an administrative register. Although all were similar in terms of economic, demographic, and social characteristics, they were ethnically different. Each district had a medical center, with a maternal and child health center, one medical post, and one physician as well as rural dispensaries.

Four quality and management improvements were instituted in the two treatment districts; none was implemented in the control district. In particular, initial stocks of drugs were delivered; personnel were trained in diagnosis and treatment; a drug stock and financial management system was installed and staff were trained in its use; supervisory capacity was increased to reinforce management.

The two different pricing mechanisms were introduced at the same time. The first was a fee-per-episode, with a fee of 200 FCFA (US$0.66) for a user over age five, a fee of 100 FCFA (US$0.33) for a user under five. The second combined an annual tax of 200 FCFA paid by district taxpayers and a fee of 50 FCFA per user over five and 25 FCFA for children under five. Annual income was under US$300 per capita. Each scheme included exemptions for targeted groups. The funds were managed at the district level.

III. Data

The three districts were chosen from administrative data. Two household surveys were implemented, one of which was a baseline, and these were combined with administrative records on facilities. Each survey collected demographic household and individual information from a randomly selected sample of 1,800 households. The baseline survey had information on 2,833 individuals who had been sick the two weeks before the survey and 1,770 childbearing women; the final survey had data on 2,710 sick individuals and 1,615 childbearing women. The administrative data consisted of quite detailed information on monthly expenditures on drug consumption and administration, personnel maintenance, and fee receipts together with the utilization of the health facilities. This information was collected in the year before the intervention, the base year (May 1992–April 1993), and the year after the intervention.

IV. Econometric Techniques

The study combines comparisons of means with simple logit techniques, the latter being used to capture utilization changes. In particular, the individual response of whether the health care facility was used (PI) to specify the following model:

Logit $(P_I) = X\exists + {}^* (A + B)$.

This model, which controls for a vector of individual characteristics X as well as dummy variables A and B, was compared with

Logit $(P_I) = X\exists + {}^*_a A + {}^*_b B$.

The dummy variables A and B are variously defined. In the first battery of regressions, A refers to the period during treatment, B refers to the period before treatment, and the regressions are run by subgroup (the specified target groups) and by district. In the second battery of regressions, A and B are used to make six pairwise comparisons of each district with each other district during the treatment. In each case, the authors test whether $({}^*_a + {}^*_b) = {}^*$. The effects of geographic and financial access are captured in the X matrix by distance measures of walking time and income quartiles, respectively. It is unclear from the discussion what the omitted category is in each case. It is also unclear whether the standard errors of the estimates were corrected for the clustered nature of the sample design.

Although the logit techniques are an efficient way of addressing three of the four research questions—utilization patterns, the effect on subgroups, and the effects of geographic and financial access—the fourth question, the effect of changes in cost recovery, is addressed by administrative data and simple comparisons of means. One obvious concern in the latter approach, which was not explicitly addressed, is the possibility of bias in the reporting of the posttreatment results. In particular, there is some moral hazard if administrators are evaluated on the successful response to the treatment.

The effect of the treatments on the use of alternative health systems was addressed through econometric techniques described elsewhere.

V. Who Carried It Out

The Ministry of Public Health carried out the survey with the financial and technical assistance of the U.S. Agency for International Development and the World Bank. The evaluation itself was carried out by Francis Diop, Abode Yazbeck, and Ricardo Bitran of Abt Associates.

VI. Results

The study found that the tax plus fee generated more revenue per capita than the fee-based system, in addition to being much more popular. The tax-based fee system also had better outcomes in terms of providing access to improved health care for the poor, women, and children. However, because geography is a major barrier to health care access, a tax-based system effectively redistributes the cost of health care from people close to health facilities toward people a long way from such facilities.

The district that implemented fee-for-service saw a slight decline in the number of initial visits but an increase in demand for health care services—compared with a dramatic increase in both in the tax-plus-fee district. Much of this could be attributed to the increase in the quality of the service associated with the quality improvements, which more than offset the increase in cost.

The cost containment—particularly of drug costs—associated with the quality and management reform also proved to be effective and sustainable. Cost recovery in the tax-plus-fee district approached and exceeded 100 percent but was substantially less in the fee-for-service district. In addition, there was much higher willingness to pay in the former than in the in latter.

The major result is that the tax-plus-fee approach is both more effective in achieving the stated goals and more popular with the population. The evaluation also demonstrated, however, that lack of geographic access to health care facilities is a major barrier to usage. This suggests that there are some distributional issues associated with going to a tax-plus-fee system: households that are a long way away from health care facilities would implicitly subsidize nearby households.

VII. Lessons Learned

There are a number of useful lessons in this evaluation. One is the multifaceted way in which it assesses the project's impact on multiple dimensions related to sustainability: not only on cost recovery but also on quality and on the reaction of affected target groups. Another is the attention to detail in data collection with both administrative and survey instruments, which then bore fruit through the ability to identify exactly which components of the intervention worked and why. Finally, the analysis of the impact on each target group proved particularly useful for policy recommendations.

VIII. Sources

Diop, F. A Yazbeck, and R. Bitran. 1995. "The Impact of Alternative Cost Recovery Schemes on Access and Equity in Niger." *Health Policy and Planning* 10 (3): 223–40.

Wouters, A. 1995. "Improving Quality through Cost Recovery in Niger." 10 (3): 257–70.

Annex 1.14: Schooling Outcomes in Philippine Elementary Schools: Evaluation of the Impact of Four Experiments

I. Introduction

Project Description. In most developing countries high dropout rates and inadequate student learning in primary education are a matter of concern to policymakers. This is certainly the case in the Philippines: almost one-quarter of Philippine children drop out before completing sixth grade, and those who leave have often mastered less than half of what they have been taught. The government embarked on a Dropout Intervention Program (DIP) in 1990–92 to address these issues. Four experiments were undertaken: provision of multilevel learning materials (MLM), school lunches (SL), and each of these combined with a parent-teacher partnership (PTP). The first approach allows teachers to pace teaching to different student needs and is much less expensive than school feeding. Parent-teacher partnerships cost almost nothing but can help with student learning both at home and at school.

Highlights of Evaluation. The evaluation is noteworthy in that it explicitly aimed to build capacity in the host country so that evaluation would become an integral component of new initiatives, and data requirements would be considered before rather than after future project implementations. However, there are some problems that occur as a consequence, and the evaluation is very clear about what to expect. Another major contribution of the evaluation is the check for robustness of results with different econometric approaches. Finally, the benefit-cost analysis applied at the end is important in that it explicitly recognizes that significant results do not suffice: inexpensive interventions may still be better than expensive ones.

II. Research Questions and Evaluation Design

The key research question is the evaluation of the impact of four different interventions on dropping out and student outcomes. However, the evaluation design is conditioned by pragmatic as well as programmatic needs. The DIP team followed a three-stage school selection process:

- Two districts in each of five regions of the country were identified as a low-income municipality. In one district the treatment choices were packaged as control, MLM, or MLM-PTP; in the other control, SL, or SL-PTP. The assignment of the two intervention packages was by a coin flip.

- In each district the team selected three schools that (a) had all grades of instruction, with one class per grade; (b) had a high dropout rate: and (c) had no school feeding program in place.
- The three schools in each district were assigned to control or one of the two interventions based on a random drawing.

Each intervention was randomly assigned to all classes in five schools, and both pre- and posttests were administered in both 1991 and 1992 to all classes in all 20 schools as well as in 10 control schools.

III. Data

The data collection procedure is instructive in and of itself. Baseline data collection began in 1990–91, and the interventions were implemented in 1991–92. Detailed information was gathered on 29 schools, on some 180 teachers, and on about 4,000 pupils in each of the two years. Although these questionnaires were very detailed, this turned out to be needless: only a small subset of the information was actually used, which suggests that part of the burden of the evaluation process could usefully be minimized. Pretests and posttests were also administered at the beginning and end of each school year in three subjects: mathematics, Filipino, and English.

The data were structured to be longitudinal on both pupils and schools. Unfortunately the identifiers on the students turned out not to be unique for pupils and schools between the two years. It is worth noting that this was not known a priori and only became obvious after six months of work uncovered internal inconsistencies. The recovery of the original identifiers from the Philippine Department of Education was not possible. Fortunately, the data could be rescued for first graders, which permitted some longitudinal analysis.

IV. Econometric Techniques

The structure of the sampling procedure raised some interesting econometric problems: one set for dropping out and one for test score outcomes. In each case there are two sets of obvious controls: one is the control group of schools, and the other is the baseline survey conducted in the year prior to the intervention. The authors handled these in different ways.

In the analysis of dropping out, it is natural to set up a difference-in-difference approach and compare the change in the mean dropout rate in each intervention class between the two years with the change in the mean dropout rate for the control classes. However, two issues immediately arose. First, the results, although quite large in size, were only significant for the MLM intervention, possibly owing to small sample size issues. This is not uncommon with this type of procedure and likely to be endemic given the lack of funding for large-scale experiments in a developing-country context. Second, a brief check of whether student characteristics and outcomes were in fact the same across schools in the year prior to the interventions suggested that there were some significant differences in characteristics. These two factors led the authors to check the robustness of the results via logistic regression techniques that controlled for personal characteristics (PC) and family background (FB). The core result was unchanged. However, the regression technique did uncover an important indirect core cause of dropping out, which was poor academic performance. This naturally led to the second set of analysis, which focused on achievement.

A different set of econometric concerns was raised in the evaluation of the impact of the intervention INTER on the academic performance of individual I in school s at time t (AP_{ist}), which the authors model as

$$AP_{ist} = \delta_0 + \delta_1 AP_{ist-1'} + \delta_2 PC_i + \delta 3\ FB_i + \delta_4\ LE_{st} + \delta_5\ CC_i + \delta_6\ INTER_{jt} + \varepsilon$$

where LE is learning environment and CC is classroom conditions.

First among these issues is accounting for the clustered correlation in errors that is likely to exist for students in the same classes and schools. Second is attempting to capture unobserved heterogeneity. And the third, related, issue is selection bias.

The first issue is dealt with by applying a Huber-White correction to the standard errors. The second could, in principle, be captured at the individual level by using the difference in test scores as an independent variable. However, the authors argue that this is inappropriate because it presupposes that the value of δ_1 is 1, which is not validated by tests. They therefore retain the lagged dependent variable specification, but this raises the next problem—one of endogenous regressor bias. This is handled by instrumenting the pretest score in each subject with the pretest scores in the other subjects. The authors note, however, that the reduction in bias comes at a cost—a reduction in efficiency—and hence report both least squares and instrumental variables results. The authors use both school and teacher fixed effects to control for unobserved heterogeneity in LE and CC.

The third problem is one that is also endemic to the literature and for which there is no fully accepted solution: selection bias. Clearly, because there are differential dropout rates, the individual academic performance is conditional on the decision not to drop out. Although this problem has often been addressed by the two-stage Heckman procedure, there is a great deal of dissatisfaction with it for three reasons: its sensitivity to the assumption of the normal distribution, the choice and adequacy of the appropriate variables to use in the first stage, and its frequent reliance on identification through the nonlinearity of the first stage. Unfortunately, there is still no consensus about an appropriate alternative. One that has been proposed is by Krueger, who assigns to dropouts their pretest ranking and returns them to the regression. Thus the authors report three sets of results: the simple regression of outcomes against intervention, the Krueger approach, and the Heckman procedure.

V. Who Carried It Out

The data collection was carried out by the Bureau of Elementary Education of the Philippines Department of Education, Culture, and Sports. The analysis was carried out by a World Bank employee and two academic researchers.

VI. Results

The study evaluates the impact of these interventions on dropping out in grades one through six and on test score outcomes in first grade using a difference-in-differences approach, instrumental variable techniques, and the Heckman selection method. The effect of multilevel materials—particularly with a parent-teacher partnership—on dropping out and improving academic performance is robust to different specifications as well as being quite cost-effective. The effect of school lunches was, in general, weak. An interesting component of the study was a cost-benefit analysis—which makes the important point that the story does not end with significant results! In particular, a straightforward calculation of both the direct and indirect (opportunity) costs of the program leads to the conclusion that the MLM approach is both effective and cost-effective.

The lack of effectiveness of school feeding might be overstated, however: it is possible that a more targeted approach for school feeding programs might be appropriate. Furthermore, because there is quite a short period of time between the implementation and the evaluation of the program, the evaluation cannot address the long-term impact of the interventions.

VII. Lessons Learned

Several lessons were learned through this evaluation procedure. One major one was that the devil is in the details—that a lot of vital longitudinal information can be lost if adequate information, such as the uniqueness of identifiers over time, is lost. A second one is that very little of the information that is gathered in detailed surveys was used and that a substantial burden to the respondents could have been reduced. Third, the study highlights the value of different econometric approaches and the advantages of finding consistency across techniques. Fourth, this study is exemplary in its use of cost-benefit analysis—both identifying and valuing the costs of the different interventions. Finally, although errors were clearly made during the study, the authors note that a prime motive for the study was to build evaluation capacity in the Philippines. The fact that the DIP was implemented and evaluated means that such capacity can be nurtured within ministries of education.

VIII. Source

Tan, J. P., J. Lane, and G. Lassibille. 1999. "Schooling Outcomes in Philippine Elementary Schools: Evaluation of the Impact of Four Experiments." *World Bank Economic Review,* September.

Annex 1.15: Assessing the Poverty Impact of Rural Roads Projects in Vietnam

I. Introduction

Project Description. Rural roads are being extensively championed by the World Bank and other donors as instruments for alleviating poverty. The Vietnam Rural Transport Project I was launched in 1997 with funding from the World Bank for implementation over three to five years. The goal of the project is to raise living standards in poor areas by rehabilitating existing roads and bridges and enhancing market access. In each participating province, projects are identified for rehabilitation through least-cost criteria (size of population that will benefit and project cost). However, in an effort to enhance poverty targeting, 20 percent of each province's funds can be set aside for low-density, mountainous areas populated by ethnic minorities where projects would not strictly qualify under least-cost criteria.

Impact Evaluation. Despite a general consensus on the importance of rural roads, there is surprisingly little concrete evidence on the size and nature of the benefits from such infrastructure. The goal of the Vietnam Rural Roads Impact Evaluation is to determine how household welfare is changing in communes that have road project interventions compared with ones that do not. The key issue for the evaluation is to successfully isolate the impact of the road from the myriad of other factors that are changing in present-day rural Vietnam as a result of the ongoing transition to a market economy.

The evaluation began concurrent with project preparation, in early 1997, and is in process. No results are available yet. The evaluation is compelling in that it is one of the first comprehensive attempts to assess the impact of a rural roads project on welfare outcomes—the bottom line in terms of assessing whether projects really do reduce poverty. The design attempts to improve on earlier infrastructure evaluation efforts by combining the following elements: (a) collecting baseline and follow-up survey data, (b) including appropriate controls so that results are robust to unobserved factors that influence both program placement and outcomes, and (c) following the project long enough (through successive data collection rounds) to capture its full welfare impact.

II. Evaluation Design

The design of the Vietnam Rural Roads Impact Evaluation centers on baseline (preintervention) and follow-up (postintervention) survey data for a sample of project and nonproject communes. Appropriate controls can be identified from among the nonproject communities through matched-comparison techniques. The baseline data allows before-and-after ("reflexive") comparison of welfare indicators in project and control group communities. In theory the control group, selected through matched-comparison techniques, is identical to the project group according to both observed and unobserved characteristics so that resulting outcomes in program communities can be attributed to the project intervention.

III. Data Collection and Analysis Techniques

Data collected for the purposes of the evaluation include commune- and household-level surveys, along with district-, province-, and project-level databases. The baseline and follow-up commune and household surveys were conducted in 1997 and 1999, and third and fourth survey rounds, conducted at two-year intervals, are planned. The survey sample includes 100 project and 100 nonproject communes, located in 6 of the 18 provinces covered by the project. Project communes were selected randomly from lists of all communes with proposed projects in each province. A list was then drawn up of all remaining communes in districts with proposed projects, from which control communes were randomly drawn. (Ideally, controls differ from the project group only insofar as they do not receive an intervention. And for logistical reasons, it was desirable to limit the fieldwork to certain regions. Controls were therefore picked in the vicinity of, and indeed in the same districts as, the treatment communes. Districts are large and contamination from project to nonproject commune is therefore unlikely, but this will need to be carefully checked.) Propensity-score matching techniques based on commune characteristics will be used to test the selection of controls, and any controls with unusual attributes relative to the project communes will be dropped from the sample. A logit model of commune participation in the project will be estimated and used to ensure that the control communes have similar propensity scores (predicted values from the logit model).

The commune database draws on existing administrative data collected annually by the communes covering demographics, land use, and production activities and augmented with a commune-level survey conducted for the purposes of the evaluation. The survey covers general characteristics, infrastructure, employment, sources of livelihood, agriculture, land and other assets, education, health care, development programs, community organizations, commune finance, and prices. These data will be used to construct a number of commune-level indicators of welfare and to test program impacts over time.

The main objective of the household survey is to capture information on household access to various facilities and services and how this changes over time. The household questionnaire was administered to 15 randomly selected households in each commune, covering employment, assets, production and employment activities, education, health, marketing, credit, community activities, access to social security and poverty programs, and transport. Owing to limited surveying capacity in-country, no attempt is made to gather the complex set of data required to generate a household-level indicator of welfare (such as income or consumption). However, a number of questions were included in the survey that replicate questions in the Vietnam Living Standards Survey. Using this and other information on household characteristics common to both surveys, regression techniques will be used to estimate each household's position in the national distribution of welfare. A short district-level database was also prepared to help put the commune-level data in context, including data on population, land use, the economy, and social indicators. Each of these surveys is to be repeated following the commune survey schedule.

Existing information was used to set up two additional databases. An extensive province-level database was established to help understand the selection of the provinces into the project. This database covers all of Vietnam's provinces and has data on a wide number of socioeconomic variables. Finally, a project-level database for each of the project areas surveyed was also constructed in order to control for both the magnitude of the project and its method of implementation in assessing project impact.

The baseline data will be used to model the selection of project sites by focusing on the underlying economic, social, and political economy processes. Later rounds will then be used to understand gains measurable at the commune level, conditional on selection. The analytical approach will be "double differencing" with matching methods. Matching will be used to select ideal controls from among the 100 sampled nonproject communes. Outcomes in the project communes will be compared with those found in the control communes, both before and after the introduction of the road projects. The impact of the program is then identified as the difference between outcomes in the project areas after the program and before it, minus the corresponding outcome difference in the matched control areas. This methodology provides an unbiased estimate of project impacts in the presence of unobserved time-invariant factors that influence both the selection of project areas and outcomes. The results will be enhanced by the fact that the data sets are rich in both outcome indicators and explanatory variables. The outcome indicators to be examined include commune-level agricultural yields, income source diversification, employment opportunities, land use and distribution, availability of goods, services and facilities, and asset wealth and distribution.

IV. Evaluation Costs and Administration

Costs. The total cost of the evaluation to date is $222,500, or 3.6 percent of total project costs. This sum includes $202,500 covering the first two rounds of data collection and a $20,000 research grant. World Bank staff time and travel expenses are not included in these costs.

Administration. The evaluation was designed by World Bank staff member Dominique van de Walle. An independent consultant with an economics and research background in rural poverty and development was hired to be the in-country supervisor of the study. This consultant has hired and trained the team supervisors, organized all logistics, and supervised all data collection.

V. Source

van de Walle, Dominique. 1999. *Assessing the Poverty Impact of Rural Road Projects*. World Bank, Washington, D.C. Processed.

Annex 2
Sample Terms of Reference

Example I: The Uganda Nutrition and Early Childhood Development Project

Terms of Reference for Consulting Firm to Assist in the Project Evaluation

I. Background

The Government of Uganda has applied for a credit from the International Development Association toward the cost of a Nutrition and Early Childhood Project. The project focuses on improving the quality of life of children under six years of age and building the capacity of families and communities to care for children. Specifically, the project will aim at achieving early child development through improving the nutrition, health, psychosocial, and cognitive status of children under six years of age in Uganda.

II. Rationale for Investing in Early Childhood Development

Investing in early childhood development (ECD) has tangible benefits not only for the children and parents but also for entire communities and the country. Rapid physical growth and mental development occur during infancy and early childhood; at two years of age, a child's brain is nearly fully grown. Cognitive abilities are also developed to a large extent by four years of age. Adequate physical and mental growth and development during early childhood enhance school readiness, improve school retention, and contribute to human capital dependency. Children from disadvantaged backgrounds can particularly benefit from early child care, thus bridging the gaps and inequalities associated with poverty.

Good health and nutrition are crucial, as is mental stimulation, if the child is to develop secure conceptual structures in later life. The synergy between nutrition, health, and mental stimulation is so crucial that tangible positive effects on child growth and development can only be achieved through an integrated approach.

169

III. Project Objectives and Strategies

The development objective of the project is to improve growth and development of children under six years of age in terms of nutrition, health, psychosocial, and cognitive aspects. The achievement of these objectives at the end of the five-year implementation period will be measured by the following markers: (a) reduced prevalence of underweight preschool children by one-third of the 1995 levels in the project districts; (b) reduced prevalence of stunting on entry into primary schools by one-fourth of the 1995 levels in the project districts, (c) improved children's psychosocial and cognitive development, (d) reduced repetition and dropout rates at the lower primary school level, and (e) development of entrepreneurship skills and economic empowerment of mothers and caregivers.

The project supports the Ugandan National Program of Action for Children and the Poverty Eradication Action Plan. The project particularly enhances school readiness of young children and thus contributes toward reaching the goal of universal primary education. The main project strategy is to enhance the capacity of families and communities to take better care of preschool-age children (zero to six years) through enhancing knowledge on child growth and development, parenting, nutrition and health care, and income-generating activities for women.

IV. Project Approach

The project is a process-driven, locally prioritized program rather than a blueprint package. Inputs are to be phased into communities as a result of a participatory planning process to ensure ownership and sustainability. The program will involve collaboration between government and nongovernment entities, including local and international nongovernmental organizations (NGOs), and communities. As a multisectoral program involving health, nutrition, early childhood education, child care, savings and income generation, the approach will involve linking various government departments and nongovernment entities to provide a comprehensive service directed toward the development of children. The project will support a range of options—a program menu—relating to the needs of preschool children and their families.

V. Project Components

Project Component 1—Integrated Community Child Care Interventions. This component supports the government's goals (a) to improve parental awareness on major aspects of child care, growth, and development through parental education, child growth monitoring and promotion, training, and sensitization; and (b) to empower communities to support child development programs through capacity building, through skills for income generation, and through support grants. The objective is to reduce malnutrition (low weight for age) of children by a third at the end of the five-year period in the project districts and increase readiness of children for primary schooling and thereby contribute to the drive for universal primary education. The government plan is to eventually cover all districts; however, interventions in this phase will be implemented in 25 districts chosen by the government based on the level of malnutrition, infant mortality, and rate of primary school enrollment. The project includes the following interrelated interventions:

(a) Parental Education. This subcomponent will increase parents' and caregivers' understanding of major aspects of child care, growth, and development, including child nutrition, health, and cognitive and psychosocial development. A range of related competencies will be strengthened in parents. Building parental skills and knowledge will in turn improve the health, psychosocial development, and well-being of children and, ultimately, their receptiveness to education at the primary level. The program will mobilize groups of mothers (and parents) at the community level, supported by project materials in local languages, technical supervision, and communications. Simplified learning materials for adults with low literacy have been tested successfully in Uganda. Emphasis will be on the enhancement of child care practices that promote proper growth and development of children, including childhood nutrition and health (exclusive breastfeeding and appropriate weaning practices—particularly the period of introduction of weaning foods, as well as the type of foods given, and food preparation, child growth promotion, and deworming), psychosocial development, cognitive stimulation and social support, and hygiene and improved home health practices.

The above interventions will be strengthened and supported by an outreach activity (children's day) organized at the parish level to enable communities to access a number of child-related services by means of one-stop shopping. A study of the impact of providing the anathelminth albendazole to young children in selected parishes will also be conducted in the course of parish-based child days and will measure the effect of every-six-months treatments on weight gain.

(b) Community Capacity Building and Empowerment for Child Care. This subcomponent comprises two interrelated activities: (a) community capacity building conducted through community planning and sensitization workshops, and (b) training in entrepreneurship to increase incomes of mothers and caregivers.

Project Component 2—Community Support Grants for Child Development. Two types of grants would be available to communities:

(a) Community Support Grants—grants to communities offered on the basis of matching contributions from communities. These grants and contributions from communities will cover activities designed to support interventions for child development that fall within the guidelines and menu contained in the project implementation manual. To qualify for this grant, communities will provide counterpart contributions, which may be in the form of goods, works, or services. Examples of the uses of such grants are construction and operation of community child care centers, home-based child care centers, or the production and marketing of weaning foods. The support grants component will be implemented in the same 25 districts included in component 1.

(b) Innovation Grants—grants made available to communities to address child-related problems. The innovation grant will aid in implementing interventions outside the menu of interventions described by the community support grants (a) above. As the term implies, the "innovation" fund will be used to support communities at different levels in implementing "innovative ideas" on improving the lives of children within their communities. The innovation grants will be accessed by communities in the same manner as the community support grants: that is, proposals will be prepared by communities following a participatory planning exercise, will then be screened by a subcounty committee, and forwarded for funding by the project.

Project Component 3—National Support Program for Child Development. This component consists of central program activities and policy initiatives designed to support the district-level programs in components 1 and 2 and provide quality assurance for the front-line project activities at the community level. This component includes (a) program monitoring and evaluation, (b) support for prevention of micronutrient deficiencies, (c) ECD curriculum development, (d) training of trainers for ECD, and (e) information, education, and communications.

VI. Implementation Arrangements

The implementation of the project is the responsibility of the government of Uganda assisted by nongovernmental organizations within the decentralization framework and devolution of powers to lower levels as stipulated in national policies. The community (LC-1) is the unit of operation for service delivery, although the coordination structure will also involve the parish (LC-2), the subcounty (LC-3), and the district (LC-5) levels.

In addition, the project hopes to use stakeholder sensitization and consultations, community mobilization, participatory community planning, capacity building for sustainability at all levels, together with strengthening of complementarity with existing national programs and structures. Existing political and institutional structures should be made use of in a multisectoral manner. Transparency and accountability should also be ensured at all levels.

VII. Project Coordination

National. A project steering committee composed of line ministries, donors, and NGO representatives will be responsible for overall guidance of project implementation.

The committee, to be headed by the permanent secretary in the Ministry of Finance, Planning, and Economic Development will provide guidance to the project on policy issues and review and approve the quality and efficiency of implementation. The project steering committee will also make suggestions to improve the district annual budget and work plans for the project.

A small project coordinating office (PCO), composed of a coordinator, a deputy coordinator, a qualified accountant, and a small support staff, will be based in the social services sector of the Ministry of Finance, Planning, and Economic Development and will take responsibility for the day-to-day coordination of project activities at the national level.

District. An existing multisectoral committee—the district coordinating committee (DCC)—will be identified by the Chief Administrative Officer (CAO) to take on the responsibility of coordinating the project at the district level. The CAO will identify a focal person from among the government officers who will coordinate NGO-related and other activities in the project. The lead NGO will be included as a member of the DCC. In districts where no NGO with adequate or appropriate capacity and skill base can be identified or strengthened to take over as the lead NGO, the implementation will be through the district administration.

Subcounty. An existing sectoral committee similar to the one at the district level will be responsible for coordinating the project activities at the subcounty level. This subcountry coordination committee will also facilitate linkages between existing structures and those of the project, and along with the lead NGO for the district, approve the subcounty NGO/CBOs' (Community-Based Organizations) annual work plans and funding requirements for the project in the subcounty.

VIII. Project Impact Evaluation

The government of Uganda is interested in assessing the impact of various aspects of the project in order to ascertain its effectiveness and to guide the design of further NECD projects. Moreover, as the World Bank considers this project to potentially inform other countries regarding NECD services, it has included the project in a three-country evaluation of ECD programs and will provide technical assistance on a grant basis to the PCO to assist specific research activities. In particular, two studies to evaluate the impact of specific project interventions will be undertaken as part of the overall project:

- Parish Child Health Day Study for assessing the coverage of anthelmintic treatments given at parish-level child health days and their impact on the weight gain of children under age six by using a randomized experimental design.
- Survey research using baseline and resurvey methodology for assessing (a) the impact of anthelmintic treatments and of overall project activities on the cognitive development, health, and nutrition of children under six years of age; (b) the impact of the caregiver education component and mass media communication campaign in the knowledge, attitude, and child-rearing practices of the principal caregivers; and (c) the impact of grass-roots management training, income-generating activities and credit savings group formation, and provision of community grants in household and community welfare.

The selected firm will provide technical and logistical support for the above studies and will be invited to participate as local research implementers in the design, data collection, and analysis necessary to complete the two studies of impact assessment. This firm will be the primary counterpart of the PCO, local researchers, and the researchers from the World Bank and the University of Oxford who will be undertaking the impact assessment.

IX. Overview of Studies

Study One: Impact of Deworming at Parish Child Days. There have been a number of studies indicating the impact of treating school-aged children with anthelmintic medicine. However, there is only one large-scale, randomized trial that shows a large effect on weight gain for pre-school-aged children. This has raised the question of whether such an effect could be achieved in African children. Thus, the NECD project will include a randomized study of the impact of providing the deworming agent, anthelminth albendazole, to young children in 25 selected parishes in the course of parish-based child days and to measure the effect of every-six-months treatments on weight gain. Data will be collected from these parishes as well as 25 control groups that will also organize child health days but will not administer albendazole on a routine basis. If the anthelmintic treatments are delivered successfully and are shown to have beneficial effects on Ugandan children, then the program of anthelmintic treatment may be recommended for all districts.

Because this is a scientific controlled trial, the selection of parishes that will be asked to administer albendazole will be undertaken by the PCO from a list of parishes where child days will be organized (this list will be provided by the NGOs working in the districts). The PCO will also select parishes that will serve as the control group. This experimental design is key to a successful evaluation.

The firm will ensure that the local NGOs responsible for the organization of the child health days in the parishes are aware of the rationale for the experimental design and that they comply with the strategy. Each child aged 12 months or older and under 6 who attends the fair in the 25 designated parishes will be given a single 400-milligram tablet of chewable, proprietary albendazole. The albendazole will be administered every six months; in the event that the NGOs choose to organize child days on a more frequent basis, the anthelmintic will still be administered on a six-month schedule and not more often.

Children in parishes where albendazole is administered as well as children in the 25 designated control parishes will be weighed at each child day, and their weights will be recorded both on their own health card and on the community register. Children who are too small to stand on the scale unaided will be weighed in their mother's arms after the scale has been set to zero with the mother standing alone on the scale. These weights will be recorded to the nearest tenth (0.1) of a kilogram. The data on the community registers are the responsibility of the local NGOs, although the firm will work with the NGOs to ensure that the data collection system is compatible with the full range of objectives of the study.

The firm consultant will transcribe these weights on a pro forma to be designed in collaboration with technical advisors from the World Bank and the University of Oxford. This data transcription will be undertaken every six months after the child day in the project area. In addition to the child's ID (a unique combination of the parish ID, the village ID, and the individual ID recorded on both the child's own card and the community register), the data on the pro forma will include the child's gender; the date of birth of the child taken from the child's health card or, if that is not available, the age of the child taken from the parish register; the date of the child fair at which the weights were recorded; and whether or not the child took a dose of albendazole. These data will be entered in a computerized record in Kampala. The individual ID will provide the basis for merging the data from different periods, and thus the ID must be recorded each time the data are transcribed and must remain constant for a child over the entire project.

The local circumstances and conditions at each child day that may deter mothers from attending will also be recorded. These include data on the state of the harvest and the weather conditions, both of which may deter mothers from attending. Any special methods and opportunities used to advertise each child day will be recorded because different forms of advertising may affect attendance. The record should also include an estimate of the number of children who visited the child day from other parishes and who did not have ID numbers obtained from the organizers of the child day.

The experiment will last two years. Thus, the firm consultant will record the data five times for each parish. That is, the firm consultant will collect the data at the beginning of the project and at 6, 12, 18, and 24 months after project initiation.

A complete copy of the data will be sent to the PCO every six months. These copies of the data will be considered the deliverable services of the first study of the project. Preliminary analysis will be undertaken at the University of Oxford on a semiannual basis. However, the firm is requested to nominate a representative who will participate in the main analysis to be performed at the end of two years. This representative will be provided travel and living expenses to work on the analysis at Oxford. The funds for this travel are budgeted in a separate line item and therefore need not be included in the contract covered by the request for proposals.

Study Two: Overall Impact of NECD Interventions. Household surveys and community surveys will collect baseline and follow-up information needed to evaluate the impact of the various project activities. The surveys will have several modules, which will measure:

- Cognitive development and growth of children under six years of age resulting from anthelmintic treatments and of overall project activities—Study Two will assess longitudinal growth and psychosocial and cognitive development outcomes in a cohort of children in communities participating in the project (with and without anthelmintic treatment) compared with a cohort of children in nonparticipating communities. Both cohorts will be followed for two or more years. The study will therefore complement the study of deworming at the parish level by allowing a greater understanding of the decision to take children to child days and to measure whether, over time, participation leads to an increase in measures of cognitive development. Moreover, by including communities that do not receive any ECD services, the study will assess whether the package of services leads to improvements in nutritional status and cognitive development.

- Changes in knowledge, attitude, and child-rearing practices of the caregivers resulting from project parental education and the mass media campaign.
- Improvement of the health and nutrition of children under six years of age resulting from growth-monitoring activities, preventive health and nutrition education, anthelmintic treatments, and overall project activities.
- Household welfare resulting from community grants, grass-roots management training, income-generating activities, and credit savings group formation.
- Community characteristics and changes resulting from the project interventions (or otherwise) that could have an impact on child well-being during the duration of the project.

Sample Selection. The basis for this study will be a baseline survey collected at the time services are first delivered to the communities and a follow-up survey collected from the same households two years after the initial survey. One-third of the sample will be drawn from the same 25 parishes in the treatment (anthelmintic) group and another third from the control groups studied in Study One. In addition, one-third of the sample will come from villages in 25 parishes in the same districts as the treatment groups but that are not expected to receive services from the NECD project. Thirty households will be selected from each parish. This implies 750 households per strata (2,250 total) in the initial survey. Given expected sample attrition, 5–10 percent fewer households are expected in the resurvey.

To collect the sample in the treatment and control parishes, all households in each parish (there are approximately 700 households in a parish on average) will be listed, possibly by a resident of the community. This list will contain the name of the household head, an indication of the location of the household, and the number of children under age six in the household. This list will serve two purposes. First, a sample of 30 households containing at least one child under the age of six per parish will be selected by a random draw. Second, the total number of children under six will serve as an estimate of the potential coverage of children in child days and thus assist in determining the rate of attendance.

Because the NECD project will have less contact with the communities that have no current NECD activity, the selection of households that receive no ECD service should use cluster sampling to reduce the costs of sample listing. In particular, one subcounty that is not in the project should be selected for every subcounty that is in the treatment group, preferably one that is adjacent to it. All parishes in these subcounties should be listed and a random draw of 25 parishes from the total list will be selected. Two villages from each parish selected will then be chosen, again using a list of all the villages in the parish. This step reduces the number of villages where a census will need to be conducted. The census—similar to the one used in the treatment and control parishes—will form the list of households used to draw the sample of 30 households per parish. This will be the third stratum of the survey.

The initial baseline survey should be undertaken in mid-1999. This timing is based on the need to know the subcounties and parishes in which the NGOs will be operating in order to employ the suggested sample design. This timing is also based on the assumption that the selection and training of lead NGOs will not be completed until late 1998.

The development and pretesting of the questionnaire, however, should be undertaken much earlier than this (early 1999) in order to be ready to implement the survey as soon as the NGOs have identified the parishes in which they will be working. As the baseline needs to be fielded before the first deworming, the ideal time for the baseline survey is concurrent with the initial community organization that will lead to a child day. Because the sample of 30 families in each parish is small relative to the total population, it is unlikely that the survey data collection will disrupt other activities or overburden the communities. The data collection in the control groups (those with NGO activity but no deworming and those with neither) should be simultaneous with the data collection in the treatment group.

Survey Instruments. The basic questionnaires to be used for the survey project are household questionnaires (which gather data at the level of the household and individuals) and community questionnaires.

X. Household Survey

Household data will be collected by using a precoded schedule. This will be drafted on the model of the Living Standards Surveys used in more than 30 countries. A first draft will be provided by researchers from the World Bank. However, the instrument will be both abridged to accommodate the particular needs of the project and adapted to local conditions by using focus groups and a pretest procedure undertaken by the firm. The household questionnaire will contain modules to collect data on:

1. Sociodemographic characteristics: A roster of individuals residing in the household in the past 12 months, their age and gender, as well as their schooling and type of employment (if any). The coding format

will indicate the parents of all children, if present—if not present, whether the parents are still living. A detailed list of assets will be collected to serve as an indicator of socioeconomic status.

2. Knowledge, attitude, and practices: The questionnaire will also collect information on the knowledge, attitudes, and child-rearing practices of the principal caregivers.

3. Anthropometric data: Weights will be recorded to the nearest tenth (0.1) of a kilogram for all children under the age of six by using digital scales that are to be provided. In addition, heights will be collected for all children between the ages of two and six. The pretest will be used to determine whether it is feasible to collect the weights of the mothers of these children (if living in the households) as well.

4. Cognitive assessment: The firm will work with other local and international research consultants to the PCO to integrate tests of child cognitive development into the overall field data collection. In the baseline survey an internationally recognized test of cognitive development will be administered to children aged 4.0–5.99 years. This test will also be administered to the same age group in the second round of the survey, allowing a comparison of cohorts. In addition, a subset of children aged 6–7.99 years at the time of the second round will be administered this test. (Annex table 2.1 summarizes this strategy.)

   In addition, knowledge assessments based on specific content from the program and a dynamic assessment may be developed for the second round of the survey. The inclusion of these measures will be evaluated during the course of the project. Finally, a school performance measure will be developed for assessing knowledge acquired in the first year of school and administered to a subset of older children in the resurvey. Existing tests might be adapted.

5. Child health: Morbidity data (including number and kind of symptoms, levels of severity, length in time), patterns of access to and utilization of health services, sanitation, and so forth.

6. Household economy: The best approach to collecting this information will be extensively explored in the pretest phase and assessed jointly with advisors from the PCO prior to finalizing the questionnaire. The variables may include food expenditures; agropastoral activities; consumption of home production; nonfood expenditures; housing characteristics; inventory of durable goods; employment; economic activities; income; land; crops and animals; income from project activities; household enterprises; asset ownership; credit and savings information on amount of money and goods lent and borrowed, if money and goods have been borrowed in the past 12 months; savings and net debt the day of the interview; information on loans, including the schedule, reason for borrowing, and number of loans from the same source; and

location of savings, if any, including bank, housing savings bank, rural savings bank, and so forth. This information will be part of the baseline and final surveys only.

XI. Community Survey

Community questionnaires will be used to gather information on local conditions that are common to all households in the area. The best approach to collecting this information will be extensively explored in the pretest phase and assessed jointly with advisors from the PCO prior to finalizing the questionnaire. The variables may include:

1. Demographic information: number of households, total population, population under six, ethnic groups, and religions;
2. Economic information, including principal economic activities and patterns of migration for jobs;
3. Infrastructure: access to roads, electricity, pipe water, market, bank, and public transport. Condition of local infrastructure, such as roads, sources of fuel and water, availability of electricity, and means of communication;
4. Local agricultural conditions and practices: type of crops grown in the community, how often and when they are planted and harvested, how the harvest is generally sold, and qualitative data on rainfall, climate conditions, and seasonality;
5. Education: number and types of preschools, formal and informal ECD arrangements, distance to schools, number of classes, enrollment rates (gross and by gender), attendance, grade progression, health and nutrition services provided at school (for example, school health programs, school lunch);
6. Health: type of health facility and distance and travel time to the nearest of each of several types of health facilities (hospital, pharmacy, health post, and so forth). Distance and travel time to the nearest of each of several types of health workers (doctor, nurse, pharmacist, midwife, community health worker, and so forth); and
7. Other: number and type of active local NGOs/CBOs, other child related projects or interventions (for example, government vaccination campaigns), and other community development projects.

Suggested Survey Staff. The survey staff should be constituted as follows:

• Core survey staff: composed of the survey manager, the field manager, the data manager, and the data entry staff who will be responsible

for overall field supervision, coordination, and monitoring of data collection and data entry and data management activities.
- Field survey staff: the field operations will be conducted by teams composed of a supervisor, two (or three) interviewers responsible for the main questionnaire and the anthropometric measurements, and a driver. A similar number of specialists who will participate in administering tests of cognitive development to the children will be selected and trained in collaboration with local and international experts.
- Coordinator for the randomized trial: the coordinator will assist in the development of the data collection instruments, training of local NGOs responsible for the organization of the child days in the parishes on the experimental design, data collection, and data transcription. He or she will oversee data entry and management of the study data set and will participate in the main analysis to be performed at the end of the study.

Organization of Fieldwork. The firm will participate in the drafting of the field instruments prior to the pretesting of the survey and will have primary responsibility for the pretest. After the pretest the questionnaire will be redesigned (in partnership with researchers from the World Bank) and then translated into local languages.

The firm will work with other local and international research consultants selected by the PCO to integrate tests of child cognitive development into the overall field data collection. The local ECD researcher, assisted by international consultants, will select and adapt the principal cognitive test to be used and will train the testers.

The following organization of fieldwork is suggested. This is based on international experience and designed to ensure quality control. Some variation of this approach might be agreed upon in consultation with researchers from the World Bank based on the experience of the firm and other advisors to the PCO and information gained during the pretest.

The fieldwork will be organized into small teams consisting of a supervisor, two (or three) interviewers responsible for the main questionnaire and the anthropometric measurements, and a similar number of specialists in administering tests of cognitive development to the children. These staff will be trained in Kampala by the local ECD researcher in coordination with international advisors on psychological testing. The training will include a discussion of the research objectives, a review of each step of the interview, practice training in the office, a dry run in the field, and a recap of experience after this dry run.

Once teams are trained they should be retained for the entire round of the survey, if possible. However, because a few staff may prove to be unsuitable during the fieldwork, it is advisable to train a few extra staff. It is not advisable to hire staff to work for a few days only in one parish and then new staff in the next parish because this results in inexperienced staff. All staff should receive new training at the beginning of the resurvey.

During the administration of the cognitive test, children should, to the degree possible, be alone with the interviewer. In no case should another person (adult or child) respond to the questions asked of the child. However, during the resurvey the test for the subset of eight-year-olds may be administered in a group format if it proves convenient.

The supervisor will be responsible for ensuring that the interviewers undertake the survey in the households chosen for the sample without substitution and that all children in the appropriate age groups are administered the tests of cognitive development. In addition, the supervisor will review each questionnaire after completion (prior to the team moving to a new parish) to ensure that there are no gaps in the questionnaire and to see that seemingly inconsistent information is verified.

The firm will enter all survey data as soon after collection as possible. Copies of the household- and child-specific data and rating scales along with the documentation necessary to access the data will be provided to the PCO in a computerized format at the end of the baseline survey. The original questionnaires should be retained by the firm because the original data will generally need to be accessed during the course of the analysis.

The child-level data must contain accurate identification codes that can be matched with the household survey codes. Although the unique individual and household codes provided to the PCO need not contain the names of the households or their exact location, this information must be stored by the firm in a manner that makes it possible to revisit the household at a later date. Because one step in the analysis will link individuals in the resurvey with their test results from the baseline, all individual and household codes must be held constant over the three surveys.

XII. Specific Tasks for Survey Specialists

The firm will participate in the following activities in collaboration with the PCO, local researchers, and researchers from the World Bank and the University of Oxford and implementing NGOs:

- Revision of work programs.
- Development and adaptation of the data collection instruments and support documentation, including listing materials, questionnaires, coding guides, interviewer and supervisor manuals, manual of operations, data entry manual, and field procedures.

- Revision of various drafts of documents, layout, translation, back-translation, and field testing. Provide hard copies and electronic versions of all documentation to PCO. Forward questionnaires to the World Bank researchers for their review and revision prior to the pilot test.
- Dwelling listing and cartographic updating. The responsibilities for listing of households and dwellings in each selected parish include obtaining base maps, preparing listing materials, contacting local officials to inform them about the listing operation, identifying boundaries, drawing maps, listing households in a systematic manner, obtaining preliminary information on households, including name of the household head, an indication of the location of the household, and the number of children under age six in the household; documenting procedures at the time of the sample design, at the end of the fieldwork, and at the completion of the data file.
- Preparation of sampling framework (with sampling specialist), training of staff to implement the designed sample, supervision of the implementation stage to ensure the quality of the sample selected, and provision of a detailed report outlining all the steps involved in the design and implementation of the sample.
- In consultancy with the World Bank, participation in determining an appropriate strategy for identifying comparison groups (that is, non-project parishes).
- Selection and training of field workers. This activity consists of all the work necessary to develop training materials and manuals for all persons involved in fieldwork. Training will be required for interviewers, supervisors of interviewers, supervisors of teams, data entry personnel, and anthropometric personnel.
- Field operation, including logistical arrangements for data collection and obtaining household and individual consent; keeping a study household register.
- Production of progress reports: The firm will prepare fieldwork progress reports (at six-month intervals) copied to the PCO and the World Bank. The firm should also prepare a basic description of the survey. This should include the survey content, the sample plan and its implementation, and the fieldwork techniques used. A full questionnaire and basic documentation should be included as appendixes.
- Development of a data entry program using software that can check for ranges and consistency of the data and generate reports indicating missing data, data outside of the accepted ranges, and inconsistent answers.
- Data cleaning, data entry, database management, and tabulation plans, including development of data entry program, data entry manual, data entry operator training, data quality checks, and guidelines

for using the data. Also, coding open-ended questions, verification of the data, checking anthropometric data against standard reference tables.

- Enforcing data use policy agreement: The firm and researchers involved in the process of data collection and analysis will sign a memorandum of understanding with the PCO that will explicitly state the policy regarding issues such as access to data, intended users, procedures for obtaining copies of the data sets and documentation, and publication and authorship rules.
- Conducting data analysis: The firm will conduct exploratory data analyses (for example, frequencies, percentage tabulations, and cross-tabulations) of key survey variables and their correlates. The firm will conduct modern statistical modeling of impacts after rounds 2 and 3 to determine overall progress in social indicators (for example, nutrition, health, incomes, and community development) and the factors that account for the changes or lack of changes.
- Producing analyses reports: The firm will report on the findings after rounds 2 and 3 of the surveys based on the analyses of the social indicators and the covariates. The firm will coordinate with the PCO and the World Bank on the Parish Child Health Day Study and on the collection of impact on cognitive development but will not be responsible for the final reports on the result of these studies.

Specific tasks for the community survey include the following:

- Work with advisers from the PCO in the development of the community questionnaire and extensively explore in the pretest phase the best approach to collecting this information;
- Work closely with the implementing agencies (lead and local NGOs) in the collection of the community data;
- Contact local officials and community leaders to explain the project impact evaluation approach and obtain communal consent for survey research and the child health day study;
- Interview key informers and obtain maps, lists, and other community records;
- Obtain lists of health and education facilities (pre- and primary schools), including geographic location, catchment area, and type of establishment (for example, private or public);
- Obtain community demographic information, including number of households and population by gender and age; and
- Obtain other data required in the community questionnaires.

Specific tasks for the child day study include the following:

- Participation in the development of the study protocol,
- Development of data collection instruments,
- Training of local NGOs responsible for the organization of the child days in the parishes for the experimental design,
- Supervision of data collected during child day,
- Data transcription,
- Data entry and management, and
- Participation in the main analysis to be performed at the end of the study.

Annex Table 2.1 Proposed Sample Sizes for Impact Evaluation of Nutrition and Early Child Development Project, Uganda

Category	Deworming and parent education		No deworming and parent education		No deworming and no parent education		Total
No. of parishes	25		25		25		Total
Time	Baseline	Second round[a]	Baseline	Second round	Baseline	Second round	
No. of households	750	700	750	700	750	700	2250
No. of children weighted at child days[b]	5000	5000	5000	5000			20000
No. of children aged 0–5.99 with anthropometry in the home (mean two per family)[c]	1500	1395	1500	1395	1500	1395	11580
No. of children given cognitive tests: test all children aged 4.0–5.99 in households	500[d]	465[e]	500	465	500	465	2895
No. of children aged 6.0–7.99 given cognitive test and anthropometry		subset[f]	—	subset	—	subset	subset

(Table continues on the following page.)

Annex Table 2.1 *(continued)*

Category	Deworming and parent education		No deworming and parent education		No deworming and no parent education	
School enrollment rates	25 commu- nities	25 commu- nities	25 commu- nities	25 commu- nities	25 commu- nities	25 commu- nities

a. Assuming a small loss to attrition of 8 percent in two years.

b. Assuming that about 200 children will attend each child day.

c. Two children per family are assumed, but families will be recruited if they have *any* children under six. Family refers here to a pair that consists of a mother (or substitute) and child.

d. This is a maximum; the actual number can vary according to the number of four- to five-year-old children encountered.

e. Assuming the same loss of 8 percent over two years; only children whose parents were interviewed will be tested.

f. Number will be a subset of the children in the age range whose parents were interviewed. They will be linked with the earlier score. Even though the number of children tested increases in the second round, the time for the interviews may decrease because much information will not need to be assessed again. It is also possible that the size of this group will be reduced.

Source: World Bank Project Document.

Validity Study. In addition to the above, one small longitudinal study will be added to examine the predictive validity of the preschool measure for school performance at the end of the first year of school. In the baseline survey, two children per community aged 6.0 to 6.9 (not yet in school) will be tested, for N = 150. These children will be located at the posttest and given a school performance test two years later, at ages 8.0 to 8.99.

Task Schedule. The tentative timetable for the task schedule is as follows:

Month 1. Begin the process of constructing indicators of cognitive development in conjunction with international consultant and in accord with terms of reference. This process may take up to six months.

Month 2. Initial pretest and revision of the questionnaire.

Month 5. Begin listing of households for sample selection. This step is dependent on the selection of the lead and local NGOs. It cannot be done until the PCO and NGOs choose the parishes where child days will be organized and then select the sites for the initial deworming program. At the same time the questionnaire should be translated and field tested again.

Month 7. Begin collection of data at child fairs for the deworming study. Data will be collected at these fairs at six-month intervals. As above, the timing of this step is dependent on the selection of the lead and local NGOs.

Month 8. Training of field staff for household survey and initiation of survey. The survey should take approximately three to four months depending on the number of teams employed. Data entry should be concurrent with data collection.

Month 14. Initial analysis of baseline data. This will be an ongoing process.

Month 20. Staff from the firm visit the University of Oxford to participate in analysis of initial data.

Months 20–36. Collection of data for round 2 for deworming study.

Midterm and final household surveys will be conducted two and four years after baseline.

Support to Firm

No specific support will be given to the firm to carry out assignments. Firms are advised to include all requirements for effective carrying out of the assignment in their proposals.

Example II: Rural Roads Impact Evaluation: Vietnam 1997 Baseline*

Terms of Reference: Baseline Survey for Rural Roads Impact Study

I. Background

The study aims to assess the impact on living standards of the World Bank–financed Vietnam rural transport project that were implemented in 15 poor provinces over three to five years starting in 1997. The study's overall focus will be on how the determinants of living standards are changing over time in communes that have road project interventions compared with ones that do not. This requires the collection of preproject baseline data for both project ("treatment") areas and nontreatment control areas and a number of further data collection rounds of postintervention data at two-year intervals. A detailed commune level database will be created in part by drawing on annually collected records at the commune level. The latter will be augmented by the collection of retrospective commune-level data and the collection of various other key supplementary data. A short district-level survey will help put the commune-level data in context. Finally, 10 to 15 households will be randomly sampled from commune-level household lists and a short household questionnaire will be administered. The study will be conducted in 6 provinces out of the 15 that will benefit from the project. The 6 provinces will be representative of the 6 geographical regions of Vietnam. A random sample of about 200 or so project and nonproject communes will be drawn. Six teams will be set up to simultaneously survey each province. The survey should begin in April and finish about August. Data should be available about October or November.

II. Survey Design

Sampling. Sampling will be done in three levels:

1. Provinces: The 15 project provinces are located in Vietnam's six geographical regions. Criteria for selection of survey provinces will be the

---

* These terms of reference were prepared by Dominique van de Walle.

following: (a) one province will be selected in each geographical region; and (b) when there is more than one possible project province in each region, a random selection will be made.

2. Communes: The aim is to survey 200 or more communes, which are randomly selected. About half or less (not more) should be communes with road link projects, the rest controls. A list will be drawn of nonproject communes in the six provinces (or alternatively one list for each province) and a random sample will be drawn. Similarly, a list will be drawn of all communes benefiting from road projects in the six provinces (or by province). This may be more than one commune per road link; all will be included in the sampling frame. From these a random sample will also be drawn. The sample will not necessarily include both communes linked by a road project. If access to certain sampled communes is impossible, it will be replaced with another commune in the district that is similar.

3. Households: In each sampled commune, a household survey will be administered to 15 households. These (plus perhaps a few replacement households) will be randomly selected from the commune household lists. After selection, the commune authorities will be asked about where the households fall in the very poor, poor, average, not poor, and rich classifications.

III. Survey Process

Six survey experts will be hired to conduct the surveys in the six provinces. After their training and the field testing of the questionnaire, they will begin surveying simultaneously in each province. In the districts, surveyors will need at least one local staff from the district project management unit to help with contacting local authorities and in some cases to help find suitable guides and interpreters in minority areas. Survey assistants or assistance from the provincial project management units will be hired as required.

Each surveyor will collect data from 35 communes on average, the districts they belong to, and 15 or so households per commune. Three to four days will be needed for each commune. The time spent in the field will be about 100 to 140 days (four to five months). The total time will be six months.

During the survey period, the supervisor will conduct field visits to all six provinces to supervise data collection and ensure high quality.

The collected data will be cleaned and entered by using a data entry program.

Annex table 2.II.1 gives an estimated timetable for the study.

Annex Table 2.II.1 Timetable for Impact Evaluation Study, Vietnam

	Jan.	Feb.	Mar.	April	May	June	July	Aug.	Sept.
Design question-naires	****	****							
Field test survey		****							
Revise question-naires			****						
Adapt data entry program, translate and print question-naires			****						
Hire and train surveyors			****						
Survey in field				****	****	****	****	****	
Check data								****	****
Perform data entry									*****

IV. Other

Equipment. The equipment purchased under the project will belong to the project as long as the study continues (through future rounds) but when not in use by the team it will be housed in the Project Management Unit for the team's use.

Budget Disbursements. The budget for the study (excluding payments to the main investigator, who will receive monthly installments) will be disbursed in three installments. The first, upon signing of the contract, will consist of 20 percent of total funds. The second installment, consisting of 50 percent of the total budget, will be disbursed once the commune, household, and district questionnaires have been finalized and approved by the World Bank task manager. This is expected to be sometime in late March. The third and final installment will be disbursed in late July or halfway through data collection. Estimated budget details are shown in annex table 2.II.2.

Annex Table 2.II.2 Estimated Study Budget

		No.	Time	Amount (US$)	Total (US$)
1.	Main investigator	1	9 months	1,000	9,000
2.	Survey experts	6	6 months	400	14,400
3.	Travel allowance for six surveyors, six local guides and interpreters	12	125 days	8	12,000
4.	Car and other transport for six survey teams	6	125 days	40	30,000
	Car rental for main investigator	1	30 days	50	1,500
5.	Air tickets Hanoi-Ho Chi Minh-Hanoi	6			
	For surveyors (south provinces)	3 persons		200	1,200
	For main investigator	3 trips			
6.	Training of surveyors	12			1,338
	Payment		1 week	50	
	Travel to field		3 days/ 3 cars	50	
	Allowance		3 days	8	
7.	Field test of questionnaire (South and North communes)	1	2 weeks		2,000
8.	Data cleaning and entry	2	2 months	200	800
9.	Survey materials				2,000
10.	Communications (fax, phone, email, Xerox)				2,000
11.	Equipment				5,000
	Computer (PMU18)	1		1,700	
	Printer (PMU18)	1		1,000	
	Fax machine (study team)	1		500	
	Laptop computer (study team)	1		1,800	

(Table continues on the following page.)

Annex Table 2.II.2 *(continued)*

	No.	Time	Amount (US$)	Total (US$)
12. Translation (questionnaire, manuals, documentation) 200 pages			8/page	1,600
13. Printing, Xeroxing				800
14. Contingencies				1,362
Total				85,000

Terms of Reference: Survey Supervisor or Main Investigator

I. Job Description

The in-country survey supervisor or main investigator will be responsible for the study's baseline survey work within Vietnam. Responsibilities include determining availability of information at the commune level; helping to revise and finalize the district-, commune-, and household-level questionnaires; field testing the questionnaire; incorporating revisions to the questionnaire; arranging for the questionnaire to be translated; hiring and training the assistants; planning the field work logistics; preparing survey implementation and questionnaire documentation; supervising survey implementation and ensuring quality control; and supervising the project database and arranging for data cleaning and entry. The person will also act as the liaison with the Ministry of Transport's Project Management Unit PMU18, the World Bank resident mission, the Canadian International Development Agency representative in Hanoi, and the project task manager at the World Bank in Washington. The person will report directly to the task manager. The person will start as soon as January 1997; the contract can be processed for a period of nine months at a rate of $1,000 per month.

II. Specific Tasks.

Specific tasks include the following:

1. Assuming responsibility for hiring, drafting detailed terms of reference, training and supervising six main assistants who will work with

local assistants (possibly from the local transport office) in the field and will be responsible for the collection of the district-, commune-, and household-level data;

2. Explorating of data availability at the commune level and working closely with the World Bank task manager to design the final versions of the questionnaires;

3. Carrying out a field test of the questionnaires in both South and North rural communes; reporting back on potential problems and necessary revisions; revising the questionnaires when needed;

4. Arranging for the questionnaires to be translated, printed, and Xeroxed (the final versions of the questionnaires will be available in both English and Vietnamese);

5. Choosing the six provinces to be included in the survey so that there is one province to represent each geographical region—when there is more than one such province, the sampled province is chosen randomly; drawing up a random sample of around 200 rural communes in the six provinces, including about half with projects and the rest without projects;

6. Planning all fieldwork logistics, including arranging for transport, drivers, travel allowances, the schedule of commune surveys, and alerting commune administrations of team arrivals and purpose;

7. Participating in survey implementation, alternating between the teams in a supervisory role; ensuring quality control; identifying problems affecting survey implementation, checking quality and completeness of data collected, suggesting ways to solve problems, and implementing them following consultation with the study leader;

8. Ensuring that future survey rounds can replicate the baseline survey, which requires (a) preparing detailed documentation of all survey implementation design and logistics (how the sampling of provinces, communes, and household was done; how the survey teams were trained and organized; how fieldwork was organized; what procedure was followed when a sampled site was not accessible or a sampled household not found; problems, issues raised, and solutions found); and (b) preparing a detailed manual on definitions of terms (for example, unemployment, income, primary occupation, child or adult, distance), units, currency amounts, codes used in the questionnaires; how the questionnaires are to be administered and to whom; how prices were collected, and so forth; the former should ensure that future rounds of the survey can reproduce the baseline's organization and logistical details, and the latter should be used in training of surveyors and for their work, as well as to aid future users of the data (there will be both English and Vietnamese versions);

9. Procuring the necessary equipment as itemized in the study budget;

10. Establishing good relations and ensuring close cooperation with PMU18. Keeping them abreast of the study and monitoring project developments; supervising the setting up of a database of project-specific data (the World Bank task manager will identify the data to be included);
11. Arranging and supervising data cleaning and entry by using the provided data entry program; and
12. Acting as liaison and communicating often with the task manager.

Annex 3
A Sample Budget from an Impact Evaluation of a School Feeding Program

Phase I: July 1999–December 2000[a]
School Feeding Research Proposal—Baseline and Cross-Sectional Evaluation
(July 1999–December 2000)
Draft Budget—7/14/1999—US$

	Staff weeks/Activity		Source of funds/Costs			
	FY2000	FY2001	BB	RPO	Other	Total
World Bank staff						
Economist	4	2	17,640			
Evaluation specialist	5	3	23,520			
Nutrition specialist	5	3	23,520			
Peer reviewer	0.2	0.2	1,948			
Peer reviewer	0.2	0.2	1,948			
						68,577
FES staff						
Study coordinator	4	4			12,000	
						12,000
International consultants						
Situational assessment (incl. travel)					7,000	
Cognitive test development (incl. travel)				6,000		
Sampling specialist				2,000		
Cost-effectiveness study				25,000		
						40,000
Regional consulting firm[b]						
Design, sampling, administration				42,000		

(Budget continues on the following page.)

	Staff weeks/Activity		Source of funds/Costs			
	FY2000	FY2001	BB	RPO	Other	Total
Fieldwork				25,000		
Data orocessing				3,500		
Analysis				30,000		
						100,500
Travel to country						
Trips	4	2		12,000		
						12,000
Contingencies						
Communication				1,000		
Software				2,000		
Translation				2,000		
						5,000
TOTALS			68,577	150,500	19,000	238,077

Total Requested from RAD: $150,500
Total Requested from Bank budget: $68,577
Total Provided by outside sources: $19,000

a. Budget estimates for phase II of the evaluation are not included in this proposal.

b. A breakdown of these costs is provided on the next page.

Estimated Budget—Local Data Collection and Analysis for Phase I
School Feeding Impact Evaluation
Costs in US$

	# People		# Staff weeks	Weekly rate	Total
Professionals					
Director	1		12	2,000	24,000
Education specialist	1		8	1,500	12,000
Nutrition specialist	1		8	1,500	12,000
Statistician/sampling	1		12	750	9,000
Fieldwork manager	1		8	750	6,000
Programmer	1		10	300	3,000
Data processing supervisor	1		8	300	2,400
Assistant – surveys	1		10	100	1,000
Assistant – anthropometrics	1		10	100	1,000
Assistant – cognitive tests	1		10	100	1,000
Data quality control	1		8	100	800
Subtotal—Professional staff					72,200
Fieldwork staff					
Supervisor	4		6	200	4,800
Cognitive tester	4		6	120	2,880
Anthropometrist	4		6	120	2,880
Interviewer	4		6	120	2,880
Driver	4		5	100	2,000
Fieldwork equipment	**People/units**			**Cost per week or unit**	
Vehicles (4 vehicles for 5 weeks)	4	5	350	7,000	
Gasoline (4 vehicles for 5 weeks)	4		5	80	1,600
Scales; rulers (5 sets)	5			20	100
Cognitive test equipment (for 4 testers)	4			20	80
Survey equipment (for 4 interviewers)	4			20	80
Subtotal – Fieldwork					24,300
Data orocessing	**People**				
Data coding	3		7	75	1,575
Data entry	4		7	75	2,100
Subtotal—data processing					3,675
Total					**100,175**

Annex 4
Impact Indicators—Evaluation of Bolivia Social Investment Fund

Developed November 1997

I.   **Formal Education—Schools Type "A" and "B"
     (multigrade and regular)**

   1.   **Final Impact Indicators**
        Achievement in Mathematics and Language tests[a]
        Repetition rate
        Dropout rate
        Enrollment
        Instruction level
        Demand for education (percent of students rejected from
          school)[a]

   2.   **Intermediate Impact Indicators**
        Regularity in student attendance
        Regularity in teacher attendance
        Students' time allocation/hours spent studying
        Classroom teaching method[a]
        Turnover in teaching staff[a]

   3.   **Intervention Indicators**
        Infrastructure
                Ratio students/classroom
                Number of classrooms in "good shape"
                Number of missing classrooms
                Availability of multifunctional area
                Availability of basic services
                        – Electricity
                        – Source of main water supply
                        – Type of sanitation service; condition of the sanita-
                          tion service
        Furniture
                Ratio students/desk
                Ratio teacher's tables/classroom
                Ratio teacher's chairs/classroom

198

Ratio "adequate blackboards"/classroom
Ratio shelves/classrooms
Texts and didactic material
Ratio texts/student
Quality of mathematics, language, social studies, and natural sciences texts
Availability of teachers' texts
Availability and condition of maps and charts
Didactic games by school cycle (prebasic, basic, and intermediate)
Availability of an abacus
Education Reform Indicators[b]

4.   **Factors Affecting Outcomes Not Linked to the SIF Project (Exogenous)**
Nutrition
Availability of school breakfast program
Cost of the school
Teachers' characteristics
Educational background
Years of service
Training received
Methods applied in teaching (in a period of classes)
Training received, by topic and course
Student evaluation practices (frequency of homework and its correction)
Evaluation of the teachers by the students
Rationale for dropping out
Students rejected by the school
Distance between the house and the school
Ratio students/teacher

5.   **Identification Indicators**
Whether school was prioritized by the Education Reform
Programmed cost by project component
Actual expenditures by project component

II.   **Health**

1.   **Final Impact Indicators[c]**
Infant mortality rate
Childhood mortality rate

Rates of incidence and prevalence of main diseases
Prevalence of malnutrition (general, slight, moderate, and severe)

2.   **Intermediate Impact Indicators**
Use of government health centers
Prevalence of tetanus vaccination
      Place where vaccine was received
Prevalence of prenatal control
      Number of prenatal controls
      Quality of control
Prevalence of births attended in health centers
      Quality of attention
Prevalence of home births attended by medical personnel
Height at birth
Weight at birth
Anthropometric assessments
      Place where assessment is held
      Age when first assessment is made
Incidence of disease and prevalence of immunization by number of doses received
      Polio
      Diptheria-tetanus-pertussis (DPT)
      Measles
      Tuberculosis vaccine (TB)
Knowledge of places to go for immunization
Incidence and treatment for coughing
Incidence and treatment for diarrhea
Prevalence of the knowledge and use of oral rehydration packets
Clinics' knowledge of prevalence of pregnancy
Attendance of high-risk pregnancies
Prevalence of good hygiene habits and use of water
Duration of lactation

3.   **Intervention Indicators**[d]
Quality of infrastructure by type of health center
Availability of basic services in the health center (drinking water, sewage system, and electricity)
Adequacy of infrastructure based on established norms by type of health center
Adequacy of equipment based on established norms by type of health center

Number of beds in the health center
Availability of essential medicines by type of health center
Availability of essential medical instruments by type of health center
Availability of essential furniture by type of health center

4.   **Factors Affecting Outcomes Not Linked to the SIF Project (Exogenous)**
Characteristics of the household
        Quality of household
        Type of household
Basic Services in the household
        Electricity
        Source of water
        Type of sanitary service
Accessibility to basic services
        Distance between the household and the closest health center
        Distance between the sanitary service and the source of water
        Distance between the household and the main source of water
        Hours of availability of water per day
        Sufficiency of amount of water per day
        Availability of water throughout the year
        Cost of consultation in the health center
        Household head's perception of the quality of:
                "Service" in the health center attended by the household
                "Infrastructure" of the health center attended by the household
                "Availability of medicines" in the health center attended by the household
Household expenses
Personal characteristics of the members of the household
        Age
        Language
        Education level
        Occupation
Geographic characteristics
        Health district
        Health area
        Health sector

> Province
> Locality
> Human resources in the health center (doctors, odontol-
> ogist, nutritionists, nurses, nurses' assistants, techni-
> cians, administrative staff)
> Population under the influence area of the health center
> by age groups
> Cost of consultation in the health center
> Health interventions not financed by the SIF

5.   Identification Indicators
Programmed cost by project component
Actual expenditures by project component

III.   Water

1.   Final Impact Indicators[e]
Infant mortality rate
Childhood mortality rate
Rates of incidence and prevalence of diarrhea in house-
holds
Prevalence of malnutrition (general, slight, moderate,
and severe)

2.   Intermediate Impact Indicators
Incidence and treatment for diarrhea in health centers
Prevalence of use and knowledge of use of oral rehydra-
tion packets
Prevalence of good hygiene habits and use of water

3.   Intervention Indicators (of Input)
Prevalence of training in health topics
Accessibility to basic services
> Main source of water
> Existence of and type of sanitary service
> Distance between the sanitary service and the
> source of water
> Distance between the household and the main
> source of water
> Hours of availability of water per day
> Sufficiency of amount of water per day
> Availability of water throughout the year
Quantity of water consumed by the household[a]

Quality of water[a]

4. **Factors Affecting Outcomes Not Linked to the SIF Project (Exogenous)**
Use of government (MSSP) health centers
Size at birth
Weight at birth
Duration of lactation
Characteristics of the household
    Quality of household
    Type of household
Accessibility to basic services
    Distance between the household and the closest health center
    Cost of consultation in the health center
    Household's expenses
Personal characteristics of the household's members
    Age
    Language
    Education level
    Occupation

5. **Identification Indicators**
Programmed cost by project component
Actual expenditures by project component

a. Not considered in baseline.
b. To be developed in coordination with Education Reform staff; will be considered exongenous to the intervention unless the SIF Education Reform interventions are considered jointly.
c. General mortality rate, birthrate, global fertility rate, adult mortality, and life expectancy at birth deleted.
d. Training in health topics deleted.
e. General mortality rate, birthrate, global fertility rate, adult mortality (male and female), life expectancy at birth, prevalence of acute respiratory infections, and treatment of coughing deleted.

Annex 5

Template of Log Frame for Project Design Summary for the Project Completion Document or Project Appraisal Document

Hierarchy of Objectives

Sector-Related Country Assistance Strategy Goal:
Provide a one-sentence statement of the long-term strategic goal (as reflected in the CAS) to which the project is designed to contribute. The statement should describe substantive development change in the sector(s) of interest.

Key Performance Indicators

Sector Indicators:
1. Indicators accompanying the sector-related CAS goal involve measurements that are not generally funded by the project but that may be funded by the Bank as part of other work.
2. Normally the borrower would monitor these indicators as part of good-practice sectoral management.

Monitoring and Evaluation

Sector and Country Reports:
1. This column identifies where the information for verifying each indicator will be found, and the process involved.
2. Indicators accompanying the sector-related CAS goal are generally monitored and evaluated via various sector or country reports generated outside the project.

Critical Assumptions

(From Goal to Bank Mission)
• Assuming that the sector-related CAS goal (stated in the far left box) is achieved in the long term, list any additional assumptions needed to link this goal to the Bank's mission (that is, poverty alleviation).
• These assumptions often involve conditions, actions, or responses outside of the

Project Development Objective:

1. Provide a one-sentence statement of the behavioral change expected from the target beneficiary group or institution(s) by the end of project implementation. Achievement of the objective serves as a simple test of demand for project outputs. The objective should express a single development purpose that is realistic, specific, measurable, and demand-driven. For a guide to setting the project objective, see "Do's and Don'ts for Setting a Project Development Objective" (call x37065 or e-mail M&EHelp@worldbank.org for a copy).

Outcome / Impact Indicators:

1. Outcome indicators relate to the results to be achieved by the end of project implementation, while impact may not be fully achieved until five or more years after project implementation has been completed.
2. Indicators at the outcome (PDO-level) are not a restatement of those at the output level.
3. Collection of data for measurement of these indicators is generally funded by the project.

Project Reports:

1. This column identifies where the information for verifying each indicator will be found, and the process involved.
2. Indicators accompanying the project development objective are generally monitored and evaluated via various project reports, supervision mission reports, and evaluation (midterm and final) reports.
3. When data collection is required, specific mention should be made of methods and responsibilities, which may include inquiries from beneficiaries.

project and outside of the sector.

(From Project Development Objective to Sector-Related CAS Goal)

• Assuming that the project development objective is achieved, list any additional assumptions needed to justify the project's contribution to the stated goal.
• These assumptions refer to the contribution(s) of additional projects, additional inputs, or additional responses from beneficiary groups and institutions that are critical to the achievement of the stated goal.

(Annex 5 continues on the following page.)

Annex 5 *(continued)*

Output from each Component:

1. State here (in the past tense) the value added by the completion of each component.

2. A correct statement of output value added will be easy to measure (as reflected in the indicators to the right).

3. For simplicity and clarity of the logic, there should be one output statement for each corresponding project component.

4. Each output should correspond in number to its respective component.

5. The project team is generally responsible for ensuring the delivery of the outputs as part of good project design and good implementation, planning, and delivery.

Output Indicators:

1. Output indicators have quantity, quality, and time attributes. If time is not stated, the end of project is assumed.

2. Output indicators generally include measures of cost-efficiency.

3. Collection of data for measurement of output indicators is funded by the project.

4. For complex projects, a separate table (perhaps an addendum to annex 1) may be used to provide a more detailed listing of output indicators.

5. It is better to have only a few meaningful and easily measured output indicators than an abundance of indicators for which data collection is problematic.

Project Reports:

1. Output indicators are generally monitored and evaluated via various project reports, supervision mission reports, and evaluation (midterm and final) reports.

2. Sources of data for monitoring and evaluating these indicators typically include administrative and management record-keeping systems and summary reports generated by the project.

(From Outputs to Project Development Objective)

• Assuming that the outputs listed in the far left box are achieved by the end of the project, list any additional assumptions needed to achieve the project objective.

• These assumptions may encapsulate conditions, policy changes, or expected behaviors of beneficiary groups or institutions that are necessary for project success.

• These assumptions are critical to the achievement of the stated project objective but are outside the direct control of the project.

206

6. The output indicators are agreed on with the borrower during PCD stage (as to the availability of data and ease of collection), and a baseline is obtained prior to appraisal.

Project Components/ Subcomponents:

1. A component is a cluster of subcomponents or activities that are designed to produce a single project output.

2. List each project component as a main heading, followed by the major subcomponents, if any, that are funded as a part of it.

Project Inputs (budget for each component):

1. List component inputs in terms of the total cost of each component including contingencies (for example, US$____).

2. For large or complex projects, the costs for subcomponents may also be shown (indented, to separate them from the component costs).

Project Reports:

1. Inputs are generally monitored via progress reports and disbursement reports (both quarterly).

2. Inputs are generally evaluated via supervision mission reports (semiannual) and audit reports (annual).

(From Project Components to Project Outputs)

• Assuming that the components and activities listed in the far left box are implemented successfully, list any additional assumptions needed to achieve the stated outputs.

• These assumptions are conditions outside the direct control of the project and are required if the stated project outputs are to be achieved.

• The project itself should not be spending money to achieve any of these conditions (since such assumptions are included in the components themselves).

Source: Operational Core Services Department, World Bank. For completed examples of this annex, visit the M&E Help Desk on the Bank's internal Web at http://Lnts012/helpdesk.nsf.

Annex 6

Matrix of Analysis

Nicaragua Emergency Social Investment Fund Impact Evaluation — 1998

A. Poverty Targeting

Issues	General Indicators	Methodologies	Comments	Source of data
Poverty levels of SF communities/districts	• Percent of households in community or district below poverty line or consumption levels of extreme poor	Requires household income and consumption survey and identification of SF activities by community and district	To compare across countries, need similar definitions of poverty lines	Oversampling national household survey (LSMS) in SF communities—only for education, health, water, and sanitation projects
	• Mean consumption level in social fund participant communities versus consumption level in country	Requires household income and consumption survey and identification of SF activities by community and district		Oversampling national household survey (LSMS) in SF communities—only for education, health, water, and sanitation projects
	• Poverty map index (as used by SF)	Maps usually use proxy measures, like a compos-	Disadvantages are that it arbitrarily chooses indi-	SF uses poverty map based on LSMS93 data

Indicator	Sub-indicator	Data collection method	Comments	Data source
	ite poverty index based on mix of variables	cators and weights, and each country has different index. Advantage is that it often provides more geographical disaggregation than income and consumption surveys—the two can be linked to derive predicted consumption levels at dissaggreggated levels		using composite poverty index; will update using LSMS98 and Census data to predict consumption at subnational levels
Poverty levels of SF beneficiaries (household level)	• Percent of beneficiaries below poverty line or in extreme poverty	Income and consumption survey that picks up SF beneficiaries either by size of SF or by oversampling in SF communities	May vary widely by SF project type	Oversampling national household survey (LSMS) in SF communities
	• Mean consumption level of beneficiary households versus national average for similar households per project type (for example, with children in primary school, with access to piped water, who use latrines)	Income and consumption survey that picks up SF beneficiaries either by virtue of size of SF or by oversampling in SF communities; can also oversample in "match" communities without SF interventions		Oversampling national household survey (LSMS) in SF communities

(Matrix continues on the following page.)

Matrix (*continued*)

Issues	General Indicators	Methodologies	Comments	Source of data
Distribution of SF resources	• Percent of SF projects and resources in bottom quintile of districts	Need consistent ranking methodology across countries		Need to review ranking system and recalibrate
Institutional design features that affect SF targeting performance	• Use of poverty map • Promotional efforts • Direct access by beneficiary groups • Share of projects by requesting agency • Decentralized offices • Target resource allocations • Subproject menu	Develop standard institutional variables that can be used to explain targeting outcomes—variables easily obtained from SFs		Information available from SF
Other factors affecting targeting performance	• Age of SF • "Social capital" of community • Distance to SF headquarters • Highest education level of beneficiaries • Presence of government or NGO interventions	Also need standard definitions for variables—variables obtained from SFs, household surveys (with identification of SF beneficiaries), and national surveys		Only indicator in doubt is the "social capital of community"

Issues	General Indicators	Data sources/ methodologies	Comments	Case Study: Nicaragua
	• Degree of country income inequality			
Comparison of alternatives	• Percent of SF projects and resources in bottom quintile of districts versus other comparable programs and delivery mechanisms	Compare targeting performance based on geographical location or poverty levels of beneficiaries, depending on survey design, scale of SF and other programs	Difficult to find viable comparators; need separate information gathering from comparator programs	Planned for cost-efficiency analysis

B. Benefits

Issues	General Indicators	Data sources/ methodologies	Comments	Case Study: Nicaragua
Physical capital	• Extent to which subprojects respond to community priorities	Community-level survey, beneficiary assessment, or household survey with oversamples in SF areas		Covered in IDB-financed Beneficiary Assessment and Facilities Survey
	• Beneficiary perception of benefit level and improvements to welfare	Household survey or beneficiary assessment in SF communities		Covered in household survey and IDB-financed Beneficiary Assessment
	• Improvement in access to social and economic	Household survey of SF beneficiaries	Need to have either baseline or recall ques-	Some recall questions in household survey,

(Matrix continues on the following page.)

Matrix *(continued)*

Issues	General Indicators	Data sources/ methodologies	Comments	Case Study: Nicaragua
	infrastructure (before and after)		tions; need to develop separate indicators per type of SF project	also possible ex ante from previous LSMS; can compare SF beneficiary with characteristics of national population and with match communities
	• Improvement in access to social and economic infrastructure versus comparator projects	Household survey of SF and comparator project beneficiaries	Need to have either baseline or recall questions; need to develop separate indicators per type of SF project	Can compare SF beneficiary with general characteristics of national population as well as match communities
	• Improvement in quality of infrastructure and services (before and after)	Facilities survey and household survey, some coverage from beneficiary assessment	Need to have either baseline or recall questions; need to develop separate indicators per type of SF project	For education, health, water and sanitation, recall plus historical information from facilities survey and SF ex ante appraisal
	• Improvement in quality of infrastructure and services versus comparator projects	Facilities survey and household survey, some coverage from beneficiary assessment (in SF and comparators)	Need to have either baseline or recall questions; need to develop separate indicators per type of SF project	For education, health, water and sanitation, SF and non-SF facilities through household and facilities surveys

Human capital		
• Improved educational status: school attendance, years completed, dropout and retention rates (before and after and versus comparators)	Household survey and information from school	Household survey and information from school for SF and non-SF schools and households
• Improved health status: for example, incidence of disease, infant mortality, malnutrition, increased breastfeeding (before and after and versus comparators)	Household survey with health module. Anthropometric measures if malnutrition included	Household survey and information from health center for SF and non-SF centers and households
• Improved economic status: increased income, reduced time spent fetching water, lower cost of services, increased employment (before and after and versus comparators)	Household survey	Household survey for SF-beneficiary and non-beneficiary match communities

(Matrix continues on the following page.)

Matrix *(continued)*

Issues	General Indicators	Data sources/ methodologies	Comments	Case Study: Nicaragua
Social capital	• Increased community capacity to address problems (versus comparators)	Household survey, community survey, and/or beneficiary assessment		Not addressed
	• Increased participation rates in community-initiated changes (versus comparators)	Household survey, community survey, or beneficiary assessment	Need to develop indicators	Information in household survey on participation

C. Sustainability of Benefits

Issues	General Indicators	Data sources/ methodologies	Comments	Case Study: Nicaragua
Sustainability of operations	• Conditions under which SF projects are operating after SF intervention (absolute sustainability)	Facilities survey	Can get some additional information from beneficiary assessment	For education and health project surveys, have both SF and non-SF
	• Conditions under which SF projects are operating after SF intervention versus comparator projects (relative sustainability)	Facilities survey	Can get some additional information from beneficiary assessment	For education and health project surveys, have both SF and non-SF

Sustainability of maintenance	• Maintenance of infrastructure and services over time (absolute)	Facilities survey	Can get some additional information from beneficiary assessment	For education and health project surveys, have both SF and non-SF
	• Maintenance of infrastructure and services over time versus comparator projects (relative)	Facilities survey	Can get some additional information from beneficiary assessment	For education and health project surveys, have both SF and non-SF
Sustainability of impact	• Quality and quantity of infrastructure and services over time	Facilities survey and household survey	Can get some additional information from beneficiary assessment	For education and health project surveys, have both SF and non-SF
Sustainability of community effects	• Tendency of SF communities to submit other proposals (to SF and others) over time	SF database, community survey, or beneficiary assessment		Would need additional work
	• Community participation in social and economic infrastructure needs over time	Community survey, household survey, or beneficiary assessment		Include in *next* beneficiary assessment; impact evaluation

(Matrix continues on the following page.)

Matrix *(continued)*

D. Cost-Efficiency Issues

Issues	General Indicators	Data sources/ methodologies	Comments	Case Study: Nicaragua
Cost-efficiency of subprojects	• Average cost per new school, health post, water system versus alternative approaches versus comparator projects	SF database and information from government ministries and municipal governments	Costs change over time and comparator projects must be identical	SF and non-SF data from facilities survey. Non-SF cost estimates may not be reliable
	• Unit costs: cost per square meter of construction, per kilometer of road, and so on, versus comparator projects	SF database and information from government ministries and municipal governments		Can calculate SF averages. Will include in cost-efficiency analysis
	• Average cost per beneficiary per SF project type versus comparators	SF database and information from government ministries and municipal governments		Can calculate SF averages. Will include in cost-efficiency analysis
	• Average cost of employment generated versus comparators	SF database and information from government ministries and municipal governments		Can calculate SF averages. Will include in cost-efficiency analysis

Cost efficiency of delivery mechanism	• SF institutional costs (investment and operating) as share of SF projects versus comparator projects	SF database and information from government ministries and municipal governments	Need to develop standard definitions of institutional costs; specify time period	Can calculate SF averages. Will include in cost-efficiency analysis
	• Average completion time versus comparator projects	SF database and information from government ministries and municipal governments		Can calculate SF averages. Will include in cost-efficiency analysis